Music Business Research

Series editors

Music business research is a new multidisciplinary field that puts a number of different analytical approaches into mutual dialogue. It is located at the intersection of economic, artistic, musical, cultural, social, legal, and technological understandings of this cultural industry and it aims to generate a better understanding of the creation, distribution and consumption of music as a cultural good. As a field it is therefore characterised by methodological diversity and involves linking academic research with music business practices. The book series welcomes monographs and edited volumes that feature groundbreaking research into this dynamic and exciting field.

More information about this series at http://www.springer.com/series/15800

Anita Jóri • Martin Lücke
Editors

The *New* Age of Electronic Dance Music and Club Culture

Springer

Editors
Anita Jóri
Vilém Flusser Archive
Berlin University of the Arts
Berlin, Germany

Martin Lücke
Macromedia University of Applied Sciences
Berlin, Germany

ISSN 2522-0829 ISSN 2522-0837 (electronic)
Music Business Research
ISBN 978-3-030-39004-4 ISBN 978-3-030-39002-0 (eBook)
https://doi.org/10.1007/978-3-030-39002-0

This Springer imprint is published by the registered company Springer Nature Switzerland AG.
The registered company address is: Gewerbestrasse 11, 6330 Cham, Switzerland

Contents

List of Contributors

Benedikt Brilmayer studied musicology and psychology. In his dissertation, he focused on the transfer of technology in making musical instruments. He has published articles on electronic instruments, curated several exhibitions, and edited the exhibition catalogue *Good Vibrations: A History of Electronic Musical Instruments*. Currently, he works at the Musikinstrumenten-Museum SIM PK in Berlin.

Lukas Drevenstedt studied Arts and Media Administration in Berlin and Amsterdam. He founded a DJ collective after graduating from high school in Berlin and began to tap into urban space through cultural events. He is General Manager at Clubcommission Berlin, the pioneering bottom-up organization for club culture and nightlife advocacy.

Anita Jóri is a research associate at the Vilém Flusser Archive, Berlin University of the Arts (Universität der Künste Berlin, UdK). She studied applied linguistics and history and finished her PhD thesis "The Discourse Community of Electronic Dance Music" in 2017 at Eötvös Loránd University, Budapest, Hungary. Her research interests include electronic dance music cultures, gender and diversity issues in EDM scenes, and applied linguistic methodologies. Jóri is also a chairperson of the German Association for Music Business and Music Culture Research (GMM).

Kata Katz is a research assistant at the Macromedia University of Applied Sciences (Berlin, Germany). She is currently working on her PhD thesis about the genealogy of the image of the "other" in the medium of photography. She studied philosophy, literature theory, and film history and theory at the University of Szeged, Hungary.

Martin Lücke is Professor for Music Management at the Macromedia University for Applied Science in Berlin. Since 2018, he is also the Berlin campus's Associate Dean. Lücke studied musicology, modern history, and political sciences at the Ruhr-University of Bochum. He finished his studies with a doctoral thesis about jazz in totalitarian systems, which was published in German in 2004. After that he began to focus on popular music and the music industry. Another focus of his work is educational research. Lücke was a cofounder and chairman (2016–2018) of the

German Association for Music Business and Music Culture Research (GMM). Currently, he is publishing the *Lexikon der Musikberufe* at Laaber Verlag.

Bianca Ludewig is a cultural activist and anthropologist. Since 2012, she has been a PhD candidate at the University of Innsbruck (Austria). Her research focuses on avant-garde festivals where music, art, technology, precarity, and urban transformation processes intersect. Ludewig studied philosophy and cultural anthropology at the University of Hamburg and continued her studies at Humboldt University—Institute for European Ethnology and Institute for Musicology. She has taught at Humboldt University Berlin and the University of Vienna. Her research interests include pop culture, popular music, precarity, gender, urban studies, and ethnographic methods. Previous to her academic studies, she has worked as a freelance music journalist, DJ, DIY festival curator, and radio activist (http://bl.wiseup.de).

Ewa Mazierska is Professor of Film Studies at the University of Central Lancashire. She has published over 30 monographs and edited collections on film and popular music. They include *Popular Viennese Electronic Music, 1990–2015: A Cultural History* (Routledge, 2019), *Poland Daily: Economy, Work, Consumption and Social Class in Polish Cinema* (Berghahn, 2017), and *Popular Music in Eastern Europe: Breaking the Cold War Paradigm* (Palgrave, 2016). She is currently working on a book about Polish popular electronic music. Mazierska's work has been translated into over 20 languages. She is principal editor of the Routledge journal *Studies in Eastern European Cinema.*

Josef Schaubruch studied music education, German, and philosophy in Mainz and Heidelberg. Currently, he is working on his PhD thesis studying the practice of liveness in electronic dance music cultures with a scholarship from the Leuphana University (Lüneburg, Germany). He has been teaching drums and live electronics for many years, tours as a musician, and has released several recordings.

Patrick Valiquet is a British Academy Postdoctoral Fellow in Music at the University of Edinburgh, where he also teaches the construction of music as an artifact of science and technology. He is currently preparing a monograph on the governance of experimentalism in Cold War British and French music education and research policy. His writing has appeared in *Twentieth-Century Music*, *Music and Letters*, *Organised Sound*, and *Contemporary Music Review*.

Botond Vitos is a cultural anthropologist and research assistant on the project *Burning Progeny: The European Efflorescence of Burning Man.* Supported by the University of Fribourg and the Swiss National Science Foundation, *Burning Progeny* is a 4-year comparative, multisited ethnography focused on the European chapters of the Burning Man movement. Vitos' research interests include event cultures, popular music studies, electronic dance music culture, and the mediations of aesthetic experiences. He is part of the editorial team at *Dancecult: Journal of Electronic Dance Music Culture*.

Chapter 1
Introduction

Anita Jóri and Martin Lücke

On June 21, 2017 at Kantine am Berghain, the external floor of the famous Berlin club Berghain, the editors of this anthology organized a symposium with the title *Summer Solstice in Berlin: The "New" Age of EDM and Club Culture* (see more in Resident Advisor 2017). The aim of this conference was to bring together scholars and practitioners from as many varied research and practice fields as possible to discuss actual EDM-related topics and issues.

The one-day event was divided into five interconnected sessions: (1) academic, (2) practice-oriented, (3) workshop-based talks, (4) a panel discussion, and (5) a music program. For the academic session, the cultural studies scholar Botond Vitos; the sociologists Jan-Michael Kühn and Christine Preiser; and the applied linguist Anita Jóri were invited to speak. They all live in Berlin and are avid scholars of electronic dance music culture. Vitos wrote his PhD thesis on techno and psytrance scenes in Melbourne, Australia. At our symposium, he introduced his new research project on experiencing electronic dance floors in Berlin. Kühn published his doctoral thesis at Springer entitled *Die Wirtschaft der Techno-Szene. Arbeiten in einer subkulturellen Ökonomie* (*The Economy of the Techno Scene: Working in a Subcultural Economy*), and he mainly focused on the economical questions of the scene. Preiser gave an overview on her research on the door policies at clubs and she presented her interview results with bouncers. It is getting ever more increasingly important to discuss this topic in Berlin, especially if we think of, for example, the door policy of the world famous Berghain. Finally, Jóri elaborated her new linguistic discourse analytic methodology, which she applies to online communities of EDM scenes.

A. Jóri (✉)
Berlin University of the Arts, Berlin, Germany
e-mail: a.jori@medienhaus.udk-berlin.de

M. Lücke
Macromedia University of Applied Sciences, Berlin, Germany
e-mail: M.Luecke@macromedia.de

A. Jóri, M. Lücke (eds.), *The New Age of Electronic Dance Music and Club Culture*, Music Business Research, https://doi.org/10.1007/978-3-030-39002-0_1

In the practice-oriented second session, Aiko Okamoto, from the networks of female and nonbinary artists female:pressure and Meetup Berlin, talked about diversity problems within the local electronic dance music scene. Lukas Drevenstedt, the commercial director of Clubcommission Berlin, highlighted the most striking issues in the club culture of Berlin such as gentrification, cultural changes, and new political and economic policies. Last but not least, Benedikt Brilmayer, researcher and curator at the Berlin Musical Instrument Museum, introduced the exhibition *Good Vibrations: A History of Electronic Musical Instruments*.

With the support of the company Native Instruments, the third session of the day was a DJ workshop with the Berlin-based DJs Camille Darroux, OANA, Red pig flower, and White Lie. The audience could try out digital and analog DJing techniques in a friendly atmosphere, thanks to the four DJs. It was an important point for us to invite female DJs only, with whom women in the audience could feel more comfortable communicating and interacting [see more on this topic in Rodgers (2010) and Farrugia (2012)].

After the workshop, a panel discussion of the most poignant political and economic issues of the local scene closed the symposium part of the day. Our panelists were Katja Lucker, managing director of Musicboard Berlin; the abovementioned sociologist Jan-Michael Kühn; and the Berlin-based musician Roxy from the techno live act PHROND. The musicologist and music economy scholar Martin Lücke moderated the discussion. From this talk, we realized even more that academics and practitioners in the field do not interact and cooperate with each other enough. One of the best examples was the terminology discussion of the panel: Katja Lucker questioned the term EDM in the title of the event. For the present academic scholars it was clear that by EDM one means the umbrella term that includes all music genres of electronically produced danceable or not danceable, mainly club-oriented music (see more in McLeod 2001; Collins et al. 2013). For Lucker, it rather referred to a mainstream electronic music that was popularized after the early 2000s, mostly by the US American music industry. She is, of course, not alone in this opinion—many other protagonists in the scene use this term with that meaning. We also have to add here that the German term Techno is used as an umbrella term for "underground" electronic music. Therefore, in a German language context, EDM means mostly the opposite: a mainstream and business-oriented music genre.

But this was only one of the examples where we realized that scholars and practitioners should work more closely with each other in order to create a common language amongst them, thereby aligning research and practical fields. The panel discussion also showed that being an electronic musician in Berlin is not as easy as it may seem from most of the cases described. The competition is getting more heated since a lot of artists move to the city in hope of a better life.

After the talks and workshop, we closed the day with a music program. We believe that an event on electronic dance music cannot come to a close without listening to music. This last part of the day was opened with a techno DJ set by Tom Talenberg, then the techno live act PHROND played. Right at the end, Nina Pixel closed the evening with her eclectic DJ set.

During the day, Echo Bücher, a Berlin-based bookstore specializing in electronic music, which unfortunately has shut down now, provided us with the latest publications on contemporary music, sound, and club culture.

It was a productive and at the same time eye-opening day in many ways. And it is why we decided to publish this volume about electronic dance music with a main focus on the city of Berlin—to document this fruitful day and also to invite other authors for contributions.

The subject of this volume is broad, and one could also say that it is vague, but our aim was to create an anthology that is as interdisciplinary as possible on the topic of electronic dance music cultures (henceforth EDMCs) in general. This is why one can find very different methodological systems, analyses, and subjects in this book. Also, the authors of this volume have very diverse backgrounds: some of them are scholars in the field of EDMCs or cultural studies in general, some work in the music business, and some have backgrounds as journalists too, thus providing insights from various perspectives. We thought that these different backgrounds might help each other's work.

Every published paper presents actual research or practice-based results. Based on the diverse topics of these articles, the following chapters were divided into three parts: (1) Electronic Dance Music and Club Culture in Berlin, (2) Musicians and Musickers, and (3) Electronic Musical Instruments and Their Users.

In the first part, Berlin is marked as an important epicenter of EDMCs. In the second part we shift this aspect specifically to musicians and musickers (Small 1998). Finally, in the third part, the technological and instrumental background of this culture is highlighted.

Lukas Drevenstedt in his text *Dimensions of Club Culture—Learning from Berlin*, gives a general overview on Berlin's club culture and its diverse dimensions. Drevenstedt also writes about the new regulations and changes in the city that completely shifted the profile of the local club culture in recent years.

In *Only the Echo is Left (Alive)*, Kata Katz analyzes the cultural input of the Berlin-based bookstore Echo Bücher that specialized in electronic (dance) music. Even though the shop was shut down several months ago, it is still important to show how Echo Bücher contributed to the local EDM scene during its active years. Katz also argues in her chapter that this store was a cultural (third) space where new ideas and models in the field of electronic music could be formed.

The cultural activist and anthropologist Bianca Ludewig gives, in *The Berlin Techno Myth and Issues of Diversity*, an overview about the issue of diversity in the field of electronic (dance) music and Berlin club cultures. To do so, she also takes specific examples from German and Austrian avant-garde or transmedia festivals and analyzes the structure of the Berlin-based platform female:pressure. Ludewig's research results also highlight some actual political and economic issues in Berlin that affect the city's club culture and its diversity.

Martin Lücke in his chapter *Club Culture and Electronic Dance Music in Berlin: An Economical, Social and Aesthetical Perspective* summarizes the most striking economic issues in Berlin's present EDM scene. He analyzes Clubcommission's

2019 published comprehensive study of the Berlin club scene, which presented economic, social, and aesthetic aspects.

Botond Vitos introduces his postdoctoral research proposal in *Researching Informal Musical Expertise and Mediations of Aesthetic Experiences Among the Berlin Techno Audience*. The purpose of his study is to identify and compare segments of techno club audiences in Berlin based on their forms of engagement in music-related activities such as audio media and recreational drug use. Vitos' aim is to identify the ways different audience segments attempt to recreate the distinctive socio-aesthetic experience of the electronic dance floor in their everyday life by means of audio media and other arrangements. We thought that it is interesting to also include a proposal like this in order to see what type of new ideas and topics are (or are going to be) discussed in the field nowadays.

The professor of film studies, Ewa Mazierska, in her text *The Influence of Berlin on Austrian and Polish Electronic Musickers* discusses the meaning of Berlin for Austrian and Polish electronic musicians and people involved in the scene. It examines their real and symbolic connections to the city, reflected in such activities as traveling to Berlin for business, playing there, using booking agents from there, collaborating with Berlin musicians, as well as being influenced by the city's music and atmosphere.

Patrick Valiquet, a musicologist specializing in historical and anthropological approaches to experimental music and music technologies, in his text *"100% Expert!" Mastery and Equality in Darsha Hewitt's Sideman 5000 Adventure* examines the tutorial video series *A Sideman 5000 Adventure*, in which the sound artist Darsha Hewitt presents her research on early drum machine technology. The chapter brings Hewitt's work into dialog with the educational philosophies of Pierre Bourdieu and Jacques Rancière.

In *Sound Visions and Visible Sounds: Electronic Musical Instruments and Their Power to Change* Benedikt Brilmayer reports on the abovementioned exhibition at the Berlin Musical Instrument Museum through the history of electronic musical instruments. This history he introduces from an organological point of view, meaning that electronic instruments and their development could be seen from the perspective of not only functionality but also handling and playing.

In her chapter *The Discourse Community of Electronic Dance Music Through the Example of the TB-303 Owners Club*, Anita Jóri presents a new type of methodology system based on the linguistic computer-mediated discourse analysis, which she applies to a sample of the online community *TB-303 Owners Club*. She analyzes the community and identity construction processes within a "virtual scene" (Peterson and Bennett 2004) through its language use and discourse processes. Furthermore, her results also add up-to-date information to the research on computer-mediated communication.

Finally, Josef Schaubruch writes about the Austrian techno band's individual performance styles in *The Human Modular Synthesizer—The Musical Design and Live Performance of Elektro Guzzi's Pentagonia*. The text focuses on Elektro Guzzi's specific constellation of musical production, musical design, and live performance as key elements of electronic dance music. This chapter provides new insights into the challenging musical practice of the performance of liveness, as exemplified by Elektro Guzzi. Schaubruch is an expert on this theme because his PhD thesis also deals with the practice of liveness in electronic dance music cultures.

As presented in this anthology, the subject of electronic dance music continues to be full of exciting research topics. From our point of view, the connection between theory and practice always remains important, as it is a living, constantly developing field. On the other hand, it is still worthwhile to look at electronic dance music from different disciplines and perspectives. The insights gained from these different perspectives underline the importance of EDM for the scientific community. Electronic dance music is valuable from an entertainment as well as an economic standpoint, and it is a living mirror of societies.

This volume is addressed to a broad audience: from academic scholars, through musicians, to other protagonists of the scene. As mentioned before, we would like to create a bridge between these actors in order to make possible a multifaceted discussion about actual issues of electronic dance music cultures, or in other words "techno cultures."

References

Collins, N., Schedel, M., & Wilson, S. (2013). *Electronic music*. Cambridge: Cambridge University Press.

Farrugia, R. (2012). *Beyond the dance floor. Female DJs, technology and electronic dance music culture*. Bristol: Intellect Books.

McLeod, K. (2001). Genres, subgenres, sub-subgenres and more: Musical and social differentiation within electronic/dance music communities. *Journal of Popular Music Studies, 13*, 59–75.

Petereson, R. A., & Bennett, A. (2004). Introducing music scenes. In A. Bennett & R. A. Peterson (Eds.), *Music scenes: Local, translocal and virtual* (pp. 1–15). Nashville: Vanderbilt University Press.

Resident Advisor. (2017). *Summer solstice in Berlin: The "new" age of EDM and club culture*. Accessed June 20, 2019, from https://www.residentadvisor.net/events/980677

Rodgers, T. (2010). *Pink noises: Women on electronic music and sound*. Durham: Duke University Press.

Small, C. (1998). *Musicking: The meanings of performing and listening*. Middletown, CT: Wesleyan University Press.

Part I
Electronic Dance Music and Club Culture in Berlin

Chapter 2
Dimensions of Club Culture: Learning from Berlin

Lukas Drevenstedt

Abstract Over the last 30 years, Berlin has become known worldwide for its vibrant club culture and nightlife. The city used to have lots of free space and not much regulation, but real estate speculation and gentrification have led to drastic increases in prices driving independent cultural activities out of the city. Club culture is an essential part of metropolitan nightlife and luckily this has been widely understood, even among politicians. The question remains, however, how to foster and govern a sustainable and yet dynamic, high-quality and diverse club cultural landscape. This chapter sketches an approach to understanding club culture as a multilayered phenomenon which can only be fully understood by combining different disciplinary perspectives or dimensions. Club culture always emerges from subcultures, it functions on an entrepreneurial basis, it is embedded in local scenes and it produces (collaborative) esthetics. The club culture model bridges the gap to other discourses and is supposed to serve policy makers and public administrators for good governance and to spark a more in-depth discourse and further research.

2.1 Introduction

Over the last 30 years, Berlin has become known worldwide for its vibrant club culture and nightlife. At the same time, Berlin is dealing with the same challenges as every other major city: an enormous influx of people combined with real estate speculation has led to shortages of space and drastic increases in prices. Opera houses, theaters, and museums funded by the state are not affected by this because they are located in publicly funded buildings. Clubs, on the other hand, have to compete on the commercial rental market, making it increasingly difficult for them to obtain leases. Club culture is gradually being driven out of central Berlin.

Politicians have realized that club culture in Berlin plays a special role in life in the city. Locals, newcomers, and tourists go to clubs to hear music, dance, socialize,

L. Drevenstedt (✉)
Clubcommission Berlin, Berlin, Germany
e-mail: ld@clubcommission.de

A. Jóri, M. Lücke (eds.), *The New Age of Electronic Dance Music and Club Culture*, Music Business Research, https://doi.org/10.1007/978-3-030-39002-0_2

have fun, and be inspired. Encounters outside of the confines of everyday life, physical experiences in a digitalized society, and the collective esthetic experience fascinate people from all over the globe.

Alongside clubs, open-air events and festivals also shape club culture. Aspiring new collectives are increasingly appropriating spaces that have not been used for cultural purposes before, such as old basements in Kreuzberg, unused sites in Spandau, or ruins in Zehlendorf. The outskirts of the city are becoming more attractive, but central Berlin remains the beating heart of the city's club culture. Similarly, theaters, museums, opera houses, and other institutions are experimenting with moving further out, while knowing that their centrally located facilities still enjoy special protection. Denying a state-funded cultural institution its building and sending it to possible locations in the city's outskirts would be scandalous. In the same way, it should also be regarded as scandalous if a club is forced to shut down and offered an alternative location in a remote part of the city.

There is an urgent need for a strategy to preserve Berlin's club culture in the city center. In this chapter, I will outline an approach that aims to do justice to the phenomenon of club culture in its structures and to create a foundation for political action in order to save the club scene in Berlin from a slow demise. There is still a very heterogeneous mix of people involved in creating club culture who are located all over Berlin and who produce a broad spectrum of esthetic attitudes and cultural practices. We need to preserve this sensitive ecosystem.

2.2 Defining the Phenomenon

Club culture initially flourishes in spaces where there is little state control. The enjoyment of loud music, dancing, and a sense of community brings people together for concerts or other club events. Every event requires a space, and the more often a series of events takes place in a specific space, the more it becomes associated with it. The appearance of the space is often changed in its esthetic and functional aspects to meet the needs of the specific community. The space gradually becomes more and more suitable.

Space, however, has become rare and is regarded as a valuable commodity. The upgrading of neighborhoods and subsequent increase in rents (gentrification) pushes clubs out. Local crowds become more cost-sensitive and often cannot afford to go out anymore. Without subsidies from the state, a high standard and variety in club culture probably cannot be maintained. In order to start this conversation, however, some questions need to be answered first: What exactly is club culture? What are the standards used to evaluate the quality of club culture? How can club culture be facilitated and supported?

Club culture is a phenomenon whereby people meet at events in a protected space to dance, listen to music, and socialize. The exact way this plays out—e.g., what music is played, the people who make up the audience, the price structure—can be referred to as *a specific club culture*. A multitude of reports and studies have been dedicated to identifying and classifying various specific club cultures (Thornton 1995; Goetz 1998; Garratt 1999; Nieswandt 2006; Rapp 2009; Hook 2012; Eberle 2013; Denk and von Thülen 2014).

However, this definition is not enough to evaluate the quality of a specific club culture; it merely differentiates one phenomenon from others. The term club culture is often mistakenly used for styles of music (e.g., techno, house, dance music), but club culture is not the same as techno or EDM culture—even if the techno movement helped to turn club culture into a global phenomenon (Mathei 2012; Denk and von Thülen 2014; Feser and Pasdzierny 2016). To this day, electronic styles of music dominate club culture, but jazz, hip-hop, and other genres are also represented. The various scenes often overlap, as can be observed at festivals such as *Fusion* or *X-Jazz Festival* (Kirchner 2011).

Similarly, club culture should not be equated with "nightlife," which is defined in the dictionary as "the activity of or entertainment provided for pleasure-seekers at night" (Merriam-Webster)—which also includes gambling and prostitution. Today, club culture often takes place during daytime. Nonetheless, the night remains an important symbol of the myth of club culture. Summing up Louis-Manuel Garcia's article on Resident Advisor from 2014: *Specific* club cultures are music scenes located within nightlife (Garcia 2014).

To evaluate the quality of a *specific* club culture, its context needs to be observed too. The meaning of club culture for society can best be understood by looking at it in terms of three different dimensions: the economical dimension, the social dimension, and the esthetical dimension. Each of these three dimensions is characterized by different competing paradigms that can serve as a basis for judging individual standards of quality.

The term "club culture" is often used synonymously with "subculture," "youth culture," and "pop culture," so it is important to illustrate the differences at this point. Subculture theory has become a broad interdisciplinary field with a resulting abundance of definitions. Without going into further detail, the concept of subculture as a social practice often entails a differentiation of "underground/mainstream" with regard to esthetic and stylistic elements as semiotic features to delineate these subcultures from the mainstream (Thornton 1995; Schwanhäußer 2010; Kühn 2017).

Youth culture on the other hand can be defined as "the cultural activities and styles of adolescents within a shared culture scene" (Wyneken 1914). This defines youth cultures as subcultures practiced predominantly by adolescents. The concept of youth culture does not seem fitting in the context of club culture because clubs do not allow admission to minors.

As club culture is practiced in spaces protected from the general public—the mainstream—it can be considered a subculture; however, specific club cultures may reproduce a subcultural mythology even when they have long become part of the pop-culture mainstream themselves. *Berghain*, *Watergate*, and *Kater Blau*—just to name a few clubs in Berlin—have attracted large numbers of visitors from all over the world, but have also left their mark on musical styles, (club) architecture, fashion, and lifestyle. What differentiates club culture from pop culture? The answer is the necessary involvement in specific communities and the importance of life encounters: "The club experience can't be translated into *one* huge event, *one* TV show or *single* tracks on the radio. It becomes *something else*." (Kühn 2017: 16–17).

I have developed the following definitions based on my experiences as a DJ, event organizer, and club-goer, from my work at Clubcommission Berlin, my research and the definitions of the LiveDMA (2018). They will be used in the following chapters and are intended as starting points for further discussion.

- Definition *club*

A club is a venue that is characterized by a program focused on live music, restricted access of a certain nature to create a protected space with its own rules, and a community that meets there to listen to music, dance, and socialize.

- Definition *club culture*

Club culture describes the phenomenon of people meeting in clubs or in similar spaces (e.g., open-air concerts, warehouse raves, or festivals) characterized by a program focused on live music, restricted access of a certain nature to create a protected space with its own rules, and a community to listen to music, dance, and socialize.

2.3 Elements of Club Culture

2.3.1 Space

Club culture is characterized by a high intensity of bodily physicality. An event is always experienced in a physical space together with other people who are present in a very analog way. Virtual attendance of a club event is not a possible option. Space is the primary essential resource for club events, which can take place indoors or outdoors. It just has to be ensured that the space is protected from unwanted outside intruders as good as possible.

The result is a semipublic venue that suggests exclusivity and intimacy while still being permeable to the outside world. Accordingly, the membrane that regulates entrance plays an important role. This membrane is usually a door guarded by bouncers. That is why it is commonly referred to as *the door*. Admittance is managed using a door policy that is not explicitly formulated but is implicitly defined by the bouncers' actions. There are also other, more subtle mechanisms to regulate attendance: a secret location for an event taking place at a time when few people are likely to randomly pass by can minimize the risk of unsolicited guests. This of course means that the event has to be communicated only via selected channels—especially if the event takes place in a public area where entry cannot be denied, e.g., in a park or out in a field. The program certainly influences the type of audience that is attracted too—this connection will be explored later in this chapter.

The door is not the only element that serves an important function in club culture. Several other typical areas can be found in almost all clubs: the cloakroom, bar, dance floor, stage and backstage, toilets and chillout area (Rapp 2009: 183). The character of each area influences the perception of the club event as a whole. According to Gerhard Schulze (2000), a club can be portrayed as a "scenery of happiness." A club is turned into a heterotopia, a concrete utopia, by employing various stylistic techniques derived from architecture, interior design, stage construction, sculpture, decoration, lighting, video art, special effects, etc. (Foucault 1993).

Club space also functions as a means of socialization: the family home nurtures a family spirit among children, and a club space nurtures a family spirit as well, with the latter family referring to the club community. In fact, many clubs become something approaching the living room of young urban dwellers or—with regard to interior style—a nostalgic version of it.

2.3.2 *Scene*

Every club has a community that is made up of three groups: the organizers, the artists, and the audience. The organizers (or promoters) provide the framework for a club event. They procure all the relevant resources such as renting a space, supplying materials, deciding on and communicating the date of the event, etc. Everything artists and audience need has to be taken care of, be it the bar, equipment, or the toilets. The artists make an event unique: they define the look of the space through lighting, decoration, performances and, of course, music. Finally, all of this is put on for one group: the audience. The club-goers are at the center of it all—and everyone is part of the audience, including the organizers and artists. Gerhard Schulze defines an audience as "every collective of people characterized by the consumption of an experience offering" (Schulze 2000: 460).

When members of a specific audience become regular visitors at a venue, they form a group called the core audience. A network of several core audiences is called a scene (Schulze 2000: 463). Club culture is typically created by members of a scene for the scene (Schwanhäußer 2010). The attendance rate of an event is an important criterion for its success. The club audience "demands an at least moderately attended event to feel comfortable" (Kühn 2017: 173–174).

If a club event takes place in a prominent space or a series of events has reached a certain level of prominence, guests who are not familiar with the values of the specific scene are to be expected. This brings up the question of how to organize the process of familiarizing newcomers with the value system of a specific scene. Typical undesirables are tourists and proles ("Touris und Prolls", Rapp 2009: 49) and techno fans ("Techno-Atzen", Kirchner 2011: 83), who are feared for being ignorant of the rules of a specific club scene and for being difficult to integrate. These drastic stereotypes of people from outside the scene illustrate how sensitive the club scene is about influences from the outside that might endanger the atmosphere at an event. Many clubs employ a door policy to regulate access for people that might dominate an event with aggressive behavior. Bouncers guard the door to protect the club as a safe space for the scene.

The exclusivity of access to a club plays a major role in the creation of myths around a specific club scene and increases the appeal of affiliation to a given scene. This so-called *seductive power* is important for the preservation and evolution of a scene (Kühn 2017: 176). The knowledge of the codes necessary to get past the door and into a club can be seen as subcultural capital (Thorton 1995) that is passed on from one person to another.

2.3.3 Program

Every club event features a musical program. Often there will be live performances and concerts. Club culture is not limited to specific musical styles. Some events have an explicit focus on music with rather linear programming (e.g., label showcase, release party), others have a thematic focus (e.g., body positivity party, queer party, fetish party) and sometimes there is a focus on a political issue (e.g., solidarity party, fundraiser). The program of an event will be published in some form, usually in advance of the event on a platform that is public to a greater or lesser degree.

The program expresses an artistic attitude. It can be regarded as a statement within the context of a discourse. At the same time, the program has an influence on the composition of the audience. The quality of the program is an important indicator of a club's societal significance: a challenging program targeted at a niche audience can be regarded as especially valuable. On the other hand, a big turnout is undeniably a symbol of successful programming.

Club culture does not function with linear programming alone. Spontaneity and improvisation are always part of events. In fact, interaction with the audience is often encouraged in one way or another.

2.4 Dimensions of Club Culture

It is helpful to identify what club culture actually is: a space with a program and an audience, as I illustrated in the last section. This, however, does not say anything about the value of a specific club culture. The economic, cultural, and social importance of club culture to society cannot be ignored. The corresponding standards and underlying paradigms are the key to correctly observing this phenomenon. Due to the multilayered nature and complexity of club culture, comprehensive dimensioning of this phenomenon is essential. These dimensions must be considered together in order to comprehend club culture in its entirety. Nevertheless, it can be useful to deconstruct the phenomenon first and take a more detailed look at its parts—also to make its relevance more visible for administrative areas and government departments.

2.4.1 Economic Dimension

The organization of a club event always begins with an entrepreneurial impetus: it is about starting something (together). Someone has to take the initiative and provide some kind of input. Club culture always develops bottom-up. Every event is a project and a series of events can lead to an evolution from collectives into organizations over time. The production of a club event is a collaborative process of creating value.

The creative industries regard creativity as their main resource. Creativity, however, cannot be exploited like other resources—it cannot be grown like potatoes or mined like iron ore. Creativity is a form of thinking outside the box. If there is constant pressure for profit, there is no space left for creativity to flourish. Clubs offer a refuge for creative thinking and creative practices. There have always been attempts by big brands to appropriate club culture for their commercial interests. These attempts, however, are bound to fail if the club culture landscape offers enough scope for alternatives. Revenues from entrance fees and the bar allow clubs to cover costs for infrastructure and to realize their creative visions.

A number of resources are needed to put a club event together. It all begins with a suitable space: this space can either be a room, a hall, an old warehouse or even an open-air area or a place in a public park. Secondly, there needs to be electricity to power instruments, playback equipment, amplifiers, and speakers. People are needed to carry out organization and financing of the operation and to set up installations, etc. All these aspects can be characterized in the form of procurement markets. These are usually implicit markets, meaning one must already have access to the structures of the scene. This is also known as a "scene economy" (Kühn 2017).

The sales market for club culture is the event market. The market volume is relatively small compared to other sectors. If clubs make profits at all, these profits are small. Only a few institutions in metropolitan areas can make big profit margins. However, the knock-on effects for other industries can be immense. The main benefactor is tourism, and other sectors such as retail and transport enjoy positive effects too. When examining the figures in Berlin, 168 million euros of direct revenue can be compared with a staggering 1.48 billion euros for tourism (Damm and Drevenstedt 2019). Club culture is a location factor and an indicator for the attractiveness of a city, especially for the creative class (Florida 2003; Landry 2008).

2.4.2 Social Dimension

What does a specific club culture mean for society or a societal group? Clubs offer the potential to create safe spaces for marginalized groups, so it is not surprising that the history of club culture is black and queer (Mühlenhöver 1999; Buckland 2002). Breaking away from conventions and social norms has been an integral part of the emergence of specific club cultures. Excess—meaning the deliberate denunciation of reason, partially aided by drugs—makes it easier to collectively turn away from societal norms and creates a state of ecstasy. This process can be turned into a ritual leading to a form of controlled loss of control. Schmitz describes this ecstasy as a situation, "[. . .] when you fully immerse yourself in something or are enraptured by it, be it in suspenseful fascination or relaxed devotion" (Schmitz 2014: 80)—all the while keeping your identity intact, while not being congruent with external factors. It is the basis for the innovative potential emerging from club culture (Garcia 2017: 72).

An important function of clubs is providing a safe space for their communities. Artists and audience are two groups that benefit equally from this. For many artists, a club is an intimate location for experimentation: new tracks get tested, sometimes even a completely new style. A new stage performance can be tried out and the artist does not have to be afraid of being filmed and shown on social media. The club is at the intersection between the private and public spheres. The informal setting is considered inspiring for many (Lange and Bürkner 2010: 62).

A club's function as a safe space is equally important for the audience. Many people who do not feel comfortable expressing themselves in majority society need places to socialize and build their identity.

Certain ways of living and expression are publicly frowned on not only in countries with less liberal laws than those in place in the western world. Homophobia and transphobia are major problems in Germany even to this day. Ideally, clubs are spaces where members of marginalized groups can move freely. This protection can only be guaranteed as long as it is actively upheld. The mentor principle facilitates exchange with the outside environment, rejuvenation of scenes, and the socialization of newcomers: "sometimes the ways of access can change drastically through mediation of a single person. [The mentors] assume responsibility for introducing new people into the community, spread important information about the scene and its values, provide access to their social and professional networks or lend support in other ways" (Garcia 2017: 79–80).

For some people, clubs are also simply a place to meet others in an analog manner. The increasing density and intensity of cities is resulting in more stress in our everyday lives: city-dwellers encounter more and more people—on public transportation, for example—without really interacting with one another. Most people constantly stare at their smartphones and are busy taking selfies and posting them on social media. Our interactions with our surroundings take place through an electronic filter. As a result, the digitally saturated public sphere is increasingly unsuitable as a space for interacting with others. Clubs serve as an escape from this everyday urban life. They are screened off to the outside. It has become broadly established that photos are not allowed to be taken in clubs—some clubs like infamous *KitKatClub* even ask guests to hand in their mobile devices at the cloakroom for the duration of their visit. This simple measure makes visitors more open to others—something that has become more seldom in everyday urban life.

In recent times, increasingly explicit rules for interacting with others have been formulated in club culture. The aim here is to foster an awareness that certain types of societal behavior are also reproduced in club culture and that privileges continue to exist, and ultimately to counteract these behaviors and privileges (Reclaim Club Culture Netzwerk 2017). Everyone should feel comfortable and should respect everyone else—on equal terms, regardless of background or gender. Whether club culture is—or should be—broadly political is a matter of debate: "After all, the partying ultimately does not follow a political objective. You can interpret it in a political manner, and everyone has their own political position—but the fact that people come together to dance doesn't allow one to draw any conclusions about common political positions. Unless you want to pull the dancefloor from under the dancers." (approximate translation of the German original in Rapp 2009: 48).

2.4.3 Esthetic Dimension

An esthetic consideration of club culture will naturally first examine the music that is played in clubs. The history of club culture is one of the developments of pop culture and is intimately connected with the emergence of a number of genres. Ultimately, there is not just one type of music that is played in clubs (Mühlenhöver 1999; Porschardt 2015; Sub Opus 36 e.V. 2016). Each specific club culture has its own musical style. There are no predefined genres—every style of music is theoretically possible in a club context. This platform offers a range of media for musical discourses that are often carried out in the public domain.

Clubs are also a working environment for artists from other areas. In particular, clubs serve as a workshop, laboratory, and presentation space for the visual arts. The artist Wolfgang Tillmans exhibits his work at *Berghain* and has said: "For me, going out in clubs, with their interplay of light, music, desire, social interaction and dance, has always touched on many things that are important to me as a person and artist who thinks about life [. . .] This was always extremely inspiring for me." (approximate translation of the German original in *Berghain* 2015: 32). In this regard, he is part of a distinguished tradition: back in the 1980s in New York, clubbers danced in front of a large-scale mural by Keith Haring (López Munuera 2018: 117).

Club culture has also been the source of esthetic input into the areas of fashion and design, as illustrated in visual form by the *Night Fever* exhibition at *Vitra Design Museum* in 2018. The great importance of clubs as an arena for differing personalities, gender identities, and sexual orientations make them an important space for experimentation in the fashion world. In 1980s, the *Antwerp Six* had a decisive influence on a form of unisex streetwear that had its origins in the Belgian underground club scene and that later attracted major international intention (Serulus 2018: 283). Clubs not only served as a source of inspiration in this regard, but also acted above all as a platform for new creations.

A fourth important area of esthetic interaction is the field of architecture: clubs usually emerge in locations where architects and town planners have not been involved. Deserted warehouse halls, damaged buildings, empty sites, and derelict areas in industrial estates offer ideal prerequisites for stimulating the visions and fantasies of pioneers in terms of locations for club culture. In rare cases, clubs are built from scratch or integrated into new buildings. *Berghain* in Berlin is located in an old power plant building. The industrial esthetic and morbid charm of the club are the work of studio karhard, a successful architecture practice. The architects designed important parts of the building, and even include the toilets (!) as an individual project on their website.

Finally, the performance aspect of club culture is also noteworthy. Interactions between artists and audiences are often part of the artistic process. Erika Fischer-Lichte (2004) describes theater as a performance that everybody present in the room participates in. Without the audience, the experience cannot take place. The audience thus becomes a creator in the art of theater (Fischer-Lichte 2012: 20, borrowing from Max Hermann 1931). The same thing can be said of the club experience: it cannot be created without the club-goers themselves.

2.5 Outlook

Club culture falls under a number of areas of political responsibility by its very nature. The city-state of Berlin has progressed to such a point that the current coalition government is cooperating in an intradepartmental manner in a number of areas—such as that of sustainable and city-friendly tourism. Club culture initially emerges as a result of entrepreneurial initiative. It takes business thinking to organize an event. Anyone who cannot assemble the necessary resources and does not have a feel for what people want to experience will quickly fail. The same applies to those trying to make a quick profit: the scene is sophisticated and very sensitive to any perceived sell outs. If the lineup is not good, prices are too high or if an event turns out to be a promotional event, the scene will stay away, and the club's reputation will be damaged. Only clubs that offer high-quality programming will be successful in the long term.

It is the task of business policy to create positive framework conditions for club culture—particularly as a result of the indirect effects on other sectors such as tourism. According to the current tourism policy of Berlin's Senate Department for Economics, Energy and Public Enterprises (Senatsverwaltung für Wirtschaft, Energie und Betriebe), over 80% of Germans regard the city of Berlin as an attractive destination because of its lively social scene (Senate Department for Economics, Energy and Public Enterprises 2018: 10).

It is the task of arts and cultural policy in Germany to safeguard the freedom of the arts as enshrined in Germany's constitution (Art. 5 para. 3 of Germany's Basic Law) and to promote culture by all for all (Hoffmann 1984). A public need must first exist as a foundation for action in the area of arts and cultural policy (Scheytt 2008: 114). The multifaceted societal significance of club culture has been described above in this chapter. Calls for action from arts and cultural policy are increasingly being heard. For example, people ask why there is support for programming in clubs only at federal level and not at state level (the *APPLAUS* award for programming)?

The main area of activity is in urban development policy. Club culture requires locations in central areas of cities in order to develop in a diverse, interesting manner. As a result of the boom in the real estate market, such locations can only be secured in the medium to long term through cooperation with government. The main goal here must be the preservation of diversity and dynamism in the club landscape. The main barometer for the success of a club is attendance numbers, but the importance of clubs can also be measured in terms of its programming profile. The Agent of Change principle was introduced by the Mayor of London Sadiq Khan in his London Plan in 2018. This shifts the responsibility for noise protection for residential buildings in noisy areas to building developers. Municipalities have to ensure that planning decisions reflect the Agent of Change principle and take into account existing uses.

Despite all the optimism as regards the anchoring of club culture in the political agenda, one must not forget that a healthy distance to what actually takes place in clubs is still required. The myth needs to be preserved, and a certain degree of contradiction needs to be tolerated. "There are certain things that are better left in the dark. Anyone who wants to know more will find out more. Anyone who doesn't, won't" (approximate translation of the German original in Rapp 2009: 206).

References

Berghain. (2015). *Kunst im Club*. Berlin: Hatje Cantz.

Buckland, F. (2002). *Impossible dance. Club culture and queer world-making*. Middletown: Wesleyan University.

Damm, S., & Drevenstedt, L. (2019). *CLUBKULTUR BERLIN*. Hrsg: Clubcommission e.V. Berlin. Kostenloser Download unter www.clubkultur.berlin

Denk, F., & von Thülen, S. (2014). *Der Klang der Familie: Berlin, Techno und die Wende*. Berlin: Suhrkamp.

Eberle, M. (2013). *galerie berlintokyo*. Berlin: Drittel Books.

Feser, K., & Pasdzierny, M. (Eds.). (2016). *Techno Studies: Ästhetik und Geschichte elektronischer Tanzmusik*. Berlin: b-books.

Fischer-Lichte, E. (2004). *Ästhetik des Performativen*. Frankfurt a.M.: Suhrkamp.

Fischer-Lichte, E. (2012). *Performativität. Eine Einführung*. Bielefeld: transcript.

Florida, R. (2003). *The rise of the creative class: And how it's transforming work, leisure, community, and everyday life*. New York: Basic Books.

Foucault, M. (1993). Andere Räume. In K. Barck (Ed.), *Aisthesis: Wahrnehmung heute oder Perspektiven einer anderen Ästhetik* (Vol. 39). Leipzig: Reclam.

Garcia, L.-M. (2014). *An alternate history of sexuality in club culture*. Accessed January 31, 2019, from https://www.residentadvisor.net/features/1927

Garcia, T. (2017). *Das intensive Leben – Eine moderne Obsession*. Frankfurt a.M.: Suhrkamp.

Garratt, S. (1999). *Adventures in Wonderland: A decade of club culture*. London: Headline Book Publishing.

Goetz, R. (1998). *Rave*. Frankfurt a.M.: Suhrkamp.

Herrmann, M. (1931). Das theatralische Raumerlebnis. In *Bericht vom 4. Kongreß für Ästhetik und Allgemeine Kunstwissenschaft* (pp. 153–163). Berlin.

Hoffmann, H. (1984). *Kultur für alle. Perspektiven und Modelle*. Berlin: Fischer.

Hook, P. (2012). *The Hacienda: How not to run a club*. New York: Simon & Schuster.

Kirchner, B. (2011). *Eventgemeinschaften. Das Fusion Festival und seine Besucher*. Wiesbaden: Springer.
Kühn, J.-M. (2017). *Die Wirtschaft der Techno-Szene: Arbeiten in einer subkulturellen Ökonomie*. Wiesbaden: Springer.
Landry, C. (2008). *The creative city: A toolkit for urban innovators*. London: Sterling.
Lange, B., & Bürkner, H.-J. (2010). Wertschöpfung in der Kreativwirtschaft. *Zeitschrift für Wirtschaftsgeographie, 54*(1), 46–68.
LiveDMA. (2018). *Glossary: Venues, clubs and festivals*. Accessed November 30, 2018, from http://www.live-dma.eu/live-dma-glossary/
López Munuera, I. (2018). Diskotektur: Körperregime und Erkundung der Ereignis-architektur. In M. Kries, J. Eisenbrand, & C. Rossi (Eds.), *Night Fever. Design und Clubkultur 1960 bis heute, Begleitbuch zur Ausstellung im Vitra Design Museum* (pp. 116–128). Weil am Rhein.
Mathei, D. (2012). *Oh my god – it's techno music! Definition und Abgrenzung des Technostils unter Berücksichtigung historischer, stilistischer und soziologischer Aspekte*. Osnabrück: Electronic Publishing.
Mühlenhöver, G. (1999). *Phänomen Disco: Geschichte der Clubkultur und der Popularmusik*. Bergheim: Musikverlag Christoph Dohr.
Nieswandt, H. (2006). *Disko Ramallah: Und andere merkwürdige Orte zum Plattenauflegen*. Köln: Kiepenheuer & Witsch.
Porschardt, U. (2015). *DJ culture: Diskjockeys und Popkultur*. Hamburg: Rowohlt.
Rapp, T. (2009). *Lost and sound: Berlin, Techno und der Easyjetset*. Berlin: Suhrkamp.
Reclaim Club Culture Netzwerk. (Ed.). (2017). *RECLAIM YOUR CLUB Fibel*. Accessed July 25, 2018, from http://hidden-institute.org/wp-content/uploads/2017/07/RYC-Fibel_Webansicht.pdf
Scheytt, O. (2008). *Kulturstaat Deutschland. Plädoyer für eine aktivierende Kulturpolitik*. Bielefeld: transcript.
Schmitz, H. (2014). *Atmosphären*. Verlag Karl Alber: Freiburg i.Br..
Schulze, G. (2000). *Die Erlebnisgesellschaft*. Frankfurt a.M.: Campus Verlag.
Schwanhäußer, A. (2010). *Kosmonauten des Underground. Ethnographie einer Berliner Szene*. Frankfurt: Campus.
Senate Department for Economics, Energy and Public Enterprises. (2018). Retrieved from https://www.berlin.de/sen/wirtschaft/en/economics-and-technology/branches/tourism/
Serulus, K. (2018). Clubkultur, New Beat und Mode aus Belgien. In M. Kries, J. Eisenbrand, & C. Rossi (Eds.), *Night fever: Design und Clubkultur 1960 – heute* (pp. 282–291). Weil am Rhein: Vitra Design Museum.
Sub Opus 36 e.V (Ed.). (2016). *SO36: 1978 bis heute*. Ventil Verlag: Mainz.
Thornton, S. (1995). *Club cultures: Music, media and subcultural capital*. Cambridge: Polity Press.
Wyneken, G. (1914). *Schule und Jugendkultur*. Jena: Diederichs.

Chapter 3
Only the Echo Is Left (Alive)

Kata Katz

Abstract This chapter explores the need and purpose of a niche bookstore that promoted electronic music culture and EDM-related items. Through asking and defining what is a cultural space, the bookstore as such can be identified as a "third place," an inclusively sociable field.

These social zones contribute value to the community and are also the forerunners of democratic dialog and exchange. A venue which can be the axis of artistic and civil networks has the possibility to contribute to new forms of ideas and expressions. Interestingly these thoughts and themes—even when they are not written explicitly—can be found in the books that are sold most often in the store. *Klang der Familie* and *Ghost of My Life* are shining examples of this through which we can contemplate art, society, and pop culture.

Another space closed in Berlin. This particular one, the bookstore Echo Bücher, is more special to some than to others. A store, a place, a venue, which described itself—on its still existing website—as a space for contemporary music, sound, and club culture. Its main focus was on electronic music and techno lifestyle: a place where you could experience sound, art, and clubbing all together. Books, records, magazines, sound objects, and goodies from independent labels were sold there. It hosted live-acts, exhibitions, book and magazine launches, DJ sets, and sound performances. In short, it was a gift from heaven for the more engaged members of electronic dance music culture. Some questions that came up in regards to the closing of the space were: Will this niche bookstore be missed? Will the ever increasingly gentrified Berlin miss a habitat like this? Do people even need it?

Recently I took part in a lecture given by one of my colleagues, Gernot Wolfram, in Hangar 1, a venue for artistic projects in Berlin, where he—reacting also to the fragile state of Hangar 1—contemplated the issue of how should and/or what will cultural places of the future look like and why we need these spots. Before we

K. Katz (✉)
Macromedia University, Berlin, Germany
e-mail: k.katz@macromedia.de

A. Jóri, M. Lücke (eds.), *The New Age of Electronic Dance Music and Club Culture*,
Music Business Research, https://doi.org/10.1007/978-3-030-39002-0_3

examine his argument, we should consider what is or can be identified as a cultural place and what purpose it has for society.

We could use the most conventional definition of culture, which means we define culture "in general as the totality of the services and orientations that individuals generate from their abilities to deal with their environment and which further develop, refine, and transcend their nature" (Kwiatkowski 2015: 244, translated from German by the author of this text).

Following this thought we can identify different kinds of cultural landscapes. We do not even have to dig deep into cultural studies to come to the conclusion that a place is never just a "Euclidian zone," as it depends on its inhabitant's cultural heritage and living environment. For example, to those who grew up in the mountains or in cities that are very hilly, the flat land of Berlin with its urban structure can seem constricting, while for someone who grew up on the plains themselves, Berlin's streets are spacious and not restricting at all. Space, as a human environment, is subject to cultural influences, and so can the perception of a place be determined by its meaning or atmospheric qualities. These contexts create symbolic and figurative areas for society, as for some tourists the city of Berlin stands symbolically for the—in the meantime commercialized—"Berliner freedom." Marking a territory to create a symbolic zone may not take more than drawing the line with a "special" taste for music, as Sarah Thornton describes in her book *Club Cultures*.

> One of the main ways in which youth carve out virtual, and claim actual, space is by filling it with their music. Walls of sound are used to block out the clatter of family and flatmates, to seclude the private space of the bedroom with records and radio and even to isolate 'head space' with personal stereos like the Walkman. (Thornton 1996: 19)

For this reasoning the most important characteristics of a cultural spot will be the social space—a nonspecific zone where individuals can come together and interact with each other. As Pierre Bourdieu defines it, these cultural fields reflect social and gender-specific conditions. These areas are produced by parties (or collectives as they refer to them in their course of action) (Thornton 1996). For example just think of Berlin's most known club Berghain, which would not be so significant without the reference and engagement of a queer and artisan scene. In his lecture (2019), Wolfram invokes the theory of the third place by Ray Oldenburg. The proposal suggests that for a healthy existence, citizens must live within the harmony of three realms: private life, workplace, and inclusively sociable fields, alias the third place. These spots can be really different: they can be a coffee house, a marketplace, bars, hairdresser salons, or any other place which has grown in the hearts of the people. These socializing spots are important for a lively collective dynamic and essential for democracy. In other words, these places promote not only the economy of sociability for their regulars but can play important roles in their collective history and how they organize their community (Oldenburg 1991). So the theory suggests that a bookstore can be more than walls with curated books and other items, but as Wolfram acknowledges it, most often (but not exclusively) institutions ignore how important the emotional aspect of interaction between individuals, place, and time can be. If the emotional aspects of this triangle meet, an area or spot could arise as a cultural space that becomes then a third place, a realm for socializing (Wolfram 2019).

Looking through Echo Bücher's shared pictures on Facebook (Echo Bücher 2013) we can see a lively social field, so we could assume that the level of emotional interaction between the triangle of time/store/individuals was a given. Even without these remarks, anybody who is really into a niche can comprehend how much emotional value a spot has in which you can find plenty of things related to that niche—it makes you react like Pavlov's dog. In the case of Echo Bücher we can identify the items and name the ten bestselling books in the EDM-related nerd's heaven as well as contemplate people's preferences.[1] The most sold book—not so surprisingly—was *Klang der Familie: Berlin, Techno und die Wende* (2014) by Felix Denk and Sven von Thülen published at Suhrkamp, and in tenth place we can find Mark Fisher's *Ghosts of My Life: Writings on Depression, Hauntology and Lost Futures* (2014) from Zero Books publishing.[2] Berlin is definitely a city that captured people's imaginations on a global scale in the last century and it still does now at the beginning of the twenty-first century. Meanwhile it became an undeniable truth that after the fall of the Wall the emerging techno scene was an important factor in reshaping Berlin and making it the new epicenter of a unique culture. *Klang der Familie* is about this emerging subculture, about those who stood in the center of it as well as those who interacted with its peripheries. Adding significant stories to the city's historic narrative and portraying a vibrant time when everything felt possible for its denizens. But can a scene have such a cultural effect?

As Thornton (1996) states, even though thinkers of the twentieth century like Baudrillard and Adorno dismissed the discotheque because for one it was seen as a cultural black hole and for the other as rhythmic obedience, there is more to electronic music culture than banal and standardized conformism. The book deals with subcultural ideologies—in its approach it does not trivialize the dance and nightlife behavior of young people but rather sees the behavior "as ideologies which fulfill the specific cultural agendas of their beholders. Subcultural ideologies are a means by which youth imagine their own and other social groups" (Thornton 1996: 10). Here they also create their own personas so that they can lose the image of the faceless masses: a hippie, a rocker, a punk, an emo, or even a hipster (though that was more likely in the 1940s) were/are these kind of personas. In order to navigate between the ideologies, Thornton adopted the French sociologist Pierre Bourdieu's theory about cultural capital and how personal taste correlates with social status. In her interpretation, Bourdieu's cultural capital—the sum of the entire knowledge a person gathers through their upbringing and education that then grants their social status—becomes subcultural capital, which is slightly different in that it reassures the status quo of its owner in the eye of the relevant beholder. As the protagonists of *Klang der Familie* tell their stories, and with Thornton's theory in the back of our

---

[1]Echo Bücher's founder David Armengou kindly provided me with some information about the store and its closure.

[2]The entire list of the most sold books is listed at the end of this chapter.

head, we can see how crucial these socioeconomic backgrounds and the cultural capital of the people were for in order for this scene to evolve and promote its own sociopolitical views.

But what are these ideologies that EDM culture tries to share with us, and how successful can these ideologies be? And can a third place like a bookstore be an essential part of their success?

The first question is a tricky one because answering this would in every way expand this chapter's frame, but by digging into techno's birthplace (Garnier and Brunn-Lambert 2014) and delineating the emotions, thoughts, and the cultural influences which emanated from it, we might be able to sketch a foundation for it. The Detroit connection was named as the time when the real magic happened—labels from there were already brands for the Berlin scene. Underground Resistance's first performance hooked people instantly and never let them go. As Robert Hood describes it:

> The Underground Resistance message was militant. It was about a city trying to survive and recover amidst unemployment, the crack epidemic, Reagonomics. Automotive factories were closing, people were losing their jobs and turning to drugs. We had struggling single parents just trying to survive. But the message was also about hope and rising up. It was a message against the music industry, against dependence on big, corporate music, against selling your soul to the powers that be. It was a powerful, in-your-face attack on the powers that be. Our attitude was confrontational: we make no compromises. We can't be controlled. We *take* control. (Denk and Thülen 2014: 141)

Reading further how he sensed the nexus between Berlin and Detroit at the time of their first show is alluring:

> The vault was an unusual location. It was dark and murky, a very underground, subterranean atmosphere. I remember it being very smoky—just perfect. An ideal setting for an Underground Resistance show. That was very indicative of the Detroit-Berlin connection. It was shortly after the fall of the Berlin Wall, and there was this resurgence of a new electronic sound—more brutal, more assertive. Before, it was more of a fantasy-based electronic sound; now, it was more reality-based and in tune with what was happening in the world, with the fall of the Wall and the political situation. It was about survival and mankind coming together. (Denk and Thülen 2014: 147–148)

The dark, thoughtful to its core, experimental music is a far reach from the mainstream, billion-dollar industry techno became in the 2000s and 2010s. Today, the Berlin and worldwide scene is more likely to appear as a hedonistic and apolitical audience, mostly White and European (Thornton 1996; Beta 2015). In regards to other cities worldwide, you may not find so many protest parties as in Berlin, and still you cannot shake the lingering feeling of hollowness at happenings like Zug der Liebe, CSD, or AfD wegbassen of the network Reclaim Club Culture that is against Nazis. The message is political but is their audience?

Thornton (1996) explored this question and has a very German answer to it: jein.[3] The politics of popular culture is way more complex than some research would

[3]Jein (more rarely *jain*) is a suitcase word from the words *yes* and *no* and has the meaning yes and no. It is mostly used when a question cannot be answered unequivocally or even simultaneously

suggest—probably due to its "infant years." Most researches saw it in simple dichotomies like us versus them, mainstream versus alternative, and so on (Thornton 1996). Instead of a single-minded worldview, clubbers create an alternative universe where they have the opportunity to create and redefine themselves rather than to give in to a socioeconomic order where civil possibilities devolve into hollow echoes. The "logic of subcultural capital reveals itself most clearly by what it dislikes and what it emphatically isn't" (Thornton 1996: 115). Even so, the crowd of the dance club miraculously resolves certain contradictions of society. It also recreates these structures and enjoys these benefits. Mainstream has the power to evoke and please the desire of social belonging:

> to put themselves in the big picture, imagine their social world, assert their cultural worth, claim their subcultural capital. As such the mainstream is a trope which betrays how beliefs and tastes which ensue from a complex social structure, in turn, determine the shapes of social life. This is the 'double nature' of social reality. (Thornton 1996: 115)

The discourse often turns to the feeling of liberation by the scene, but in fact this is misleading, as the line between political and affective freedom is being crossed here—these freedoms are not equal. For example, though some female vocalists use empowering lyrics, this does not change the fact that degrading/low-key music always has a female connotation. Pop is never male (Thornton 1996). In theory there is an interest for more political engagement, but how can you get an audience to listen with open ears?

If Oldenburg (1991) is correct, third places can encourage dialectic interaction between individuals in communities and so benefit social changes. Following this logic, a bookstore and other third places can be areas benefitting the discourse. So why is it that this music, this kind of resistance, does not happen anymore? Where is the music of the new era? Where is the change? As Mark Fisher puts it: frankly, it never arrived.

In his book *Ghosts of My Life* (2014) Fisher argues that we are frozen in time, as motion is suspended and the future cannot pass the standstill of the present, similar to the Jarmusch vampires—everlasting pictures of marbled individuals eagerly waiting for a new era to arrive, but constantly frustrated by the lingering and persistent sense of waiting for Godot. We are trapped in the twentieth century—we never even entered the twenty-first. "The feeling of belatedness, of living after the gold rush, is as omnipresent as it is disavowed" (Fisher 2014: 15). The feeling of a nostalgic wave is not a psychological state of the mind, as a situation of this magnitude only arises when the historical notion of time shatters. In this entropical case, nostalgia is a symptom, a craving for a form. Fischer (2014) sees the analogy, for example, in the popcultural behemoth *Star Wars*, where the only purpose for technology is to disguise the archaic form of the saga. It is the complete opposite application of technology then in, for instance, the case of Kraftwerk, where technology serves as a tool to invent a new form. He cites several interpretations of the pathology of

with yes or no, or when you want to answer a question with reservations (Bibliographisches Institut GmbH 2019).

transitoriness, and even though he has no straight answer one thing is clear, popular culture did not escape the epidemy. Electronic music—once the epitome of the future—lost its edge and has shown no sign(s) of escaping this dead end. "Music culture is in many ways paradigmatic of the fate of culture under post-Fordist capitalism. At the level of form, music is locked into pastiche and repetition" (Fisher 2014: 22). Post-Fordist capitalism takes away the space and the opportunity from an artist to pause worklife, not giving them the time to explore new forms of art (Fisher 2014).

As the capitalism of the postmodern destroys cultural places and puts them into brackets, social dialog cannot happen—society misses the chance to turn exclusion to inclusion, to let people meet eye to eye. Even though Marx's specters are lost on the blood-tripping lovers, they are the eerie manifestation of this hauntology which yearns for a new era to come. A new art, a state-of-the-art music, a unique form. To move again, to breathe again. But these changes cannot possibly be modeled without cultural spaces, third places, and that is why we need even a small niche bookstore—to spread educated resistance that understands the need for intersectionality. It not only resists but changes structures. We need new forms, and not just in music.

References

Beta, A. (2015). Electronic warfare: The political legacy of detroit techno. *Pitchfork.* Accessed September 4, 2019, from https://pitchfork.com/features/electric-fling/9588-electronic-warfare-the-political-legacy-of-detroit-techno/

Bibliographisches Institut GmbH. (2019). *Duden.* Accessed September 5, 2019, from https://www.duden.de/rechtschreibung/jein

Denk, F., & von Thülen, S. (2014). *Der Klang der Familie. Berlin, techno and the fall of the wall.* Norderstedt: BoD-Books on Demand.

Echo Bücher. (2013). *Facebook.* Accessed September 4, 2019, from https://www.facebook.com/EchoBuecher/

Fisher, M. (2014). *Ghost of my life: Writings on depression, hauntology and lost futures.* Croydon: zero books.

Garnier, L., & Brunn-Lambert, D. (2014). *Elektroschock. Die Geschichte der elektronischen Tanzmusik.* Höfen: Hannibal Verlag.

Kwiatkowski, G. (Ed.). (2015). *Philosophie-Das Fachlexikon von A-Z.* Berlin: Dudenverlag.

Oldenburg, R. (1991). *The great good place: Cafes, coffee shops, community centers, beauty parlors, general stores, bars, hangouts, and how they get you through the day.* New York: Marlowe & Company.

Thornton, S. (1996). *Club cultures – music, media and subcultural capital.* Hanover: University Press of New England.

Wolfram, G. (2019). *KIWit.* Accessed August 28, 2019, from https://www.kiwit.org/kultur-oeffnet-welten/positionen/position_10816.html

Echo Bücher's Most Sold Books from July 2013 to July 2018

Byrne, D. (2012). *How music works*. Edinburgh: Canongate.

Carlyle, A., & Lane, C. (Eds.). (2011). *On listening*. Axminster: Uniformbooks.

Chick, S. (2010). *Ninja tune: 20 years of beats and pieces (Labels unlimited)*. London: Black Dog Publishing.

Denk, F., & von Thülen, S. (2014). *Der Klang der Familie. Berlin, Techno and the fall of the wall*. Norderstedt: BoD-Books on Demand.

Fisher, M. (2014). *Ghosts of my life: Writings on depression, hauntology and lost futures*. zero books.

Keller, C., & Macias A. (2012). *Come on in my Kitchen, The Robert Johnson Book* (Traveler Edition). Geneva: JRP Ringier.

Lane, C., & Carlyle, A. (2013). *In the field: The art of field recording*. Axminster: Uniformbooks.

Lawrence, T. (2009). *Hold on to your dreams: Arthur Russell and the Downtown music scene*. Durham: Duke University Press.

Obrist, H. U. (2013). *A brief history of new music*. Geneva: JRP Ringier.

Rapp, T. (2009). *Lost and sound: Berlin, Techno und der Easyjetset*. Suhrkamp: Frankfurt am Main.

Rodgers, T. (2010). *Pink noises: Women on electronic music and sound*. Durham: Duke University Press.

Young, R. (2005). *Warp: Labels unlimited*. London: Black Dog Publishing.

Chapter 4
The Berlin Techno Myth and Issues of Diversity

About the Connections Between Techno, the Muting of Diverse Perspectives, Inequalities and the Persisting Need for Platforms Like Female:Pressure

Bianca Ludewig

Abstract In this chapter I will give an overview of diversity issues within the field of electronic (dance) music and Berlin club cultures. This perspective is taken from the viewpoint of a member of the female:pressure network and a scholar of popular music studies and cultural studies. This chapter starts out to grasp the issue of diversity within the context of my PhD research on German and Austrian avant-garde festivals or transmedia festivals (I define transmedia festivals, as urban festivals which showcase not only club and experimental electronic music, but alongside a diverse range of other art forms such as discourse, media art, sound art, sculpture/installation, or performance that are often linked to technology). By unraveling the quest for more diversity in club cultures, I will start with a discussion on gender inequality and how these are linked to technology, introduce the platform female:pressure and discuss the muting of diverse perspectives in the history of club cultures. I also point out some of the myths that have been repeatedly contested about Berlin techno, as repeating them does not make them facts, it made these tales just more suspicious; or at least incomplete (at the cost of other groups and sub-cultures). Subsequently I connect this discussion with the booming business of techno in Berlin and close with pointing out the recent rise of collectives and the challenge of collective problem-solving, and end with a bird's-eye view of the issues at stake. The title of the book *The "New" Age of Electronic Dance Music and Club Culture* is very much inviting such an investigation. This is done via a mix of personal accounts and discussing the work of other scholars, media coverage, and video documentation.

B. Ludewig (✉)
University of Vienna, Vienna, Austria

Berlin, Germany
e-mail: bianca.ludewig@wiseup.de

A. Jóri, M. Lücke (eds.), *The New Age of Electronic Dance Music and Club Culture*, Music Business Research, https://doi.org/10.1007/978-3-030-39002-0_4

4.1 Introduction

At the beginning of my PhD research project on avant-garde festivals in electronic music, I did an internship at a prominent Berlin festival of this type in 2014. One of my jobs was to help organize the magazine for the festival edition and I had to draw attention to the curator in charge that there were no female*[1] authors planned for the issue and that we should consider including female writers as well. My own awareness was not only shaped by personal experience (as a former music journalist but not limited to that) and by the conversations in the female:pressure[2] list serve. In general, female:pressure functions as an international network where members can exchange information. This might be: Where can I play a gig in a city I visit? Where can I find a place to stay? Who can make my webpage or do photos for my portfolio? Who can help to organize an event with me in city X? Or the other way around—open job offers, scholarships, workshops, and residencies are shared. Furthermore, the newest media coverage and publications about gender and diversity issues in club culture, and first and foremost the latest musical works of the members are posted into the mailing list. Through special topics of interest also discussions emerge, and artists find each other to collaborate on a project—be it an event, an article, a track, or CD compilation. In 2012, female:pressure started to count the participation of female artists within club events, labels, festivals. This was the result of continuing discussion in the mailing list on the booking situation of members, there was a feeling that women were treated and evaluated differently than men and were eventually less represented. So, the idea came up to look more precisely. The outcome was not very pleasing as it turned out that on average only about 10% of the participants at those electronic music events were female (female:pressure 2013).[3] Even more disturbing were the conversations that followed my argument about the absence of females at the festival. Females were thought of as not reliable, less professional, are just not making good music; and why are they not just solving the issue instead of complaining about it? Also, Electric Indigo[4] mentions similar experiences, referring to an interview

[1]Female* is used in this chapter to refer not only to the biological sex of women but also to trans-artists; this includes trans-men and trans-women as they usually relate (if they have to) rather to females than to males. As the following analysis aims to unmask gender stereotypes, it still relies on referring to male and female*. See also Rodgers about this dilemma in fn #5.

[2]"female:pressure is an international network of female, transgender and non-binary artists in the fields of electronic music and digital arts founded by Electric Indigo: from musicians, composers and DJs to visual artists, cultural workers and researchers. [...] female:pressure intends to strengthen networking, communication and representation—a standard instrument to obtain information about artists, contact them, and find out about other, maybe less known women in electronic music all around the globe. [...] The network comprises of almost 2400 members from 75 countries as at March 2019" (female:pressure 2019a).

[3]I remember that also media was at stake in the list discussions and counting but did not make it into statistics.

[4]Electric Indigo is a Viennese DJ and producer. In the 1990s she worked at the Hardwax Record Store in Berlin. In 1998 she founded female:pressure. Today she lives in Vienna and performs and DJs internationally.

featured in The Wire (Allan 2013: 16) where a festival curator of an avant-garde festival said that increasing the number of female artists would reduce the quality of the lineup (Vihaus 2017). Some of these arguments I have heard for years and years over and over again, but it was irritating inside the organization of an innovative avant-garde event. This was not some mainstream electronic music festival where the status quo of social conditions is usually not reflected much or challenged. This happened also constantly in more distinctive environments, as Electric Indigo and myself experienced at a female:pressure talk in a club in Innsbruck. That is why we would make ironic comments and jokes in the list serve, often about festival websites where lineups would appear with photographs and you would see 50+ white male DJs. That was the rule, not the exception.

Now about 5 years later things have changed somewhat. At least in some scenes and circles it is simply the done thing, almost fashionable to include females and nonbinary artists. This is also reflected in the facts surveys that focused after 2015 mainly on festivals (as labels, clubs, or earlier targeted music media turned out to be too brought to handle for the few troublemakers who are in charge of the facts surveys). And it is worth mentioning that the female:pressure surveys have been done without any financial support or funding. Remarkably enough, it would seem that there is no country, institution, or organization which can support such an effort financially. Seemingly, this is for bureaucratic reasons, as research like this fits in no funding scheme if done outside of academia. That is disturbing, also because it would be so important to contextualize the data and explain it, frame it through personal accounts, theories, and research studies on similar issues. Also there would be enough academics within the network who could do it; as this would be an intensive research effort no member could do this extra work on top of the rest as it is commonplace that women still earn less, do most of the family as well as care work, and are more affected by the precarious and insecure working conditions of the present, which prevails in arts and culture. Coming back to the survey: The survey of 2017 included all of the statistics on festivals since 2012, and was done for the first time with the help of a professional statistician. The outcome was that female* participation at festivals had increased to about 17%. To a large amount this is due to the facts surveys in themselves and the following media attention and distribution, the pressure it was able to build up.

4.2 Female:Pressure—Why Have Not They Been Heard All Along?

In 2018 the female:pressure network (henceforth f:p) celebrated 20 years of existence and one could wonder why only numbers and graphics started to raise attention, even though founder Electric Indigo and other active musicians who became members like Acid Maria, Tina 303, Gudrun Gut, Donna Maya, Chra, Xyramat, Monika Kruse, AGF or internationally Miss Djax have been around in the scene(s) since the 1990s. And ever since, they try to bring awareness to the static situation of invisibility (or muting) of female musicians and activists from the scenes and its histories. Why did it need numbers and graphics to raise attention for this issue? Why have not they been heard all along?

Gender matters gained more attention in the 1990s as gender mainstreaming became a public issue. The Riot Grrrl Movement was in the media or Lady Fests, later Girls Rock Camps, started to happen in Germany and different scenes started to do events focused on female musicians. In the 2000s in Hamburg, where I grew up, f:p was popping up behind DJ names more often on event flyers. Gender Studies started to appear at universities. I was part of a female radio group in Hamburg, Radio Sankt Paula, and though it was obvious that it was still a long way to go, one had the feeling that something was evolving as others also started their own groups or initiatives focusing on female* issues. I was interested in club music and also started DJing, but I was not part of any specific electronic music scene more popping in and out different club culture scenes. I had also a longer engagement within Hip Hop where the lack of females was notorious. Maybe this optimism toward the techno scenes was due to internationally prominent figures like Berlin radio host Marusha, and artists like Ellen Alien, Miss Kittin, or Kemistry and Storm, who were backed up by locally popular female DJs in Hamburg—especially in the drum and bass scene—and somehow I thought there were many more females in electronic music than in other genres.

That this was not the case became obvious throughout the years, though I have seen plenty of female musicians and DJs and bought their records. Also due to the scenes I frequented, and my personal bias, it was constantly disturbing that at some events and festivals they were not present, also their presence in the media was rare (not only in reports, reviews, or cover stories, but also as journalists. In the Hip Hop magazines that I wrote for in the 2000s, there were hardly *any* other female journalists). It became unmistakably obvious that things were not improving when I started researching electronic music and club culture at university. Ten years ago there were far fewer publications on electronic music or club culture than today, and females* were rarely mentioned in art music and club culture. The number of publications increased throughout the years, and in the 2010s there was literally a boom of documentation and publications on electronic music, especially focusing on Germany and Berlin. In those attempts to write the German history of electronic music, female* musicians were missing. For example, I was surprised that Electric Indigo is not mentioned in one of these histories of Berlin Club Culture, her having worked from 1993 until 1996 at the infamous Hardwax Record Store and having DJed several nights a week on average.

As I had seen many female DJs in different settings, it became obvious that they have been somehow deleted from music history.[5] I assumed that it could be due to

[5]Of course this is not only happening in music, as a scholar of cultural studies I was shocked that in a book released in 2006 on contemporary cultural theory out of 44 introduced important thinkers in cultural studies only 4 were women. And I add for those who do not know that the majority of

the bad reputation of feminism during the end of the 1990s and first decade of the 2000s, where feminism and its appearances in the media seemed outdated, compared to the new technology and startup mentality infused into urban mainstream. Some female artists would refuse to play at female-only lineups or events, as this could damage their reputation and market value. What seemed to be the most powerful tool in the music business were male networks of support. This is also emphasized by Electric Indigo in the article mentioned above; this is the reason why some fellow DJs and musicians do not want to join f:p—as taking a feminist stance can be a stigma in this industry sector. This is also stressed by Angela McRobbie (2007) in several articles, especially in *Top Girls?*, where she explains how young women today are forced into a "post-feminist masquerade" so that they can become hyper-active as creative workers and in consumer culture which they are encouraged to. Their pivotal role in the new global labor market coincides with a fading away of feminism and the women's movement (McRobbie 2007: 719) and young women become an "intensively managed subject of post-feminist, gender-aware biopolitical practices of new governmentality" (McRobbie 2007: 723). Women have to show-case a spectacular femininity in their quest to become part of public life, and the political sphere according to McRobbie (and we can recognize this also in the world of electronic music, where very often, successful female DJs and producers are spectacularly beautiful and feminine. Cases such as US footwork producer Jlin[6] remain an exception). But instead of the much desired independence the biopolitical practices eventually diminish activity in the sphere of formal politics and civic society, McRobbie talks of a "feminist tragedy" (McRobbie 2007: 734). Coming back to club culture, which is just as much a part of this brave new world of work paved by insecurities, other Viennese DJs and event organizers mention in the same article the unbroken importance of personal networks for bookings in the club scene and that these are still male dominated (Vihaus 2017). And it is probably no coincidence that the musician Astrid Gnosis[7] was booked by the same Austrian event organizers at Hyperreality in 2019, after describing her experiences in *Kaltblut Magazine* 2018: "The most challenging has been to learn to rely on myself alone. To see my friends turn into enemies, to have no mentors. It's been hard to be insulted and humiliated for being a strong woman. It's been the hardest to ultimately

students in cultural studies are women*. This amounts interestingly to the first ratio of the female: pressure survey, only that here more women* than men are involved, at least in the past 30 years.

[6]Jlin is an Afro-American DJ and producer from Indiana, seemingly indifferent to codes of femininity displaying a casual gender-neutral style. Her debut album of 2015 was a little sensation in the world of club and electronic music and received critical praise.

[7]Astrid Gnosis is a multidisciplinary artist working with sound, video, and performance, who has Colombian roots and grew up in Spain and now lives in London. As her main influences she mentions Dutch hardcore, hip-hop, rave and pop. As though herself and the article locate her in hardcore techno, at a presentation about my book on gabber and breakcore I quote her and play a video of hers, later some of the male attendees and musicians stress that she is not hardcore. And genre purism seems like a mechanism to exclude women eventually as a lot of female DJs and musicians do not want limit themselves to one style or genre.

understand that before my ideas people see me as a threat to an established order of things. It is more commonly expected to need others to be strong [. . .]. It's been hard to see the idiots winning. The biggest challenge to getting my work out has been to build an audience, without opportunities to play live. As a solo artist, with no representation, well it feels like screaming inside an empty well" (Hussain 2018). In the same article in *The Gap* musicologist Rosa Reitsamer, who published a book on the DIY music careers of DJs with a Vienna case study (Reitsamer 2013), mentions that men and women are both facing a tough competition, and that women still have outsider positions due to which they are facing more control and monitoring of their peers. Here quality control is much tighter than for the male peers (Reitsamer 2013). This seems closely related to the discontent members addressed in the mailing list that kicked off the facts surveys.

Scholar and musician Tara Rodgers did an in-depth study on the history of electronic music, and interviewed 24 female musicians in the field of experimental electronica in her book *Pink Noises*. In her introduction she explains that "many men were supportive, but electronic music cultures overall seemed to discourage or deny women's participation. This was made clear by the lack of substantive coverage of women in electronic music magazines and history books" (Rodgers 2010: 3). Presence and diversity of expressions by women working with sound was profoundly underestimated over the last century according to Rodgers. Questions are being raised as to who has access to tools and opportunities for creative expression, and "how women artists are represented in mainstream media," writes Rodgers (2010: 5). Tropes like noise or experimentalism in existing electronic music histories have as of yet "conjured a canon of male composers and writers" (Rodgers 2010: 5). That is why a broad critique of gender issues across multiple histories linked to electronic music is necessary, according to Rodgers. Music culture privileges planned obsolescence. Electronic music histories have been setting the parameters of who and what counts as invention, production, or making noise according to certain ideologies and politics, the author believes (Rodgers 2010: 5–6). Rodgers attempts to write a counter history of female* accounts,[8] because "some of the most important contributions to the study of electronic music and sound have positioned women as outside the scope of study" (Rodgers 2010: 11; Kahn 1999: 13–14); defined DJ cultures as distinctively masculine with relative inattention to women's participation in these cultures (Reynolds 1998: 274–275) or "used observational statistics, such as fewer than one in ten DJs is female, to explain women's absence from the text" (Rodgers 2010: 11). Reitsamer (Vihaus 2017) stresses that while there might be still less women* active in electronic music production and DJ culture, underrepresentation is not an argument to exclude them from bookings and lineups and to marginalize them further. Her study, although not focused on females* is also an attempt to write females* back into music history and represent their presence.

[8]"I rely notoriously on the terms women and men to frame the project because these social categories significantly affect the organization of electronic music histories [. . .]" (Rodgers 2010: 4).

4.3 Gender and Technology

Rosa Reitsamer (Vihaus 2017) explains that the connection of technology and masculinity structures society, and that this leads to coding expertise in the field of technology being perceived as masculine. Rebekah Farrugia, author of *Beyond the Dance Floor* did a test search with the phrases "toys for boys" and "toys for girls" on Amazon and the results featured in the top ten recommendations were "monster truck custom shop, tool kit, science kit and rocket kit" for boys and "jewellery box, tea set, cookware and bracelet-making kit" for girls (Farrugia 2012: 20). The recommended toys for girls have no connection to technology. This might be another reason why women are still largely ignored as music producers. In an interview with *Pitchfork* (Hopper 2015) Björk stated that she often does not get the credits for her production work, invited remixers and coproducers do.[9] She admits that she did not talk about the issue because she did not want to act defensive, but for the sake of other women she decided to speak up: "I want to support young girls who are in their 20s now and tell them: *You're not just imagining things*. It's tough. Everything that a guy says once, you have to say five times. Girls now are also faced with different problems. I've been guilty of one thing: After being the only girl in bands for 10 years, I learned—the hard way—that if I was going to get my ideas through, I was going to have to pretend that they—men—had the ideas. I became really good at this and I don't even notice it myself". As a possible act of prevention, she recommended taking photos in the studio of the production process so that the image of women working with production gear gets into the minds of the mainstream. This was picked up by electronic music producer Antye Greie-Ripatti (AGF) who created a tumblr blog (female:pressure 2019b) dedicated to photos of women making music. Here pioneers as well as women from all over the world are seen in the mix, in the studio and out in the world making field recordings. This is obviously necessary, and Rebekah Farrugia gives some arguments why.

Farrugia (2012) argues that the status quo relationship of gender and technology as masculine was constructed by discourses and subsequently became naturalized. This affects women's access to electronic music technology, the networks and spaces in which they circulate. Technology is not inherently masculine but has been labeled as such as a result of "constructed narratives, rhetorical devices and material practices" (Farrugia 2012: 20). She agrees with Rodgers when she stresses that women have been systematically written out of technologies' collective memory (Farrugia 2012: 20). It led to the point that femininity seemed incompatible with

[9]"I didn't want to talk about that kind of thing for 10 years, but then I thought, 'You're a coward if you don't stand up. Not for you, but for women. Say something.' So around 2006, I put something on my website where I cleared something up, because it'd been online so many times that it was becoming a fact. It wasn't just one journalist getting it wrong, *everybody* was getting it wrong. I've done music for, what, *30 years*? I've been in the studio since I was 11; [...] I've sometimes thought about releasing a map of all my albums and just making it clear who did what. But it always comes across as so defensive that, like, it's pathetic. I could obviously talk about this for a long time" (Hopper 2015).

technological competence. The innate relationship between man and technology begins with childhood and continues into adulthood and is expressed across popular music genres, the music industry, scenes, or practices (Farrugia 2012: 21). Through the marketing of radio technology to high fidelity systems, women have been distanced further from audio technology, which leads to ways of participation in music scenes that are coded as "feminine" (Farrugia 2012: 22). The classroom is another influential place where gender stereotypes about audio and music tech are reproduced. For subcultural engagement this means that in contrast to the ethos of active male rebellion, girls' involvement with music has been linked to consumerism and passiveness instead of creative practices in the history of subcultural studies: "In many cases, the efforts of women who chose to play instruments and form bands have been overlooked or written out of the picture" (Farrugia 2012: 24).

Also, Brewster and Broughton state in their celebrated book *Last Night a DJ saved my Life* on the history of the DJ that in the 94-year history of DJing, women have been largely frozen out of the picture with few exceptions (Brewster and Broughton 2000: 377). They claim that new club culture scenes offer more possibilities for women, but end there without explaining this further. Thus, for Farrugia it is not surprising that "EDM has developed as a male centric space that mirrors most other popular music genres and the mainstream music industry" (2012: 27). Angela McRobbie (1994) observed that EDM reproduced "the same sexual division of labour which exist[ed] not just in the pop music industry but in most other types of work and employment" (Farrugia 2012: 28). Referring to several authors (McRobbie 1994; Redhead et al. 1998; Reynolds 1999), Farrugia recounts that women in the 1990s would take part in EDM mainly as participants; and when women engaged in roles beyond the dance floor, they were usually in low-level positions such as helping out on the till/entrance, working behind the bar or distributing flyers. "This is not to dismiss women's participation in these capacities, but rather to highlight how women's ability to pursue both power and pleasure further up the hierarchy of rave and DJ culture was limited" (Farrugia 2012: 28).

According to Farrugia, the changing climate of sexual politics in the 1990s due to third-wave feminism, popularized in music via the Riot Grrrl movement was not noticeably reflected in EDM culture, while record collecting is another factor that she defines as "homosocial" (Farrugia 2012: 28). Referring to Sarah Thornton and her book *Club Cultures* (1996), she notes the masculine bias of subcultural capital and the gatekeeping mechanisms of club culture. Also, Simon Reynolds (1999) attests that the presence of women on the dance floor is not reflected by the proportion of women in the ranks of professional DJs. This is due to the tricks of the trade which are passed down from mentors to male acolytes which include the accumulation of exhaustive and arcane information about labels and producers. If female DJs appeared on public relations materials, Farrugia notes, they would rarely be rhetorically constructed along the same lines as their male colleagues: "despite early rave culture's philosophical grounding in peace, love, unity and respect" (Farrugia 2012: 31). These gender inequalities strengthen Reynolds' (1999) assessment that even at rave's height, the agenda of peace, love, unity, and respect was more myth than reality.

4.4 The Construction of Electronic Music History and the Muting of Diverse Perspectives

Most overviews of club culture past or present are overwhelmingly positive and note that hierarchies are less restricting and limiting than in other subcultures; they offer more freedom for women and men alike. In accordance with other scholars (Weinzierl 2000; Gilbert and Pearson 1999; Reynolds 1999) Farrugia (2012: 32) notes that this equality "does not apply to participation further up the ladder for DJs or producers". Various scholars claim (Thornton 1996; Reynolds 1998) that certain aspects shifted throughout the 1990s for EDM, e.g., the celebrity star status first absent in club and DJ culture. It also shifted location, from rave spaces to club venues—largely due to law enforcements that sought to stop illegal raves and anarchistic attitudes. Due to commodification processes, celebrity thus becomes important, as it is increasingly necessary to attract consuming visitors to clubs for revenue. While at first everybody was important to shape the party experience the attention now shifts again to stars. She concludes that "the freedom women experience on the dance floor is not reflected on the stage or in production studios" (Farrugia 2012: 33).

The erasure of females is demonstrated vividly by Rodgers through the example of the documentary *Modulations: Cinema For The Ear* (1998) about the evolution of electronic music in the twentieth century. In the credits about 80 informants are listed and all of them were men. The only time women are visible is in a factory in Japan where women engage in repetitive labor assembling and testing keyboard synthesizers: "The wide shot of anonymous female laborers contrasts sharply with the close-up angles and star treatment of the individual male experts in the surrounding scenes. [...] Women are aligned with the reproduction of mass-produced goods, while men are positioned as cultural producers and arbiters of aesthetic innovation" (Rodgers 2010: 14). Rodgers suggests in her analysis that women are not completely absent but used as contrasts and metaphors of the feminine or maternal "to establish a male subjectivity in sound and reproduce priorities of a male-defined culture" (ibid.: 14–15). This reveals a particular ideology and politics of gender.

Judith Keilbach (2016) comes to similar conclusions in her analysis of the film, *We Call It Techno!* (2008). Following Keilbach through the documentary, fragments, interviews, conversations, and statements are selected and combined in a way that they resemble a whole new narrative. This is a very popular way of documenting contemporary history. There are endless other video or film documentaries on techno [*Sub Berlin. The Story of Tresor* (2012), *Sound of Berlin* (2018), *Berlin '90s. Der Sound der Wende* (2015), *Party auf dem Todesstreifen* (2014)] and also popular books on techno in Berlin are following this "talking heads" collage pattern (e.g., Denk and van Thülen 2014). For Keilbach, this is a decontextualization and it is opposite to what oral history is trying to accomplish. Here the interviewees are transformed into witnesses of history and their role is to verify through their testament the intention of the filmmakers/directors (Keilbach 2016: 98). Keilbach sums up the narrative by some main tropes; these are: artists/producers and audience were identical, everybody could participate, techno was a democratic sound—a sort of dancefloor socialism, techno united Eastern and Western Germany, techno was a (sub)culture made in Germany. For Keilbach, techno as a democratic social experience seems more like a myth, the given evidence turning out to be ambivalent as *We Call It Techno!* hides its intention behind the words of the interviewed witnesses. This hidden narrative authority only accentuates certain selective aspects of the history.

Techno is depicted as a movement free of hierarchies, dominated by unity, equality, and democratic principles. Aspects like technology or music industry are not picked up by the directors. The concept of techno as a German pop culture has been invented too—by taking techno out of its transnational context and discussing it as a phenomenon born out of German reunification, and even mapping it as such (Keilbach 2016: 100–101). Furthermore, references to the gay scenes are not taken up. By following this narrative other groups are blanked out. The montage evokes the impression that gays entered techno after it turned mainstream, whereas gay scenes have been vital within techno since its inception (Keilbach 2016: 101–102).

In the film the early techno scene is displayed as a group of White hetero guys and as such the film undermines its own hypothesis of techno as a democratic community where everybody could participate (Keilbach 2016: 102). Out of 25 interviewees 24 are White males and German speaking; only one woman is interviewed. Keilbach shows that the interview with (and of) Elsa for Toys is different from the others as all the others are shown as music experts whereas she is introduced as a visual artist who ran into the Loveparade accidentally while shopping. After this another statement mentions that fashion designers were present at the Loveparade. For Keilbach this puts Elsa for Toys in the stereotypical role related to female interests like fashion and shopping. Whereas the guys talk about the music, she talks about the visual aspects.[10] "The selection of the interviewed and their fragments suggest that responsibilities within techno are split and distributed according to gender specific aspects: the guys did the music and the women the decoration" (Keilbach 2016: 102, translated by the author).

Keilbach believes that ambivalence is normalized through montage. She closes with the statement that documentaries like this are full of contradictions and ambivalences and thus they ask for counter-narratives, counterstatements, and opposing accounts[11] (Keilbach 2016: 103)—just like what Rodgers is trying to do regarding women* in electronic music and sound history. Rodgers concludes from her in-depth research that the question of "who is counted in electronic music historiography is inevitably informed by the politics of social and professional networks, and by

[10]This is also stated by Therese Kaiser of Femdex: "I think that this is the dynamic of a certain development: the guys do the music and the women do the entrance, the flyers or decoration" (Vihaus 2017, translation by the author).

[11]Another crucial aspect in my opinion is that always the same artists are interviewed over and over again in latter books and documentaries as if there were no other relevant protagonists involved in the making of Berlin techno. Obviously it is not about an in-depth research that brings forward new aspects but rather about attaching popular names to ones work.

limited definitions and standards of achievement" (Rodgers 2010: 15). She stresses that the public face of electronic music be it on releases, magazine covers, international festivals, scholarly publications, or films, "is typically male and does a certain kind of symbolic work" (Rodgers 2010: 15). Even though this might happen unknowingly in films or books due to a lack of awareness, the outcome stays the same and this kind of symbolic work is reproductive. For Electric Indigo society at large is reflected in scenes "nothing is isolated and thus structures are reproduced. This is only obstructed when gender justice and the like become explicit objectives of the scenes" (Vihaus 2017, translated by the author).

4.5 The Myth of Berlin Techno and the Reunification

In many video documentaries, books or journalistic essays about the emergence of Berlin techno in the 1990s club culture is portrayed as a White phenomenon. The various manifestations of Black music, which was a huge influence on the Berlin club scene due to the presence of American soldiers and the GI Discos in the city, is largely neglected. This blends perfectly into an image of a city where East and West are united and in which techno is the soundtrack of a new Berlin. In this newly constructed image as a story of German reunification and the birth of Berlin club culture, techno is described as very open and heterogeneous scene, in which all are welcome and usual prejudices are swept aside. It is presented as an upheaval of previous hierarchies, and radical openness within the arena of the dancefloor and many new liberties and opportunities. But this narrative has some blind spots. That is stressed in some analytical works of Alexander G. Weheliye, professor of African-American Studies at Northwestern University where he teaches Black literature and culture, critical theory, social technologies, and popular culture. In an interview Weheliye mentions:

> I see narrativisation of the reunification and the birth of Berlin techno and the Berlin republic as part of a much longer tradition of thinking about Germany and German-ness. [. . .] The reunification is typically imagined in mainstream histories as a seamless blending together of East and West, which leaves out the virulent racism and violence during this period, especially against non-white bodies. (Goh 2015: 41)

For Weheliye, and also for me, it is incomprehensible that in these narratives the pogroms are still largely omitted. A series of violent racist attacks took place in Hoyerswerda in 1991, Hünxe 1991, Rostock Lichtenhagen 1992, in Mölln 1992, or Solingen 1993 (and we can continue this until the present to the NSU trail[12] as a

[12]The *NSU trial* was a trial against several people in connection with the National Socialist Underground (NSU)—an extreme-right terrorist organization in Germany—and the NSU murders. It took place between 2013 and 2018 in Munich. The trial was notable for being one of the largest, longest, and most expensive in German history and made public claims of institutionalized within the German police force who for years ruled out the Neo-Nazis as potential suspects in the killings and instead focused on suspects with Turkish backgrounds.

prominent example). And these were just peaks of constant racist incidents in Germany. The seamless narrative of East and West together in harmony on Berlin's dancefloors endangers the extinction of the pogroms from the German and international collective memory of the reunification period. The ambivalent encounter of German remembrance culture and the Berlin techno narrative was also addressed by Matthias Pasdzierny in *Techno and German Contemporary History* (2016, translation by the author) where he tentatively criticizes[13] the entanglement of techno history with the construction of German identity in the 1990s and after. To him the (postcolonial) approach to deconstructing existing material (books, films etc.) which Weheliye or Keilbach are largely following does not count as evidence, but he follows Keilbach in admitting that these documents are not representing oral history and thus if we want to really analyze these entanglements we would need real oral histories that take the specific forms of remembrance through popular music into account, and thus a serious historiography of techno in Germany has not happened yet.

For Weheliye it is also problematic that these accounts "are also constructing a very particular story about musical cultures in West Berlin during the 1980s before the advent of techno. What is generally left out are the not very elaborate but nevertheless very present black music cultures in GI discos and other clubs that played black music in West Berlin" (Goh 2015: 41). In his analysis these are attempts to disassociate Berlin techno from Black musical influences. Ultimately this prevents a perspective on diverse histories of Berlin techno and of German subcultures and other forms of clubbing. Weheliye wants to highlight that there existed other forms of clubbing and musical cultures, "which are once again being written out of history. This ensures that Berlin techno, Germany, and German-ness are continually being imagined as white" (ibid.). In his argumentation it was necessary for Berlin techno to be imagined as something specific to Berlin and to Germany, "it had to separate itself from Blackness, whether imagined or real" (Goh 2015: 41). He adds that German public and academic discourse denies the existence of race because if the topic is addressed, critics are often put in the position of being too sensitive or of being racist themselves.

This is also emphasized by Paul Gilroy, who conceptualized (about the same time when Berlin techno was rising) the important idea of The Black Atlantic,[14] for him slavery is an integral component of Western civilization and this also continues in Western patterns of thought and argumentation and leads to "racialized reason"

---

[13]"Possibly this is connected with the importance of pop music for the construction of a 'new' German identity in the post-reunification period, which has increased to an unprecedented extent since the 2000s. The techno memory boom should therefore primarily be understood as an important forum for today's negotiation of national identity in reunited Germany and also for the self-image of the new and old capital Berlin as a new 'capital of lightness', whose founding myth today transfigures and commercializes the history of the techno and club scene of the early 1990s" (Pasdzierny 2016: 118).

[14]The Black Atlantic describes the historical and contemporary movements of people of African origin across the Atlantic—from Africa to Europe, in the Caribbean, to America and later vice versa.

(Gilroy 1993: X). For Gilroy the practices of The Black Atlantic describe a counterculture of modernity, which is not just relevant on behalf of Black (Atlantic) peoples "but of the poor, exploited, and downpressed everywhere" (Ludewig 2018a: 75–77; Gilroy 1993: 77). This conception helps to understand the production, circulation, and consumption of music as an elusive dynamic of "politics of race and power" (Ludewig 2018a: 77; Gilroy 1993: 105). So, if we even consider DJ techniques, which have been invented by Afro-American youth or sound system culture practices created in the Caribbean, it becomes obvious that techno culture owes a lot to the Black Atlantic and its new modes of cultural production. In an ambivalent way, tribute is given to Detroit's Underground Resistance within the history of Berlin techno. Weheyile has some, in my opinion unfinished, thoughts about this (Goh 2015), and it is up to future research to analyze this more precisely.

In the case of Berlin techno, this elimination of diverse strands of genre and subculture is not only a question of ethnicity or race, as this is also true for other "White" dominated scenes, (including female artists or gay scenes) but Germany seems to have a special tendency for "whitewashing" its own history, according to Weheyile[15] or Hito Steyerl, which I will now turn to.

The historic entanglements in the case of Berlin are illustrated vividly in an early documentation by artist Hito Steyerl (1998) focusing on the construction site Potsdamer Platz at the end of the 1990s, which was the biggest construction site of Europe at that time. It is an important analytic contribution about contemporary Berlin and questions on power and exclusion. A central theme of the documentation is that where borders are torn down, new ones immediately emerge. Using the history of the construction site as a narrative, where until the end of the Second World War the center of "German" power was located, the documentary illustrates how new manifestations of power arise and also new forms of exclusion. The film unmasks the myth that the fall of the Berlin Wall brought freedom to the citizens of Berlin or Germany (though for single individuals this might be true).

The film starts at the Potsdamer Platz construction site where Dong Yang, a Berlin student of Asian origin, who had been beaten up by Nazis, is interviewed by the filmmaker. He says, "After the fall of the Berlin Wall the Germans we're very excited, I have the feeling that they have forgotten what they are. It would be better for the foreigners if the wall would still be here" (Steyerl 1998: 03:10–03:27). The voiceover reports that after the fall of the wall, the empty strip between the walls was sold to investors. After 2 months protesters came with tents occupying the death strip, because—as one of them explains "Daimler-Benz got the site for nothing and we want to protest against this situation that only the richest of the rich get again these historical places in the city's center. There won't be any more room for people with different attitudes and life-styles, it's all about money" (Steyerl 1998:

[15]For Weyehile German history and historiography "which to a degree are due to the fact that large-scale German colonialism 'only' lasted from the Berlin Conference to the end of World War I. As a result, colonialism and the longstanding presence of people of colour in Germany can be continually disavowed, because not doing so would mean 'un tuning' the white harmonic scaffolding of German collective memory" (Goh 2015: 43).

6:10–6:34). Like Dong Yang, the squatters, who tried in vain to save a part of the empty middle for the general public, belong to the excluded of the post-reunification period.

The documentation blends present events on the construction site with retrospect on significant historical events which happened decades or centuries before near Potsdamer Platz, such as the Berlin Conference of 1875, where "a system of buffer zones, satellite and vassal states was created in the Balkans, [. . .] where the conflicts continue to this day" (Steyerl 1998: 15:40–16:10). Or a few years later, in 1884, the Congo Conference, where the borders for Africa were defined, and according to the narrator, a historic milestone in the economic plunder of Africa was planned and then implemented. And of course, events related to the Second World War, for instance the arrival of more and more forced laborers who had to work in agriculture and in the German industry—Mercedes too relied on the employment of forced laborers.

The occupiers on the construction site are interviewed again. They admit that they do not know how long they will be able to stay, because they are afraid of the increasing nationalism in Germany, which went along with the fall of the wall and grew especially in East Germany. In East Berlin, they say, many squats were attacked by organized fascists. Toward the end a young Chinese woman says that the wall has now gone, but that the purpose of this wall was to regulate territorial relations between people and in that way the wall still exists. The voiceover reports that while Germany is reuniting and the former no-man's-land is being opened for market opportunities, borders elsewhere are consolidated. Several hundred people die on the borders of Europe: they drown, suffocate, freeze to death, or die of thirst. And also within Germany national liberated zones are being put up. More than 20 years later this is still a matter of fact.

4.6 The Business with Club Culture

D. Strauss (2013), former senior editor of *Exberliner*,[16] believes that physical altercations, drugs, conspiracy, money, and reputation are the building blocks of nightlife. Today Berlin's after and before hours became a farce and are currently pure industry. "In 2013, Berlin is a 'hip' city—a brand—and this is something it has never done very well, unless mismatched H&M is one's idea of creativity. The specificity of its ugliness was, at one time, inspiring" (Strauss 2013: 207). Due to globalization, Internet, and gentrification Berlin's fall is inevitable for Strauss. As an example, he takes Bar 25 and its endless and excessive parties dedicated to its nearing end. Admitting that Bar 25 was fun nonetheless, it was to him the beginning of the end for Berlin. Soon after it expired the same people were building a luxury hotel on the same spot. And he wonders how one should respond? He argues that

[16]Berlin Magazine in English, originally for Ex-Pats, founded in 2002.

money laundering investments created the breeding grounds of Berlin as a lifestyle city: "The economy of Berlin does not actually expand but resides on a series of bubbles: real estate, tech, restaurants. The only consistency is European crime money and clubs" (Strauss 2013: 207). Even the city's government is now promoting its nightlife and meanwhile it is selling off iconic symbols like the East Side Gallery to investors. He calls Berlin a *moneyed* world without money. He mentions Bar 25 also as the playground of aristocratic kids rebelling against their families. And adds that "[t]hose aristocratic manners would edge into self-satire, and then over the last couple of years, attain their mature form with Bars such as KingSize, Trust or Tausend, bars that feel like Munich [. . .]. Class is the unspoken root of all German nightlife activity" (Strauss 2013: 208). This is confusing he admits as Berlin used to be a city one fled to specifically to avoid the rich.

Ina Wudtke, who lost her apartment when the building she lived in and two adjacent houses at Prenzlauer Berg were sold to Mr. von Münchhausen in 2006, also stresses this point. Her account of many years fighting the investor includes horrible stories of unruly methods trying to get her and the other tenants out, such as lying and telling every tenant a different story, throwing away all her belongings from the basement, endless and noisy (though often aimless) construction works, gluing black plastic to the windows for months, up to taking off the roof above her, leaving her below a tarpaulin, causing rainfall to pour into her apartment and damaging her belongings, and endless parties by the Münchhausens, their kids, and their rich friends, who all moved in as time went on. And the list continues (Wudtke 2018). Wudtke mentions that Mr. von Münchhausen explained on Wikipedia that his father tried in vain to hide Adolf Hitler's former vice-chancellor Franz von Papen from allied forces. And also Heidrun von Papen moved in: "The kids usually parked their BMWs on the sidewalk right in front of the house and had parties in rotating constellations on the newly-built roof terraces and in the sanitized courtyard [. . .]. The noise of construction by day and parties at night created a horror scenario for the working residents" (Wudtke 2018: 67–68). After 7 years of fighting the investor in endless court cases she had to move out in the name of modernization, as after its modernization she would not afford the rent anymore. The adjacent apartment was sold for 360,000 €, like most apartments in Prenzlauer Berg, Kreuzberg, Neukölln, or Friedrichshain, as most of them have been bought by international investors.

For Strauss the upcoming new paradigm became obvious with a change of aesthetics. This is also reflected in sonic aesthetics, with Berlin's sonic ambition seeming extinguished as almost every bar and smaller club has a sound system ruled by limiters these days. He takes the reader on a walkabout starting in Prenzlauer Berg and Mitte and lists endless names of places now (long) gone, replaced by hotels and bagel shops. Approaching the fall of Berlin, Strauss states that whereas most Berliners did not have money and never expected that they would need it, the tourists who came to stay did not think that way: "the expats, even the poor ones, didn't plan to live as if they were coastal Pakistani fisherman with bottle pfand instead of seafood" (Strauss 2013: 212). Around 2005 he states everybody began moving West en masse, first hitting Kreuzberg at Schlesisches Tor, continuing to Kotti and then inevitably spilling over to Neukölln, formally one of the cities' poorest districts and causing the rents in these areas to increase, and the prices in Neukölln to buy flats are today more expensive than in Prenzlauer Berg and Mitte: "It was all so sudden, and felt like gentrification by confetti bomb—the quickness of the transformation has brought out a touch of nationalism and meanness in the locals, and there are spots like Sameheads, at which one probably has to buy a round every time one hears a word of German" (Strauss 2013: 212).

Strauss says that "the government attempts to promote culture—club culture—as a means of attracting investors" (Strauss 2013: 214). On the other hand it is hard to explain to American Christian Billionaires[17] that a primary appeal of Berlin is about clubbing, gay culture, and doing drugs and he believes that could be the reason why the city is just selling the existing cultural places. He also assumes that is why nightlife empires are more interested in high-end restauranteering these days. Strauss concludes "that Capitalism appears to be transforming in a sort of global Feudalism and Berlin seems to be a particularly active petri dish for the experiments that will affect future generations of potato diggers (under the guise of Soundcloud programmers)" (Strauss 2013: 214). To him, almost every spot of Berlin is now being transformed or abused in the name of marketing, where the aristocrats work hand in hand with politicians[18] which results in new venues like Soho House: "Older clubs built from relative scratch such as Cookies, Watergate or Berghain will be grandfathered in as nouveau riche: never quite respected, but allowed to sit at the Round Table" (Strauss 2013: 214). He closes with what is on its way: the imperial castle[19] that rises before our eyes "and few who pass by wish to storm its gates" (Strauss 2013: 215). Wudtke also created a video work about the resurrection of this "imperial castle," connecting it to the parallel gentrification processes: No money for social housing, but for imperial status dreams.

I wonder if Strauss still lives in Berlin; but he is not the only one painting an uncanny picture of what was, is, and will be in Berlin. I collected about a dozen texts, which also relate the city to music and club culture (e.g., Stahl 2014, collective volume; Bader and Scharenberg 2005, 2010; Henkel and Wolff 1996).

The *Tagesspiegel*, a local Berlin newspaper, recently published (2018) a report on the Berlin techno business with the teaser-title on the cover: "Techno in Berlin is a

[17]The builder-owner of the Mercedes Benz Arena (until 2015 O2 World Arena), was the Anschutz Entertainment group, one of the largest investment companies who owns and runs the biggest arenas, theaters, and entertainment places worldwide. It is owned by Philip Anschutz, a US billionaire, who owns various venues and sports teams in Berlin and against the protest of many the property at the Spree was sold to him. The protests were due to the fact that he is a conservative republican who financed, e.g., campaigns against gays and owns media and research institutes through which his conservative world views are promoted. Strauss refers here to him and the harsh contrast of the promoted image of Berlin opposed to businesses affairs of the city.

[18]For a very good overview how sleaze, corruption, and old boy-networks are ruling Berlin since a long time, unbroken by the reunification see M.D. Rose (1998).

[19]Imperial castle refers to the Berlin City Palace that was demolished in 1950 by the German Democratic Republic authorities. The Palace of the Republic was built in 1970 on that spot. In return, after the reunification, the German government decided to demolish the Palace of the Republic and rebuilds the Berliner Schloss since 2013.

million-dollar business. How do you get involved without selling yourself?" (translation by the author). For the *Tagesspiegel* it is obvious that Berlin's nightlife is legendary as it attracts people from all over the world who come "to witness this party, to celebrate, to immerse themselves once in this myth" (Afansajew and Erk 2018: 16). And they also admit "nightlife is a hard business, about a lot of money, hard work, contacts and likes" (Afansajew and Erk 2018: 16).

4.7 The Rise of Collectives and the Challenge of Collective Problem-Solving

As nightlife is tough competition a strategy for survival has always been about building bonds. Generally, for men this is a familiar practice crucial for a successful career; for women, however, this is far newer and still a bit unusual if done for the sake of career and not family. Today, almost every intimate contact is used for networking, and as insecurities like freelance work on temporary basis are increasing, there is a need for more stable bonding. Therefore, I want to argue that this is the so-called collective. Farrugia states that in response to exclusionary practices "many girls and women have since taken a do-it-yourself approach to creating girl- and women-centered spaces in male dominated music cultures" (Farrugia 2012: 25). Thus, they were able to bypass gatekeeping structures and to engage in music production. But the setup of spaces only for females* is highly contested within the music communities by males and females*. Especially when it comes to fostering female*-dominated lineups, male DJs and producers have been somewhat reluctant. It is maybe due to stress with ongoing competition which they feel both genders are exposed to or they feel that the business is just a question of professionalism, reputation and hard work that women are not willing to fully engage with. Also, competition for event funding is becoming a tight squeeze. This increases also the competition between female* collectives. Though it was a great achievement that Musicboard Berlin[20] tried to support marginalized groups in the music industry and put a focus on female*-led projects in 2017 and artists with special abilities in 2018. Furthermore, it established a 50/50 quota in 2017, which was received with a lot of anger by the music industry's representatives (see more in Ludewig 2018b). Though lots of great projects were funded, our regular event Meetup Berlin[21] applied several times without success at Musicboard. This can

[20]"The Musicboard Berlin is the only institution of its kind nationwide with the aim to fund pop music in new and creative ways, and maintain a dynamic discourse on pop music in Berlin. [...] The Musicboard provides a new and courageous form of pop music funding. [...] Since the beginning of 2013, the Berlin Senate set up Musicboard Berlin under the lead of Katja Lucker. Its task is to strengthen the local pop music scene by supporting projects of national and international scope which are able to enlarge the visibility of Berlin as a center of artistic productivity" (Musicboard Berlin n.d.).

[21]Meetup was originally an offspin of female:pressure activities in Berlin. It is a new and growing community of female* artists in the fields of music and arts in Berlin. There are 10 meetings

happen due to tight competition, because more and more temporary projects and events focus on females* after the new guidelines came out. As a feedback, we were told that the jury had a problem with exclusion as only in its first 2 hours it gives room for discussions and presentations limited to female and transgender attendees and thus the jury found our concept too restrictive and not inclusive enough as males are excluded in parts of the event.[22]

It remains uncool to offer women*-centered spaces today, and it is hard for them in many social spheres to get financial support at all. Also, within panels and public discussions inside and outside of gender aware networks, it is frequently discussed if music (still) needs those kinds of (safer) spaces, quotas or gendered groups and networks. It is disturbing: once one feels that this has advanced to a general standard, it often turns out that this is not the case and that this is still limited to personal or subcultural bubbles or mainstreaming tokenism. Or have we entered already the phase of backlash McRobbie anticipated in 2007?

One impact for Berlin funding institutions and event organizers was for sure the female:pressure survey, and it was presented prominently at the Musicboards Festival Pop-Kultur in 2017. Far beyond Berlin it induced a shock-effect to some: While gender mainstreaming, gay marriage, and antidiscrimination laws were established in some countries, it turned out that the club scene with its reputation and self-image of being progressive, democratic, diverse, and egalitarian, was not as advanced as it seemed after all. Whatever the cause has been—since 2013 many individual female* artists, groups, and female*-led networks in all areas of the arts were getting organized and have been raising their voice and became more visible: filmmakers and -directors, music industry workers, fine artists, architects, etc. Also, the 2000s saw the rise of the collective in the (fine) arts as an effective tool for more visibility and outreach. Female* musicians have also been making use of this model since the 2010s, and music groups like Discwoman (US), Femdex (AT), Bliss (AT), Mint (DE), Drömfakulteten (SE), Soundsysters (DE), Creamcake (DE), our collective Meetup Berlin, and many others have all surfaced. Most of these collectives are composed of 5–10 members and have a network that connects further.

Although female:pressure is the biggest network and platform, not all of these groups are part of f:p. This is also due to the fact that f:p is very diverse concerning styles of electronic music, political/feminist attitudes, personal agendas, or geographies/origins (which can result in different forms of expression when discussing in written form, different knowledge and access to information, educational

throughout the year to discuss and exchange ideas, develop projects, and combine forces to make things happen. Meetup provides an opportunity to meet likeminded individuals for collaborating on projects.

[22]For some of us who are dealing for two decades with gender issues, it is odd that one has to explain why this still makes sense today, especially when one applies for a funding with a gender quota. The jury, of course, includes women, but also women often do not agree with quotas or female* spaces, especially when they themselves had successful careers and male mentors or supporters (and as a matter of fact, male support seems still to be the most effective way to build a career).

backgrounds, different political and economic contexts, etc.). This is already true for the f:p group in Berlin which is member-wise the biggest hub and set up its own Facebook group to make communication easier for local issues. As obstacles for members can be fighting the flood of mails in the international list serve that can amount at times of specific discussions easily to 50 per day. In such a large community of course single members might not feel addressed anymore and pressing issues of the everyday can get lost in the shuffle. This might be a reason for inactivity. As Christina Nemec (2019) summarizes it is also a constant process of negotiation and often sensitive, especially in the connection to identity issues: *"Who is f:p?," "Who can talk as f:p?," "Who is making f:p-radioshows or events?," "Who can use the logo?," "In what language and wording are we talking to each other?," "What initiatives should we support as the f:p-collektiv?,"* or *"How do we address members?" The latter has resulted in a discussion that has been going on for several months on the mailing list, which* was caused by members being corrected for saying something as seemingly innocent as "hey ladies." A member of the mailing list was blogging via the mailing list in response anonymously about this topic under the title "stop policing my language," where they explain possible reasons for gender neutral ways of addressing each other:

> One of the main reasons (for me) is that trans and nonbinary people are already excluded from many parts of society. Many trans and nonbinary people speak languages that can't accurately express their gender, excluding them from language itself. Many can't feel safe or comfortable using public amenities such as toilets, swimming pools, fitness studios, shopping for clothes, etcetera. Complications with official documents can also cause a lot of problems in education, employment, at airport security, and more. (Unknown Author 2018)

The text offers a link to a list of privileges cis-gender people have but are mostly not aware of (Killerman 2011). The dispute went off with lots of emotions, hurt feelings, and led sadly to some long-time members leaving the group. However, it also resulted in lots of diplomatic ideas, innovative comments, and more experience and knowledge about what it means to be a community of women, nonbinary and trans-members, some notions about better practices, possible codes of conduct, and new gender-neutral vocabulary. Also, it raised again the question of what one understands as feminist practices or mindsets and what these should or could be today?

Emotional discussions or overflowing mail accounts can lead to inactivity of members which is another difficulty networks are facing; the Viennese f:p group has a separate list serve, but communication is lately limited to about five or ten mails a year. Furthermore, there have been no more local meetings happening for some years. The same is true for Berlin, where the last regular meetings have been happening connected to the planning of the Perspectives Festival around 2015. This was a reason why Aiko Okamoto and myself founded the Meetup Berlin, so we could have regular meetups again where females* can showcase their music and discuss topics related to music and/or diversity. It was also a possibility to meet women who are active in electronic music, but who are not part of f:p and to connect with other groups of similar interests. Though there have been two big international gatherings in Berlin related to the Abelton Loop summit in 2016 and 2017, born out of individual effort of single f:p members (Akkamiau, Mo Chan), as a number of international members would travel to Berlin to attend the summits and it was one of the rare opportunities to meet in person.

Also, the Heroines of Sound Festival founded in 2014 by Bettina Wackernagel, which tries to bridge electronic music as part of the art music world and the club scene, served as an annual meeting point for Berlin members and other international ones either performing there or visiting the event. Also, other female* activists organized events related to gender and music as the We Make Waves[23] (in 2017) and the following connected DICE festival[24] (in 2018) which served as meeting points. But generally, the situation in Berlin is spread out, at times it seems a bit atomized, lots of singular groups are active in the field of arts which embrace gender issues—be it the queer scene, trans-gender related or female* activism. This is also true for the club scene. This is amazing and necessary, but it also feels strange sometimes that those groups and scenes are too seldom connected and thus are not supporting each other. This might be due to the increasing networking pressures in our specific fields and agendas, as competition in the field of music and events (cultural gentrification) is increasing and thus with few resources networking with the "right" people who have impact is important. In the case of Berlin also more and more artists came to Berlin to profit of the (formally) cheap living conditions, increased network possibilities and accumulated arts and culture institutions as well as with likeminded artists. Others could simply not live this kind of life in their city, village, or country—especially gay, queer and transgender artists and for them Berlin is still a refuge.

Despite opposing needs, opinions, contexts, and situations, f:p manages a lot of projects. The most important project remains maintaining its primary tool—the mailing list—for 20 years now which has been done mainly by Electric Indigo throughout the years until today. Special projects have been realized by other individual members, such as the femalepressure.tumblr.com realized by AGF, the female:pressure radio show in Hamburg by Xyramat, and further f:p shows and podcasts done by teams in Berlin, Vienna, and elsewhere. Furthermore, other projects like events and compilations have been realized.[25]

[23]We Make Waves took place in November 2017 and is an "first-of-its-kind organization designed to support the work of women, trans and non-binary people working in the music industry. [...] Beyond its year-long activities, WMW hosts a three-day festival and conference [...]. Our work goes beyond the annual festival and conference. Our goal is to nurture a vibrant independent community not only by exhibiting the work of emerging artists but also by providing essential support systems for those who otherwise have none" (We Make Waves n.d.).

[24]Dice took place in November 2018 in Berlin and appears to be some sort of follow up to WMW: "DICE Conference + Festival is a three-day event including workshops, panels, lectures and live performances featuring female, trans, and non-binary artists and speakers" (Dice n.d.).

[25]For example, the Perspectives Festival 2013, 2015, 20 years of female:pressure in Berlin, 21 years of female:pressure in Vienna, international single and regular f:p events, solidarity cd-compilation for Pussy Riot, solidarity compilation for women of Rojava, Open Sound Vienna/Open Sound international DVDs/CDs.

Electric Indigo said in an interview in 2014 that her motivation to start f:p resulted from comments in the 1990s on her gender as a DJ and especially that people did not know about other female* colleagues. Guys could name maximum of two female* DJs (and I experienced the same in Rap/HipHop), so the incentive was to offer more knowledge and to show who is out there. Important for her was that this database was not limited to club music but that it would include fine arts as visuals, photography, or graphic design as they were crucial elements within club culture (interview 2014). Through the years also other experts like bookers, event organizers, researchers, and journalists became likewise part of the endeavor, as it is necessary to have all of what constitutes club culture within the platform.

4.8 Collectives, Individuals, and the Bird's-Eye View Perspective

2013 was the most dynamic year in the history of female:pressure, says Electric Indigo (Ludewig 2014), when 25% of new members entered and the first facts counting with its complementary press statement was realized and got a lot of media attention. This was followed by the setup of a Facebook group, Twitter account, Soundcloud and Bandcamp page. Also new f:p events and radio shows were set up and the f:p Perspectives Festival was held in Berlin where the discourse on gender equality in electronic music continued (with lots of controversial discussions[26]) and f:p artists were showcased. According to Electric Indigo the main issue was the problem that bookers said, they relied on ticket sales and thus big names and that was why they could not book unknown female artists (ibid.). This contributes to a loop as females who do not play, do not make the necessary experiences and are not talked or written about and this results again in the absence of bookings. Since Facebook and Instagram turned out as the dominating tools for artist and event promotion, you also need gigs to get more followers, and without followers you do not get gigs. This is also put forward by Sarah Farina, who says that likes and followers are the new currency of the event market (Afansajew and Erk 2018: 18). This is also confirmed by Alexa Gansera of Tailored Communication—club promoters check the Internet first: "The question is what your name is worth. How many people will come to this party to see exactly you play?" (Afansajew and Erk 2018: 20). Due to these circumstances creating alternative events where female* artist can play are needed. Those interviewed and mostly visible in the Tagesspiegel report are women: Farina, Ellen Alien, and Gansera, alongside her colleague Melissa Taylor; it can be assumed that this is because of the f:p facts counting and the following media attention as before 2013 mostly men would be presented as experts in such articles.

[26]Unfortunately the recordings that have been made are not available to the public due to internal conflicts.

Only the future will show if this is a permanent change or a tokenism used for marketing or funding opportunities. The #metoo debate, especially in the United States, spawned movements of cis-men, like the pickup artists and related groups, who love far right politicians like Donald Trump and the last thing they would do is to mentor or support women's careers (they might be accused, falsely for no reason of course). Instead women's fertility is in the center of attention and they seek to stop abortion (Smith 2019, CBS news).[27] General prejudices toward women in music can only be counteracted through educational work, says Electric Indigo (Ludewig 2014). And that is what f:p is ultimately about. She also emphasizes how much voluntary work these kinds of efforts involve.[28] And one can assume that the need for this work will not become irrelevant in the future, even though this is always the aim and great hope.

So coming together, be it in networks, collectives or platforms still seems necessary. As Christina Nemec puts it wisely: "The 'we' is contestation, it is anticipation and self-empowerment; the 'we' is always against a conservative backlash, the more in 2019" (Nemec 2019, translation by the author). Electric Indigo says that more collaborations, solidarity, and support are needed. As this would be a win-win situation for everybody in the club-circuit (Vihaus 2017). This can happen in the form of established artists using their influence toward a more diverse lineup. One of these examples is a popular Berlin-based DJ who prefers to stay anonymous, who has as a prerequisite for his bookings "that I will not play on line-ups comprising less than 20% artists who are not cis male, and that these artists must be playing on similarly sized or larger stages to myself" (e-mail exchange with artist 2019). He does not state this in public as he wants to avoid artists being booked as a result of the policy from being singled out by trolls as "only booked because of." And obviously to avoid being put into focus as opposed to those he is trying to support. To not talk about this in public also helps everybody involved to stay flexible under changing conditions and work toward the commitment nonetheless: "I feel these kinds of compromises are more productive than a hard-and-fast rule" (e-mail exchange with artist 2019).

[27]Just now many US states try to pass bills that prohibit abortion, even in the case of rape. The Republicans want to force the Supreme Court to a revision of the 1973 law which made abortion legal in the United States.

[28]This cannot be emphasized enough that collectives rest most of the time on the dedication, effort, and extra time of single individual members. Some of them are: Andrea Mayr (programing and maintaining the database), Death of Codes, Michelle Endo and Tanja Ehmann (Facts Surveys), Stephanie Roll (statistician Facts Surveys). AGF (Twitter, Tumblr, Rojava Compilation), Acid Maria (gig-collection of members for Facebook), Sonae (Facebook Page, female:pressure concerts in Cologne), Kaltès (Facts, Perspectives Festival, female:pressure @ Tresor nights), Akkamiau (Rituals × female:pressure Berlin, SoundCloud, Facebook, f:p meetups), Mo Chan/Aiko Okamoto (Perspectives Festivals, spokesperson, female:pressure visual pulse group, Meetup Berlin). Xyramat (female:pressure radio Hamburg), Rosa Danner and Anna Steiden (female:pressure radio Vienna), Aschka, Kritzkom and Rona Geffen (female:pressure radio Berlin).

Niet! (female:pressure podcast), CO/RE (f:p graphics), Olivia Louvel (Bandcamp).

Electric Indigo (Vihaus 2017) says that she could not afford to act this way, as she feels the work for f:p not only had positive effects on her career: "I know that in the past I was not booked at some festivals because of my association with female: pressure. That has changed in part, but overall my role in this respect is certainly not career-promoting," Electric Indigo explains. She adds that this is also the reason why some of her colleagues still do not want to be included in the f:p database: "It's sometimes more of a flaw in the industry to promote feminism" (Vihaus 2017). As a leading voice of f:p Electric Indigo promotes now instead of a 50/50 ratio in lineups a gendered split into thirds comprised of females, males, and mixed acts and/or nonbinary artists who resist the assignment of a certain gender (Vihaus 2017).

Since some years Berlin groups like Reclaim Club Culture or Clubs with a political self-conception like Mensch Meier or about:blank try to bring more awareness to their parties. This is focused on those who attend the party. But is it enough to make our clubs and parties safer spaces with more awareness if our cities are transformed to purely profit-orientated enterprises? This affects our housing situation, our work places, our solidarity, and the city at large. Slowly most of the clubs and event organizers understand by experience, as either their apartments or clubs are sold to investors (after their private and public activities had been helpful for valorization processes). In such a situation tougher competition might be an outcome instead of the bird's-eye view on the bigger picture. Also the latest debates about police presence at the upcoming Fusion festival 2019 (Thurm and Fuchs 2019) could be a reminder that those freedoms and achievements which are accredited to club culture, which most Berliners are taken for granted, could also be lost (especially due to the far-right entering now the parliaments and committees). Defending them, when they are in danger (and this includes of course the perils imposed by commodification and gentrification) might be vitalizing for the scenes.

While talking to Ellen Alien, the impression of the *Tagesspiegel* reporters paints a picture of an industry in which the love of music has turned into business, friendships into professional contacts, and a dandy lifestyle into a bone job (Afansajew and Erk 2018: 21). Even worse, they compare it to professional football and its mafialike-business structures: "In fact, everyone knows how much money is involved and that business is slowly but surely devouring passion. But as long as the show is good and the passion seems almost real, that's no problem. The Berlin brand works" (Afansajew and Erk 2018: 22, translation by the author). What they end up owing to the reader is how you make it in the game without selling yourself. Ellen Alien tries to produce harder sounds that do not attract the masses, Farina lives straight edge and believes in the exceptions to the rules to keep her optimism. And yes, one can also see Berlin or clubs as spaces of possibilities. Maybe there are situations, events, actions, and attitudes coming up we cannot imagine yet—by individuals, collectives, networks, and communities. What Hito Steyerl is offering at the end of her rather depressive analysis of Berlin and its long-lasting power relations is a bit of humor. And she quotes sociologist, philosopher, and historian Siegfried Kracauer, who had his most productive time in Berlin within its darkest period, shortly before the Nazis took over and whose advice is as valid today as it was back then: "There are always holes in the wall we can slip through and the unexpected can sneak in" (Steyerl 1998, final sequence).

References

Afansajew, N., & Erk, D. (2018). Die Nachtschicht. Techno in Berlin ist ein großer Zirkus – und ein sagenhaftes Business. Wie mischt man mit ohne sich zu verkaufen? *Berliner Tagespiegel, 6*, 14–23.

Allan, J. L. (2013). Additive synthesis. Female:Pressure are using hard data to urge electronic music festivals to book more women artists. *The Wire, 351*, 16.

Bader, I., & Scharenberg, A. (Eds.). (2005). *Der Sound der Stadt. Musikindustrie und Subkultur in Berlin*. Münster: Westfälisches Dampfboot.

Bader, I., & Scharenberg, A. (2010). The sound of Berlin: Subculture and the global music industry. *International Journal of Urban and Regional Research, 34*(1), 76–91.

Brewster, B., & Broughton, F. (2000). *Last night a DJ saved my life*. Headline Book Publishing.

Denk, F., & von Thülen, S. (2014). *Der Klang der Familie. Berlin, Techno und die Wende*. Berlin: Suhrkamp.

Dice Festival. (n.d.). Accessed April 10, 2019, from https://2018.dice.berlin/about/

Farrugia, R. (2012). *Beyond the dance floor. Female DJs, technology and electronic dance music culture*. Chicago: Intellect Ltd.

female:pressure. (2013). *Fempress report*. Accessed February 12, 2019, from http://www.femalepressure.net/PDFs/fempressreport-03-2013.pdf

female:pressure. (2019a). Accessed June 20, 2019, from http://www.femalepressure.net/fempress.html

female:pressure. (2019b). Accessed May 20, 2019, from http://femalepressure.tumblr.com/

Gilbert, J., & Pearson, E. (1999). *Discographies. Dance, music, culture and the politics of sound*. London: Routledge.

Gilroy, P. (1993). *The Black Atlantic: Modernity and double consciousness*. London: Verso.

Goh, A. (2015). "White Brothers With No Soul": UnTuning the historiography of Berlin Techno. Interview with Alexander G. Weheliye. *CTM Magazine Untune-Edition*, pp. 40–43.

Henkel, O., & Wolff, K. (1996). *Berlin underground. Techno und Hip Hop zwischen Mythos und Ausverkauf*. Berlin: FAB-Verlag.

Hopper, J. (2015). The invisible woman. Accessed February 5, 2019, from https://pitchfork.com/features/interview/9582-the-invisible-woman-a-conversation-with-bjork/

Hussain, A. (2018). It's Gabber time: Up close and personal with Astrid Gnosis. *Kaltblut*. Accessed May 3, 2019, from https://www.kaltblut-magazine.com/its-gabber-time-up-close-and-personal-with-astrid-gnosis/

Kahn, D. (1999). *Noise water meat: A history of sound in the arts*. Cambridge, MA: MIT Press.

Keilbach, J. (2016). We Call It Techno! Zeitzeugen und die filmische Konstruktion von Technogeschichte. In K. Feser & M. Pasdziemy (Eds.), *Techno studies* (pp. 95–104). Berlin: b_books.

Killermann, S. (2011). *List of cisgender privileges*. Accessed March 15, 2019, from https://itspronouncedmetrosexual.com/2011/11/list-of-cisgender-privileges/#sthash.Y4ZswiHP.dpbs

Ludewig, B. (2014). Soundhistories and cyberfeminism with Tara Rodgers and Electric Indigo. *Wiseupradio*. Accessed April 12, 2019, from https://www.mixcloud.com/WiseupRadioshow/wiseup-012018-rerun032014-soundhistories-and-cyberfeminism-with-tara-rodgers-electric-indigo/

Ludewig, B. (2018a). *Utopie und Apokalypse in der Popmusik. Gabber und Breakcore in Berlin*. Wien: Institut für Europäische Ethnologie.

Ludewig, B. (2018b). Kulturelle Praktiken transmedialer Festivals als Überschreitungen. In S. Alisch, S. Binas-Preisendörfer, & W. Jauk (Eds.), *Darüber hinaus…: Populäre Musik und Überschreitung(en)* (pp. 115–134). Oldenburg: BIS-Verlag.

McRobbie, A. (1994). *Postmodernism and popular culture*. New York: Routledge.

McRobbie, A. (2007). Top girls? *Cultural Studies, 21*(4–5), 718–737.

Musicboard Berlin. (n.d.). Accessed April 15, 2019, from https://www.musicboard-berlin.de/en/about-us/the-musicboard/

Nemec, C. (2019). "There are not enough women to book" – 21 JAHRE FEMALE:PRESSURE. *Mica Austria*. Accessed May 23, 2019, from https://www.musicaustria.at/there-are-not-enough-women-to-book-21-jahre-femalepressure/

Pasdzierny, M. (2016). "Das Nachkriegstrauma abgetanzt?" Techno und die deutsche Zeitgeschichte. In K. Feser & M. Pasdzierny (Eds.), *Techno studies* (pp. 105–120). Berlin: b_books.

Redhead, S., Wynne, D., & O'Connor, J. (Eds.). (1998). *The clubcultures reader. Readings in popular cultural studies*. Malden: Blackwell.

Reitsamer, R. (2013). *Die Do-it-yourself-Karrieren der DJs*. Bielefeld: transript.

Reynolds, S. (1998). Rave culture: Living dream or living death? In S. Redhead, D. Wynne, & J. O'Connor (Eds.), *The clubcultures reader: Readings in popular cultural studies* (pp. 84–93). Malden: Blackwell.

Reynolds, S. (1999). *Generation ecstasy: Into the world of techno and Rave culture*. New York: Routledge.

Rodgers, T. (2010). *Pink noises. Women on electronic music and sound*. Durham: Duke University Press.

Rose, M. D. (1998). *Berlin. Hauptstadt von Filz und Korruption*. München: Knaur.

Smith, K. (2019). *Abortion is still legal in Alabama and Georgia, despite new abortion bans*. Accessed May 20, 2019, from https://www.cbsnews.com/news/alabama-abortion-law-abortion-is-still-legal-in-alabama-and-georgia-despite-abortion-bans-2019-05-17/

Stahl, G. (Ed.). (2014). *Poor, but sexy. Reflections on Berlin scenes*. Bern: Peter Lang Verlag.

Strauss, D. (2013). Berlin falling. In W. Farkas, S. Seidl, & H. Zwirner (Eds.), *Nachtleben Berlin 1974 bis heute* (pp. 207–215). Berlin: Metrolit.

Thornton, S. (1996). *Club cultures: Music, media, and subcultural capital*. Hanover: Wesleyan University Press.

Thurm, F., & Fuchs, C. (2019). *Polizei rüstet sich für Großeinsatz*. Accessed May 28, 2019, from https://www.zeit.de/gesellschaft/zeitgeschehen/2019-05/fusion-festival-polizeieinsatz-sicherheitskonzept-interne-dokumente

Unknown author. (2018). *Stop policing my language*. Accessed April 10, 2019, from https://wemakewaves.de/blog/stop-policing-my-language/

Vihaus, Y. (2017). 20 Jahre Female Pressure. Wo stehen wir heute? *The Gap, 166*, 10–15.

We Make Waves. (n.d.). Accessed April 10, 2019, from https://wemakewaves.de/about/

Weinzierl, R. (2000). *Fight the Power! Eine Geheimgeschichte der Popkultur und die Formierung neuer Substreams*. Wien: Passagen Verlag.

Wudtke, I. (2018). The 360.000 euro view. In I. Wudtke (Ed.), *The fine art of living* (pp. 63–78). Berlin: Archive Books.

Videography

Künzel, T. (2012). *SubBerlin. The story of Tresor*.

Lambert, R. (2014). *Party auf dem Todesstreifen. Soundtrack der Wende* (Klang der Familie documentary).

Lee, I. (1998). *Modulations: Cinema for the ear*.

Lim, C. (2018). *Sound of Berlin: A journey through the capital of electronic music*.

Steyerl, H. (1998). *Die Leere Mitte*.

Ulrich, W.-C. (2015). *Berlin '90s. Der Sound der Wende*. ZDF.

Chapter 5
Club Culture and Electronic Dance Music in Berlin: An Economic, Social, and Aesthetical Perspective

Martin Lücke

Abstract Worldwide Berlin is one of the most important cities for all kinds of electronic dance music. Since the German reunification in 1989, new musical styles have developed in Berlin, and the city is frequented by numerous (foreign) guests due to its unique vibrant club scene. The Berlin club scene is of great academic interest not only due to music aesthetics or sociology, but also due to economic reasons. Because the numerous clubs (even if many have financial problems due to increasing gentrification) record high turnovers, they are an important employer and thereby a central carrier of the constantly developing electronic music scene. In 2019, the Clubcommission Berlin published the first comprehensive study of the Berlin club scene which presented economic, social, and aesthetic aspects. These are summarized in this chapter.

5.1 Introduction

It is incontestable that Berlin has a pioneering role and is home to the often quoted and multifaceted club landscape. Over the past 30 years, numerous clubs of varying size and musical orientation—but also success—have been founded in the reunited city of Berlin based on the initially available space and cheap rent. Some of them have remained, many have, however, closed again, and to this day there is a constant fluctuation within the club scene.

In the past decades, various academic disciplines have dealt with the vibrant Berlin club scene (e.g., Mühlenhöver 1999; Denk and von Thülen 2014; Stahl 2014; Heilmeyer 2015; Feser and Pasdzierny 2016; Kühn 2017). Numerous studies on all kinds of aesthetic and sociological questions have been published. One aspect, however, has long remained relatively undocumented: the economic significance of Berlin's club culture. While Jan-Michael Kühn (2017) published a comprehensive study on the subject, his research was not primarily based on any figures, although

M. Lücke (✉)
Macromedia University for Applied Sciences, Berlin, Germany
e-mail: M.Luecke@macromedia.de

A. Jóri, M. Lücke (eds.), *The New Age of Electronic Dance Music and Club Culture*, Music Business Research, https://doi.org/10.1007/978-3-030-39002-0_5

10 years earlier the city of Berlin (2007) commissioned a similar study for the club and event industry.

Based on this almost unique state of affairs—because many other musical genres are in this regard better documented—the Berlin-based Clubcommission published its first comprehensive qualitative and quantitative study on the economic significance of Berlin's club culture in 2019 (Clubcommission 2019). The study includes both club operators and visitors.

Two hundred and fifty-one clubs were contacted for the study, 75 took part (which corresponds to a response of approximately 30%). The visitor survey consisted of a panel of approximately 500 participants (Clubcommission 2019).

Club culture has economic, social, and aesthetic significance for society as a whole. For this reason, an assessment of Berlin's club culture must include all three components. Therefore, the authors of the study examined three dimensions of Berlin's club culture: the economic dimension, the aesthetic dimension, and the social dimension. These three dimensions overlap and must therefore always be linked for a complete consideration of the phenomenon of club culture. The following explanations are largely based on the mentioned study. I will first provide a general overview of the Berlin club scene's significance before individually considering the three dimensions.

5.2 Club Culture in Berlin

An initial survey of the Berlin club scene and club culture's significance financed by Musicboard Berlin is provided by Clubkataster (2019). This interactive website lists all clubs currently open as well as closed clubs up to 1900 on a map over time. Two things become clear here: (a) the geographical change club culture has undergone until today and (b) the club culture's spatial focus within the urban geography.

According to the Clubcommission's study (2019), the Berlin scene consists of 226 professional clubs and 54 professional event organizers as well as more than 400 other actors who belong to the informal scene and are active as occasional event organizers. The total number of actors in the scene can be estimated at over 700. Pure event locations and purely commercial discotheques were, however, excluded from this analysis.

The Berlin club scene is concentrated in Berlin's inner-city area. Ninety percent of all clubs are located in only 10 of Berlin's 96 districts, mainly Mitte, Friedrichshain, Kreuzberg, Neukölln, Alt-Treptow, Schöneberg, Chalottenburg, Tiergarten, Wedding, and Prenzlauer Berg. The clubs' short life span can also be seen from the fact that although only one-third of the clubs have existed in one place for more than 10 years, more than 40% still use the same name. The Berlin club scene, as usual for clubs, is small in spatial size, which means that most clubs are located in small- to medium-sized venues (up to a maximum of 1000 square meters). Only 9% of the venues use larger rooms. The club's size corresponds to its capacity: Only 13% have a capacity of over 1000 visitors.

In total, Berlin's clubs hosted almost 58,000 events annually with more than 70,000 artists. This is about 17 events per club per month of which 75% were music and dance events.

5.3 Economic Dimension

> Club culture can act like the engine of a changing city, breathing new life into wasteland and acting as a magnet for professionals. Nearly every job advertisement or career page of New Economy companies advertises clubs as part of Berlin's cultural diversity. (Clubcommission 2019: 15)

A more detailed examination of the economic dimension focuses on the question of the club scene's significance for a city like Berlin. As early as 2015, Wolfgang Seufert evaluated figures for the club culture in a Germany-wide study of the music business, in which he only included clubs up to a maximum size of 1000 square meters (which included 90% of the Berlin club scene) in the study. According to Seufert (2015), the clubs' total revenues (based on figures from 2014) were as follows (Table 5.1).

Seufert also analyzed the music clubs' total cost structure (Table 5.2).

Looking at the Berlin club and event scene, the Clubcommission (2019) was able to estimate a total turnover of 168 million € for 2017. The average turnover per club was 600,000 €, with 40% of all clubs in the 100,000–250,000 € turnover range. This

Table 5.1 Structure of total income for music clubs (Seufert 2015: 33)

Revenue type	Percentage of
Commodities (food, drinks, etc.)	37.5
Ticket sales	28.3
Government funding	7.0
Revenues from activities outside the music business	16.1
Other	11.1

Table 5.2 Music clubs' total cost structure (Seufert 2015: 33)

Expense type	Percentage of
Staff costs	27.8
Compensation for freelancers	8.4
Artist fees	25.8
KSK-tax[a]	2.7
Other material costs	35.3

[a]The Künstlersozialkasse (KSK) is part of the statutory social insurance in Germany. It provides freelance artists and publicists with access to statutory health, nursing, and pension insurance. In contrast to voluntarily insured self-employed persons, they only pay a contribution corresponding to the employee's share. Utilizers of artistic services (e.g., clubs) are obliged to pay a KSK tax

Table 5.3 Revenue structure of the Berlin clubs 2017 (Clubcommission 2019: 32)

Revenue type	Percentage of
Commodities (food, drinks, etc.)	60
Ticket sales	21
Third-party rental	11
Government funding	7
Other	6
Sponsoring	5

shows that the Berlin club scene only achieves a relatively low total revenue through its direct business activity. Just under a quarter of Berlin's clubs have a turnover of more than 1 million €, and only 4% (or 9–10 clubs) even have a turnover of up to 5 million €.

If, however, the upstream and downstream turnover, e.g., in gastronomy, logistics, music industry, etc., is added up, the Berlin club scene's overall economic turnover increases to 216 million €. An important factor is also the direct return flow from clubs to the federal government or the state of Berlin through taxes and fees. Here, the Clubcommission was able to calculate a return flow of 53 million €, in other words about a quarter of the turnover flows directly back to the state.

Despite the just described low total revenue per club, most clubs can at least cover their costs. If only 20% of all clubs have a negative cost recovery, almost 50% even make a profit. This is a positive sign and means that the Berlin club scene seems to be viable, at least from an economic point of view.

Unlike Seufert (2015) in his study on the clubs' sales structure, the Clubcommission comes to the conclusion as in Table 5.3.

In their study the gastronomic services offered by the clubs are the main source of turnover, while the entrance fees only account for one-fifth. In addition, this data from 2017 can be compared with the data from a study of the Berlin club scene from 2007 commissioned by city of Berlin (Berlin 2007): In 2007 the club scene's revenue was about 170 million €—an average of 567,000 € per club, with 65% of the revenues coming from gastronomy, 18% from sponsoring, and 17% from entrance fees. Interestingly, the figures for 2007 and 2017 differ only marginally, so from an economic point of view we can actually speak of an economic stagnation of the club scene.

Apart from that, the club scene is an important employer in the cultural and creative industries. According to the Clubcommission (2019), more than 9000 people were employed in Berlin's club culture in 2017. Their different employment conditions, however, differ: Only 28% of the employees are full-time or part-time employees with paid social security contributions, i.e., just under 2500 persons. The majority work as mini-jobbers[1] (40%) and another 20% are freelancers and thus have to cover their social security contributions themselves. The remainder are trainees and volunteers. On average, each club has 33 employees, with the majority (51%)

[1]Mini-jobbers earn a maximum of 450 € per month.

having less than 20 employees; this also means that the large clubs have large number of employees.

As shown, the clubs' main sources of income are gastronomy and entrance fees at a ratio of 3 to 1, but while the average entrance fee is about 10 € (the range is between 3 and 18 €), the gastronomy is only just over 10 € per visitor. This ratio, however, does not match the club's turnover distribution and must therefore be questioned. Based on the study an average turnover per visitor of 30 € would have been expected.

Due to this it is not surprising that in the Clubcommission's visitor survey 30 € is mentioned as the average sum spent on gastronomy.

As already mentioned in other surveys on the electronic music scene (e.g., Rapp 2009), Berlin's club culture also seems to be very attractive for Berlin visitors. In the Clubcommission's study (2019), more than a third of the respondents said they came to Berlin because of its club culture. This shows how important a vibrant scene is for the external image of the entire city and is backed in some of the figures. The overall economic effect of the so-called club tourists (arrival and departure, accommodation, gastronomy, transportation but also shopping, etc.) amounts to an estimated 1.5 billion € and thus represents an important economic factor.

In addition, club culture also seems to be a reason for moving to Berlin—which, on the other hand, endangers club culture in its present form due to the increased need for living space and the resulting gentrification of neighborhoods which thus endangers the clubs' operation due to noise ordnance policies, etc. More than 40% of those surveyed expressed that they could consider moving to Berlin permanently due to the club culture.

5.4 Social Dimension

Another central aspect of the Clubcommission's study is the social dimension:

> Within the social dimension of club culture, it is about political attitudes and discourses, about shelters and door policies, about implicit and explicit rules in the club and how they are negotiated and lived. It is about awareness, dealing with discrimination, health, safety and consumer competence, sustainability, organization, co-determination, participation, inclusion, exclusion and much more. (Clubcommission 2019: 40)

The Clubcommission's broad focus includes aspects such as the club operators' political commitment. In the following paragraph I will focus on those aspects that also enable me to draw conclusions about the economic potential.

The clubs' audience in Berlin is a diverse mix. Almost 40% of the visitors are so-called regulars (people who regularly visit the same club), a quarter are one-time visitors, probably tourists who have a club visit on their Berlin schedule. These figures correspond to that of the club culture's economic dimension already described. The published figures also illustrate that 60% of the visitors come from Berlin, and almost 22% from other European and non-European countries. The

Berlin club scene is thus (at least still) dominated by locals, who are therefore the main target group which the club managers focus on.

Interestingly, the Berlin clubbers' average age is older than expected: almost 50% are 31 years old and older, the average age being 30 years. In addition, it is especially the older audience of those over 30 who call themselves regulars.

The effective audience composition is critical to the success of a club. According to the club managers, they actively try to manage the composition through targeted promotion measures (52%) and an active, selective door policy (41%). This selective door policy, in particular, is also cause for displeasure among some of the guests. Almost half of the surveyed visitors to a (Berlin) club had once been turned away at the door, a small percentage even every time.

The reasons for visiting a club, which finally determine the revenue of the club operator, also differs: The three most frequent reasons were:

- 76%: to intensively experience/dance to music
- 69%: to meet friends
- 51%: to get away from it all/to escape everyday life

The club visit's social component (meeting friends, experiencing something) is therefore the main reason for going to clubs. It is therefore central for these institutions to create suitable rooms and opportunities to remain attractive for visitors and thus to generate and maintain the economic basis for the club's success.

5.5 Aesthetic Dimension

> In addition to booking and musical programme planning, the aesthetic dimension of club culture also includes space-related areas such as architecture, interior design, scenography, stage design, decoration, lighting, visuals/video art, performances, the overall dramaturgy of the event and, if necessary, the dress code of the event. These different aesthetic concepts and disciplines regularly follow the collaborative principle and merge into a unity through shared experience. (Clubcommission 2019: 52)

Of course, as shown in the previous section it is primarily music that attracts guests to clubs. Just as diverse as the clubs' visitors are, so heterogeneous is the choice of music. That said electronic music styles such as house, techno, minimal, drum‘n'bass as well as EDM make up a high proportion of the music played at Berlin's clubs.

Three-quarters of the clubs pursue a purposefully artistic concept and have a musical format which influences which performing artists to select. The majority (40%) of them are designed by the club owners themselves, 27% are determined by a booker. When booking an artist, the focus is primarily on the artistic quality of the act (95% very important and important), followed by aspects such as promoting young talent (77% very important and important) and booking local acts (79% very important and important).

Aspects such as sound, light, and decoration also play a central role in the aesthetic dimension, whereby the technical management or the club management is usually responsible for this. This also points to the central role the club owners as such play. As a rule, it is the owners themselves who determine the musical and aesthetic character of the club and who personally is responsible for the success or failure of a club.

5.6 Berlin Club Visitors

Around 20% of the club visitors go to the club several times a month, especially those who live in Berlin. The majority of clubgoers also visit only one club on a typical club evening (58%), while the remaining 42% visit more than two, and in some cases even more than three, clubs. Interestingly, 95% of the visitors use public transportation to reach the club, but with 82%, cars still account for a large proportion (multiple answers were possible). Certainly, the type of transportation depends on the origin of the clubgoers (whether Berliners, tourists, etc.) as well as the location of the club within the city.

The most important neighborhoods for local club visitors are Friedrichshain-Kreuzberg (36%) and Mitte (21%). Tourists, on the other hand, are more in Mitte (29%) followed by Friedrichshain-Kreuzberg (19%). These figures also correspond with the presentation of the club landscape in Berlin in terms of geographical location (Clubkataster 2019).

It is also important to note that the majority of club visitors (57%) visit other cultural institutions, ranging from entertainment to so-called high culture (classical concerts, opera, etc.) several times a month. A relevant aspect for the future is the creation of possible synergies between different cultural institutions with the aim to appeal to the same audience.

5.7 Summary

In this compact summary of the 2019 Clubcommission study of the Berlin club and events scene and its different dimensions it has become clear how diverse the approach to this scene can be. The clubs' economic situation, their revenues, the profit they can generate, etc. also depends on social and aesthetic factors that lead to a club visit, at least from the guests' point of view. It is always important to consider and further investigate how the economic, social, and aesthetic aspects overlap.

The comparison with the 2007 study of the Berlin club scene (Berlin 2007) also reveals surprising insights: According to both studies, revenues in this sector have not increased in the 10 years between the studies. Either the numbers for 2007 were too optimistic or the estimates for 2017 were too pessimistic. The club culture's economic importance for Berlin as a business location, which has grown over the last 10 years, should at least have shown an increase in revenues due to inflation alone.

Further efforts are certainly needed to analyze the economic field of the club scene in more detail. This is made more complicated by the fact that the club scene, unlike, e.g., music publishers or labels, has been changing rapidly and will continue to change. Clubs close and new clubs open at a new location. The concentration of clubs in Berlin, especially within the so-called *Ringbahn* which separates Berlin's inner and outer boroughs, ensures—in the long run—that the entire scene will—even has to—change in spatial terms. What effects this will have on the economic significance of the club scene for the city of Berlin must meanwhile be regularly examined. It should be noted, however, that the economic significance of Berlin's club culture must continue to be integrated into the consideration of the entire cultural and creative economy's significance. This is also how the demand at the end of the Club Commission's study should be understood: to establish the club scene as a separate area in the cultural and creative industries.

References

Berlin. (2007). *Studie über das wirtschaftliche Potential der Club- und Veranstaltungsbranche Berlin.* Accessed August 16, 2019, from https://www.creative-city-berlin.de/uploads/standortinformationen/8dt_studie_ber_das_wirtschaftliche_potenzial_der_club-_und_veranstaltungsbranche_in_berlin.pdf

Clubcommission. (2019). *Clubkultur Berlin.* Berlin.

Clubkataster. (2019). *Clubkataster.* Accessed August 16, 2019, from https://www.clubkataster.de

Denk, F., & von Thülen, S. (2014). *Der Klang der Familie: Berlin, Techno und die Wende.* Berlin: Suhrkamp.

Feser, K., & Pasdzierny, M. (Eds.). (2016). *Techno Studies: Ästhetik und Geschichte elektronischer Tanzmusik.* Berlin: b-books.

Heilmeyer, F. (2015). Die unfertige Stadt. Über den wechselhaften Dialog zwischen Planung und Nutzung. In A. Brandlhuber & F. Hertweck (Eds.), *The Dialogic City – Berlin wird Berlin* (pp. 165–185). Köln: Verlag der Buchhandlung Walther König.

Kühn, J.-M. (2017). *Die Wirtschaft der Techno-Szene: Arbeiten in einer subkulturellen Ökonomie.* Wiesbaden: Springer.

Mühlenhöver, G. (1999). *Phänomen Disco: Geschichte der Clubkultur und der Popularmusik.* Bergheim: Musikverlag Christoph Dohr.

Rapp, T. (2009). *Lost and sound: Berlin, Techno und der Easyjetset.* Berlin: Suhrkamp.

Seufert, W. (2015). *Musikwirtschaft in Deutschland.* Berlin: Bundesverband Musikindustrie.

Stahl, G. (Ed.). (2014). *Poor, but sexy – Reflections on Berlin scenes.* Bern: Peter Lang.

Chapter 6
Researching Informal Musical Expertise and Mediations of Aesthetic Experiences Among the Berlin Techno Audience: A Postdoctoral Research Proposal

Botond Vitos

Abstract The purpose of this study is to identify and compare segments of techno club audiences in Berlin based on their forms of engagements in music-related activities such as audio media and recreational drug use. A central focus is to identify the ways different audience segments attempt to recreate the distinctive socio-aesthetic experience of the electronic dance floor in their everyday life by means of audio media and other arrangements. Another concern is to find out how their techno club experience may change their music listening practices and their lifestyle choices in everyday contexts. The study is based on a mixed-methods design involving quantitative and qualitative methods. In the first phase, after an initial participant observation in Berlin techno clubs, survey data is collected from a sample of $n > 300$ visitors of five venues where techno is regularly played, measuring sociodemographic details, reception patterns in clubbing contexts, reception patterns in everyday contexts, and lifestyle choices. The second phase involves approximately ten qualitative follow-up interviews with participants selected from the survey respondents based on their media use and reception patterns that will help to interpret and deepen the insights from the survey statistics. It is expected that the study will enrich the study of informal musical expertise, pave new ways in club/drug research, while also providing valuable contribution to the applied fields of product engineering, marketing and design in audio technology, and electronic dance music culture.

Funding is being sought for this research with a starting year from 2020 or later.

B. Vitos (✉)
Berlin, Germany
e-mail: x@vitos.tv

A. Jóri, M. Lücke (eds.), *The New Age of Electronic Dance Music and Club Culture*, Music Business Research, https://doi.org/10.1007/978-3-030-39002-0_6

6.1 Introduction

Based on mixed-methods research design, and as continuation of my PhD and MA projects, my postdoctoral research aims to investigate informal musical expertise and related aesthetic experiences among club audiences in the Berlin techno scene[1] based on the forms of their engagements in music-related activities including audio media and recreational drug use. Techno, together with house, are among the earliest and most influential genres of electronic dance music, a popular music meta-genre that emerged in the United States during the 1980s (Brewster and Broughton 2000: 292–336). Reynolds (1999: 28) acknowledges the way certain house tracks of this period signaled a detour from the soulful influences of disco toward a "machine music (...) that turned you into a machine" by executing the functional programming of electronic dance floors. In the late 1980s the sounds of Detroit techno and Chicago house were imported to the United Kingdom, where, fueled by the drug MDMA, they gave birth to the *acid house* music scene and its illegal parties dubbed *raves*. The post-rave era of the 1990s witnessed the proliferation of subgenres and scenes, rendering electronic dance music culture a diversified global phenomenon, often discussed by scholars under the (imprecise) umbrella terms of house, techno, and rave (Butler 2006: 46).

The musical attributes of electronic dance music (sub)genres are interconnected with various socio-aesthetic sensibilities, which St John (2009: 103) situates along a spectrum of interrelated "vibes." As suggested by the term vibe, the archetypal dimension of electronic dance music cultures is rooted in the communal dance experience. This experiential component is closely related to drug consumption, an indispensable link in the drug–music–visuals–dancers ensemble of dance floors (Gore 1997). Various concepts have been offered for a somewhat loose description of the drug-induced experience, such as the "oceanic experience" (Malbon 1999), "desubjectification" (Landau 2004), or the "experience of a transcendental universality" (Rietveld 2004). These concepts are more useful in discussing dance floors from a broader perspective, and while the dance floor is recognized as the "ground zero" of electronic dance music interactions, due to the irrational nature of the experience it is often described as a black box that short-circuits further analysis. This analytical obstacle can be overcome by acknowledging that this apparent void comes from an interaction of mediations that are particular to the various genres and scenes, which draws attention to the media ecologies of electronic dance floors.

[1]Scene is a widely used concept in popular music studies that addresses the local realizations of musical taste among urban communities, with particular regard to their cultural and spatial contexts (Bennett and Peterson 2004: 8).

6.2 Previous Research Work and Proposed Directions

My postdoctoral research constitutes a continuation of my past investigations of electronic dance music cultures. My Master's project, based on ethnographic fieldwork on outdoor festivals in the Czech Republic, provided an analysis of Czech psytrance parties through an interdisciplinary application of cultural anthropology and literary theory (Vitos 2010). Drawing on ethnographic fieldwork conducted in Melbourne, my PhD project engaged in the comparative research of techno and psytrance electronic dance music scenes. During my fieldworks I was particularly interested in the micro-level, qualitative analysis of the respective dance floors, taking into account participant descriptions of the various technologies and spatial contexts mediating the dance experience. In this I followed Hennion's (2003) call for an investigation of taste and pleasure as described and experienced by actors themselves, which is facilitated by addressing the mediations from which the appreciation of music emerges and examining the social and cultural contexts interrelated with the productive moments of aesthetic pleasure. My research signaled that on the level of the individual partygoer the interplay of sonic structures, drug use, and environmental arrangements enables a state of self-virtualization that can be approached through Baudrillard's theories of simulation and virtuality. I argued that regular participation in electronic dance music events encompasses a chain of thoroughly mediated, immersive experiences akin to participation in computer-based virtual worlds but distinctly involves the ritualized and excessive consumption of specific mediating technologies in contexts that are commonly regarded as extraordinary and in which the gap between the virtual and actual is eliminated, leading to profound reconfigurations of everyday life (Vitos 2014: 3).

Influenced by the perspectives of ethnography in conjunction with media and consumer theories, my research locates the electronic dance experience in the blurred boundary between subjects and mediating technologies, emerging from technological appropriations and creative engagements with anomalies that can be traced to the early history of electronic dance music. In these formative years novel affordances (Hutchby 2001) of existing technologies were discovered, with the exploitation and exploration of accidents, the rediscoveries of misdesigned and obsolete technologies impacting upon the early evolution of electronic dance music genres just as much as the embracing of the latest innovations (Butler 2006: 67–68). A famous example is provided by one of the inventors of techno, Derrick May, who dubbed the early Detroit techno sound "a complete mistake. It's like George Clinton and Kraftwerk stuck in an elevator" (Sicko 2010: 11). The historical emergence of certain popular party drugs such as MDMA and LSD can also be regarded as technological appropriation, with both chemicals being invented as pharmaceuticals first and then appropriated for other uses (Redhead 1993; Russell 1993). Another relevant, yet little researched field of inquiry concerns the appropriation of abandoned spaces. The history of techno provides numerous examples for repurposing disused industrial and urban spaces, most notably derelict warehouses and factories (Pope 2011: 25; Reynolds 1999: 71–72).

Having moved to Berlin in 2014, I intend to revisit some of these issues in the context of a postdoctoral research conducted in the Berlin techno scene that offers significant methodological and theoretical extension to my previous work. To achieve this, I plan to collaborate with the research project *Music and Media Survey—Empirical Basic Data and Theoretical Modeling of the Mediatization of Everyday Music Reception in Germany*, led by Steffen Lepa and Stefan Weinzierl, within the Audio Communication Group of the Berlin Institute of Technology. A key contribution of this project to mediatization research is the discovery of six "audio media generation units" among German music audiences. Drawing on the concept of "media repertoires" (Hasebrink and Popp 2006; Hasebrink and Domeyer 2012), in the Music and Media Survey the audience members' class membership is assumed to be in a "fuzzy causal relationship" with their adoption of "audio media repertoires" (Lepa et al. 2014: 212). I wish to explore the possibilities of similar club repertoires among Berlin techno audiences based on their audio media and recreational drug use, as well as other music-related activities. This will close a pressing research gap in the field, since in spite of the cultural and economic impact of EDM culture in Germany there are only very few social scientific works yet concerning the structure and types of music festival and club audiences (Otte 2015). Another focus of inquiry of my project will be on the ways that media usage patterns and forms of club engagement may act as indicators of "informal musical expertise" conceptualized along the dimensions of sonic, material, and embodied expertise (Lepa et al. 2015). As part of my continuing research interest in the relations between the party and the everyday, I also aim to investigate the recreations and reenactments of the distinctive dance floor experience in everyday listening situations by means of audio media and other arrangements. In addition to these shared theoretical interests, I propose to align my methodology with the mixed research design of the Music and Media Survey. Accordingly, my project will rely not only on qualitative methods such as interviewing and participant observation, but also on quantitative survey analysis.

6.3 Location and Language of Research

The location of my research is of particular relevance. During the past decades, Berlin has solidified its position at the center of global techno music, with parties mushrooming since the fall of the Wall, and many influential producers/DJs moving in from all over the world. This leading position as *capital of techno* has been enabled by various factors including the city's post-1989 culture clash, its postindustrial readjustment toward a service-oriented entity, its unique sociocultural dynamics, its ambience of tolerance, and the adaptability of its night life economy (Peter 2014). Indeed, for many international techno fans, including some of the respondents of my PhD research, the Berlin scene is endowed with an almost mythical veneer of authenticity, as well as professionalism. A mixed-method research of informal musical expertise and mediations of aesthetic experiences among Berlin techno partygoers is therefore a valuable task that has not been addressed previously, and it also provides a logical extension to my earlier project and gives my work a wider, international scope.

As a continuation of my previous research, the study will be conducted in English, with the exception of the quantitative survey, which will be bilingual to ensure the representativeness of the sample. Berlin parties are usually attended by a variety of Germans, expatriates, and tourists (Rapp 2010: 80–84), and by means of the bilingual survey design I aim to reach this mix of groups. The survey will be followed by qualitative (in-depth) interviews with participants purposefully selected according to their media use patterns. Participants with a good command of English will be recruited for the interview sample; statistical representativeness is not a prerequisite for the qualitative research component.

6.3.1 Key Questions and Aims

- Is it possible to establish a typology of techno audiences based on their media orientations and the forms of their engagements in music-related activities?
- In what ways may such orientations and engagements act as indicators of informal musical expertise?
- In what ways may different audience segments attempt to recreate, remember, or reenact the distinctive socio-aesthetic experience of the electronic dance floor in their everyday life by means of audio media and other arrangements?
- How does their club experience change their music listening practices and experiences in daily life?
- In comparison with the research of the Melbourne techno scene, is it possible to identify archetypal experiences transcending local contexts?

6.3.2 Secondary Research Questions

- Do sociodemographic variables explain reception patterns?
- Do recreational drug consumption patterns explain musical taste and forms of engagement?
- How does the urban (Berlin) context influence music reception and taste patterns?

6.3.3 Relevance of the Research Topic and Dissemination of Results

The project aims to provide new material for the social scientific study of informal musical expertise by focusing on electronic dance music audiences and their music-related practices including audio media and recreational drug use. Based on a mixed-methods research design, the study assesses the role of technological mediations in clubbing experiences and during home listening, constituting a novel approach to the fields of club research and popular music studies. The typological classification of techno audiences is in itself an innovative project, and the subsequent qualitative research component facilitates the in-depth investigation of typifying practices and user experiences. By exploring the role and use of audio media in the everyday reenactments of club experiences, the research also aims to provide valuable contribution to the applied fields of product engineering, marketing, and design in audio technology development. The results will be disseminated to the research community through publications in peer-reviewed journals predominantly from the fields of media studies and popular music studies, as well as conference papers.

6.4 Research Examples and Theoretical Perspectives

I wish to contribute to the theorization of informal musical expertise (Lepa et al. 2015) by focusing on its distinctive particularities among visitors of techno clubs. My PhD research, although building on a different theoretical framework, offers several connections to this discourse, which I aim to develop in the Berlin context. The following section offers a few fitting examples from my PhD to the manifestations of sonic, material, and embodied expertise (Lepa et al. 2015) in electronic dance music.

Sonic expertise was highly regarded in the focus groups of my PhD, which is unsurprising given the abundance of subgenres and the emphasis on sound quality and frequency range in electronic dance music. Furthermore, my interlocutors often emphasized that good music attracts attention by posing a challenge to the mind, and in techno this challenge is connected to subtle structural changes in the music.

> Jack: Well the thing that I find about it [is] that it seems to be constant, and yet it's always changing, ever so slightly, and what I really like about it is that you have to appreciate the little changes. I feel like, if people don't listen to enough techno music, they just hear this repetitive sound, and yet you listen to this sound, and you hear something different every—like, you hear changing through a song, that's like you're appreciating the subtleties of it, and that can sort of translate when you're dancing in the club to it. You still hear all these subtleties to it, even though from the outside world it sounds as it's basically just four beats (focus group, November 2011).

Jack contends that these gradual changes in the music, which are highly valued by dancers, are almost incomprehensible to outsiders, who may lack the (informal) sonic expertise of those in the club.

At the same time, club culture is often considered as a "heady combination of dance music (...) and drugs" (Moore 2003: 138). Nightclubs hosting techno events provide contexts for the recreational drug use of partygoers who consider clubbing and drug use as a leisure activity (Demant et al. 2010: 241). Consequently, a club study approach should focus on both club and drug cultures. The synergistic fusion of electronic dance music and drugs was often emphasized among my interlocutors, and there was no general consensus whether the drugs facilitate connection with the music, or if it is the other way around.

> Sam: From the drugs and music interaction, I'd rather say: I can listen to music without drugs. But if I'm on drugs, I need music. The music helps the drugs, rather than the other way around, you know. If we were here, we were all high, I would be like: why aren't they any tunes going? [Others laugh.] So I think the question's back to front, it's not drugs helping the music, drugs are better with music (focus group, December 2012).

From a media studies perspective the drug effect is an important constituent in the media ecology of the dance floor, where drug-technologies are applied in the mediation of the music for socio-aesthetic purposes. Discourses and practices concerning the various drugs and effects belong to the *material expertise* of partygoers.

Drugs also play an important role in forming the *embodied expertise* of partygoers. They may trigger synaeshtetic perceptions of the music, traces of which may be brought back to the everyday through home listening. Furthermore, the drug effect aids the development of informal dance styles and movements, and acts as catalyst in formative experiences that create associations between hearing the sound and performing the motor event (Lepa et al. 2015: 4):

> Thomas: For me, first time experience: supposedly it was this strong kind of MD[MA], and I was just—I took it some time before, and just asking a friend: when's it gonna kick in, when's it gonna kick in? Then I said: all right, I'm gonna go get some water, I was still very-very sober. As I turn around with two bottles of water, away from the bar, it's just this: wow, I'm on a cloud, I'm on something, and wow, it was pretty amazing. And then, I think that was the first night I found my groove as well because at most of the gigs I went to before, prior, I was just standing there, sort of not really doing much. But then, then and there I found my groove, and yeah, dancing and getting into the music (focus group, July 2012).

Similar associations may develop between sound and environment: techno parties create lasting memories for the participants, in which the music is often molded into its typical, postindustrial surroundings. In the following fragment Cooper nostalgically evokes the relentless effects of the techno kick drum on the warehouse environment of a bygone techno party.

> Cooper: Yeah, there's [sic] certain sounds that I'm missing now that I know I'll never hear them again. Like the Docks, you know, Docklands, that's now been redeveloped and is all apartments and all down there, but they really just used to be drydocks, you know, docks where they were boarding all the goods for Melbourne ships, and sheds. (...) And those sounds you just don't think you'll ever hear again. Like standing outside of one of the big sheds of the docks, and hearing the kick drum inside, but just the rattle of the metal, like whoom-whoom-whoom. And it's the kind of thing where you just start thinking about whether you're going to hear it again (focus group, January 2012).

For Cooper the rattle of the metal guided by the four-to-the-floor techno beat is endowed with an emotional/symbolic significance, a memento of the sense of belonging and social aesthetics characteristic of the warehouse parties of the 1990s Melbourne. At the same time, Cooper's orientation to the embodied experience of techno music is highly functionalist, and in another part of the interview he praises the music for its rhythmic and sonic qualities that trigger kinaesthetic impulses in the listener. The fragment thus demonstrates an "embodied listening mode" that is functional and expressive at the same time (Lepa and Seifert 2016), where adrenaline-producing sound effects become symbols of identity and tokens of important biographical events. Further examples of such orientations are expected to be discovered in the Berlin context, where the claiming/repurposing of abandoned or postindustrial spaces is part of an ongoing heritage that has historically enabled the development and formation of alternative cultural clusters and has been fully exploited by techno event organizers (Peter 2014: 182–183).

The previous interview fragments and interpretations illustrate some ways to connect my past research orientations with the theoretical preoccupations of the Music and Media Survey project. Extending such trajectories of my previous work, I aim to carry out a mixed-methods research of musical expertise among Berlin techno partygoers based on the following grounds.

6.5 Quantitative Research Component

The data will be collected through a bilingual online questionnaire (respondents may choose to answer in English or German). By means of an initial participant observation I will identify and explore five Berlin clubs where techno is being frequently played. Berlin techno venues are expected to be on the forefront of global trends in electronic dance music and techno. To enrich the sample, I aim to target at least one iconic techno club (such as Tresor and Berghain), midsize clubs where techno is often played (such as About Blank and Griessmühle), as well as lesser known locations (such as Ipse and Ohm). The participant observation will involve one visit in each club accompanied by taking field notes. During the participant observation I will distribute inside or in front of these clubs bilingual flyers addressed to partygoers who listen to techno in clubs and at home, containing a suitable teaser text and a link to the online survey. My initial sample will be collected from these clubs, with each club being assigned a different Internet link (to the same questions) enabling the stratification of the sample and subsequent weighting of results. At this stage, I aim to reach $n > 300$ respondents. Furthermore, during a second phase another $n > 300$ partygoers will be recruited (resulting in a second sample) through advertisements posted on Internet forums and aimed at visitors of Berlin techno events. The survey will be divided into five main parts: sociodemographic variables; music reception patterns in clubbing contexts; music reception patterns in everyday contexts; lifestyle choices; and willingness to participate in follow-up studies. During the analysis the survey data will first be typologized using cluster analysis. Class predictions will be then performed by means of multinomial logistic regression.

Proposed variables:

1. *Sociodemographic variables*
   Age, gender, sexual preference, education, marital status, occupation, household income, town of residence, ethnicity, language spoken at home
2. *Clubbing*
   - Frequency of clubbing (in the club where the survey was distributed)
   - Frequency of clubbing (in other clubs, with the possibility to name the other clubs)
   - Continuous time (in hours) normally spent in a clubbing context
   - Frequency of drug use (ordinal scales for common recreational drugs)
   - Techno music preference in clubs (ordinal scales for common techno subgenres with 0 indicator for lack of knowledge and the possibility of adding a new subgenre)
   - Preferred equipment for DJs (turntables, notebook and controller, unimportant)
3. *Everyday techno listening*
   - Frequency of everyday techno listening (ordinal scale)
   - Techno music preference at home (ordinal scales for common techno subgenres with 0 indicator for lack of knowledge and the possibility of adding a new subgenre)
   - Frequency of audio technology use during everyday techno listening (ordinal scales for common audio technologies as well as production and mixing equipment)
   - Frequency of drug use during everyday listening (ordinal scales for common drugs)
4. *Lifestyle*
   - Is the respondent's choice of friends and partners influenced by their preference of techno? (ordinal scale from "not at all" to "very much")
   - Other music listened to (ordinal scale for: none; subgenres closely related to techno such as tech-house; unrelated electronic dance music genres; music other than electronic dance music)
   - Frequency of engagement with techno-related information such as new record releases, event listings, DJ charts, and Facebook pages
5. *Recruitment*
   Willingness to participate in subsequent in-depth interview in English, with monetary incentive of € 30 (yes/no)

6.6 Qualitative Research Component

The qualitative research component benefits from the adoption of a partial insider perspective. This is facilitated by the preliminary participant observation conducted in the five selected clubs. Even though the idea of an absolute insider perspective with total proximity to the field is problematized by the complexity and fluidity of contemporary identities and groupings, it can still be stated that insider participants of (underground) electronic dance music scenes are generally committed to relatively distinctive sets of tastes, values, activities, or other characteristics (Measham and Moore 2006: 16). Demant et al. (2010: 245) emphasize the importance of gaining access to such hidden populations and experiences, calling attention to the methodological advantages of adopting a dual position, where the participant observer is situated in between insiders and outsiders, allowing reflection on dance floor experiences during the interviews and the data evaluation.

Approximately ten (the exact number depends on the number of classes established during the survey analysis) individual in-depth interviews will be aimed at the qualitative exploration of sonic, material, and embodied expertise and related aesthetic experiences. The interlocutors will be purposefully selected, based on their class membership, from survey respondents who gave an affirmative answer to the willingness to participate question. The interviews will be conducted in English. Berlin is an international clubbing destination with a cosmopolitan techno scene (Rapp 2010), and it can be safely assumed that a sufficient number of suitable respondents will speak English at a conversational level. A monetary incentive of 30 € will be offered to participants.

Some preliminary topics:

- The role of mediating technologies and spatial contexts in the construction and intensity of aesthetic experiences (in clubs and during home listening)
- The infiltration of clubbing experiences into the everyday and their influence on lifestyle choices
- Phenomenological aspects of recreational drug effects; drug–music interactions
- Berlin as capital of techno—influence of the local context
- Partygoer biographies and clubbing careers

6.7 Ethical Considerations

The personal details of the participants will not be recorded in the quantitative survey, with the exception of the email address, which will be stored securely and used only for communication purposes, should the participant be selected for follow-up interview. In the qualitative interviews the identification of interview information/participants will remain confidential and only be known to the researcher. Pseudonyms will be used to protect the privacy of the participants. No inconvenience or discomfort is expected to follow from the involvement of the interview participants. Before the commencement of interviews, the interviewees will be notified that participation is voluntary and they are entitled to avoid answering any question which they feel is inappropriate or intrusive. Discussions or observations of illegal activity in relation to dance music activities will remain confidential to the researcher. All research data will be stored in a secure location.

6.8 Comparative Perspective

As a continuation of my earlier projects, it is my hope that the Berlin research will provide valuable contribution to a broader comparative study of two electronic dance music genres (techno and psytrance) in three countries (Germany, Australia, and the Czech Republic). This extended project would benefit from a cross-national perspective similar to some prior research of electronic dance music genres (e.g., Rietveld 1998; St John 2012), while also benefiting from in-depth, ethnographic methodology involving participant observation and qualitative interviewing.

References

Bennett, A., & Peterson, R. A. (2004). Introducing music scenes. In A. Bennett & R. A. Peterson (Eds.), *Music scenes: Local, translocal and virtual* (pp. 1–16). Nashville: Vanderbilt University Press.

Brewster, B., & Broughton, F. (2000). *Last night a DJ saved my life: The history of the disc jockey*. London: Headline.

Butler, M. (2006). *Unlocking the groove: Rhythm, meter, and musical design in electronic dance music*. Bloomington: Indiana University Press.

Demant, J., Ravn, S., & Thorsen, S. K. (2010). Club studies: Methodological perspectives for researching drug use in a central youth social space. *Leisure Studies, 29*(3), 241–252.

Gore, G. (1997). The beat Goes on: Trance, dance and tribalism in rave culture. In H. Thomas (Ed.), *Dance in the city* (pp. 50–67). Basingstoke: Macmillan.

Hasebrink, U., & Domeyer, H. (2012). Media repertoires as patterns of behaviour and as meaningful practices: A multimethod approach to media use in converging media environments. *Participations: Journal of Audience & Reception Studies, 9*(2), 757–779.

Hasebrink, U., & Popp, J. (2006). Media repertoires as a result of selective media use. A conceptual approach to the analysis of patterns of exposure. *Communications, 31*(3), 369–387.

Hennion, A. (2003). Music and mediation: Towards a new sociology of music. In M. Clayton, T. Herbert, & R. Middleton (Eds.), *The cultural study of music: A critical introduction* (pp. 80–91). London: Routledge.

Hutchby, I. (2001). Technologies, texts and affordances. *Sociology, 35*(2), 441–456.

Landau, J. (2004). The flesh of raving: Merleau-Ponty and the "experience" of ecstasy. In G. St John (Ed.), *Rave culture and religion* (pp. 107–124). London: Routledge.

Lepa, S., & Seifert, M. (2016). Embodied listening modes as part of habitual music media orientations: Relating young adults' audio technology use with their music socialization and taste preferences. *Networking Knowledge: Journal of the MeCCSA-PGN, 9*(2). https://doi.org/10.31165/nk.2016.92.430.

Lepa, S., Hoklas, A.-K., & Weinzierl, S. (2014). Discovering and interpreting audio media generation units: A typological-praxeological approach to the mediatization of everyday music listening. *Participations: Journal of Audience & Reception Studies, 11*(2), 207–238.

Lepa, S., Hoklas, A.-K., Egermann, H., & Weinzierl, S. (2015). Sound, materiality and embodiment challenges for the concept of "musical expertise" in the age of digital mediatization. *Convergence: The International Journal of Research into New Media Technologies, 21*(3), 1–7.

Malbon, B. (1999). *Clubbing: Dancing, ecstasy and vitality*. London: Routledge.

Measham, F., & Moore, K. (2006). Reluctant reflexivity, implicit insider knowledge and the development of club studies. In B. Sanders (Ed.), *Drugs, clubs and young people: Sociological and public health perspectives* (pp. 13–25). Aldershot: Ashgate.

Moore, K. (2003). E-heads versus beer monsters: Researching young People's music and drug consumption in dance club settings. In A. Bennett, M. Cieslik, & S. Miles (Eds.), *Researching youth: Issues, controversies and dilemmas* (pp. 138–153). London: Palgrave.

Otte, G. (2015). Die Publikumsstrukturierung eines Open-Air-Festivals für elektronische Musik. In Empirische Kultursoziologie (Ed.), *Jörg Rössel and Jochen Roose* (pp. 27–64). Wiesbaden: Springer.

Peter, B. (2014). Breaching the divide: Techno City Berlin. In G. Stahl (Ed.), *Poor, but sexy: Reflections on Berlin scenes* (pp. 173–190). Bern: Peter Lang.

Pope, R. (2011). Detroit techno and dystopian digital culture. *Dancecult: Journal of Electronic Dance Music Culture, 2*(1), 24–44.

Rapp, T. (2010). *Lost and sound: Berlin, techno and the Easyjet set*. Berlin: Innervisions.

Redhead, S. (1993). The politics of ecstasy. In S. Redhead (Ed.), *Rave off: Politics and deviance in contemporary youth culture* (pp. 7–27). Aldershot: Avebury.

Reynolds, S. (1999). *Generation ecstasy: Into the world of techno and rave culture*. New York: Routledge.

Rietveld, H. (1998). *This is our house: House music, cultural spaces and technologies*. Aldershot: Ashgate.

Rietveld, H. (2004). Ephemeral spirit: Sacrificial cyborg and communal soul. In G. St John (Ed.), *Rave culture and religion* (pp. 46–61). London: Routledge.

Russell, K. (1993). Lysergia Suburbia. In S. Redhead (Ed.), *Rave off: Politics and deviance in contemporary youth culture* (pp. 91–174). Aldershot: Avebury.

Sicko, D. (2010). *Techno rebels: The Renegades of electronic funk*. Detroit: Painted Turtle.

St John, G. (2009). *Technomad: Global raving countercultures*. London: Equinox.

St John, G. (2012). *Global tribe: Technology, spirituality and psytrance*. Sheffield, UK: Equinox Pub.

Vitos, B. (2010). DemenCZe: Psychedelic dementia in the Czech Republic. In G. St John (Ed.), *The local scenes and global culture of psytrance* (pp. 151–169). New York: Routledge.

Vitos, B. (2014). "An avatar … in a physical space": Researching the mediated immediacy of electronic dance floors. *Dancecult: Journal of Electronic Dance Music Culture, 6*(2), 1–21.

Part II
Musicians and Musickers

Chapter 7
The Influence of Berlin on Austrian and Polish Electronic Musickers

Ewa Mazierska

Abstract This chapter discusses the meaning of Berlin for Austrian and Polish electronic musickers. It examines their real and symbolic connections to the city, reflected in such activities, as travelling to Berlin for business, playing there, using booking agents from there, collaborating with Berlin musicians, as well as being influenced by the city's music and atmosphere. It also briefly presents the history of the relations between, respectively, Austria and Poland and West and East Berlin during the period after the Second World War up to the fall of the Berlin Wall. In her investigation, the author draws on interviews conducted with Austrian and Polish electronic musicians, as well as some secondary sources, such as journal articles and films.

7.1 Introduction

In this chapter I intend to discuss the meaning of Berlin for Austrian (chiefly Viennese) and Polish electronic musickers.[1] By meaning I understand the real and symbolic connections to the city, reflected in such activities, as travelling to Berlin for business, playing there, using booking agents from there, collaborating with Berlin musicians, as well as being influenced by the city's music and atmosphere. To do so, I draw on about 15 interviews conducted with Austrian and Polish electronic musicians, as well as some secondary sources, such as journal articles and films. Most of my interviews were not focused on Berlin, as they were conducted them for my monographs about Viennese (Mazierska 2019) and Polish (2021) electronic music.[2] For this very reason, the mention of Berlin can be regarded as testimony

[1]Following Christopher Small I use the term "musickers" (Small 1998), rather than "musicians," because here I am concerned not only with artists, but with all participants in a musical experience, all users of music, such as club managers, record labels' heads, and music fans.

[2]My book is currently in preparation, to be completed by the end of 2020.

E. Mazierska (✉)
University of Central Lancashire, Preston, UK
e-mail: EHMazierska@uclan.ac.uk

A. Jóri, M. Lücke (eds.), *The New Age of Electronic Dance Music and Club Culture*, Music Business Research, https://doi.org/10.1007/978-3-030-39002-0_7

to the importance of the city to these people. I use one city, Vienna, and talk about several cities in Poland, largely because Austrian electronic music in the period which I researched was concentrated in Vienna, while in Poland it was more widespread, and the influence of Berlin was noticeable in several towns and cities.

7.2 Cultural Exchanges Between Berlin, Austria, and Poland During the State Socialist Period

Berlin is not the closest capital city to Vienna; the closest being Bratislava. However, inhabitants of the two cities speak the same language, although in different dialects and share a large part of their history. Both suffered from depopulation after the Second World War, although Vienna did not endure bombardment and destruction as Berlin did. However, it was Vienna, rather than Berlin, which served as the setting of *The Third Man* (1949) by Carol Reed, the famous film which showed the material and moral degradation of Europe after the end of the Second World War. Subsequently both Berlin and Vienna were rebuilt, although in the case of Berlin, its division by the Berlin Wall reflected the division of Europe into the Soviet Union controlled East and the capitalist West, agreed at the Yalta Conference of 1945.

This division affected the artistic journeys of Austrian musicians after the Second World War. It was more likely for them to give concerts in West than in East Berlin. Not only were they paid more there, but arranging gigs was simpler, as it did not require dealing with the music bureaucrats and censors. Germany was the natural destination of those Austrians who had international ambitions. For example, it was the first country where Falco toured after gaining fame in his own country.

For Poles, Berlin is the closest foreign capital. From many places in the West of Poland, such as Szczecin and Poznań, Berlin is nearer than Warsaw. During the state socialist time many inhabitants of Poland travelled to East Berlin as the standard of living was higher in East Germany and the city offered more consumer goods than shops in Poland, particularly during the crisis-ridden 1980s. To be able to afford these goods, many entrepreneurial Poles sold illegally their products, such as clothes and decorated plastic bags, in Berlin.

East Berlin and East Germany at large were also regarded as the best places in the European East for Polish musicians of state socialist period to tour. The rates there were the best in Eastern Europe and the audience was enthusiastic. The biggest stars, such as rock band Czerwone Gitary, made records there and sold them in more than a million copies. This enthusiasm, however, was not reciprocated. Polish audiences were dismissive of East German popular music and especially pop-rock. Such an attitude reflected the opinion that East Germany was a much more loyal or obedient member of the Eastern bloc than Poland, which was reflected not only in its strictly political decisions, but also cultural discussions and policies, including those concerning music.

In a nutshell, in the late 1940s, both countries adopted the doctrine of socialist realism, which affected all fields of artistic production. However, as David Tompkins observes,

> By the mid-1950s, the musical worlds of Poland and East Germany looked very different from each other—in Poland, the aesthetic ideology of socialist realism collapsed, while in East Germany, a less restrictive version of this music continued to be composed and performed for decades. In both countries, initial enthusiasm for socialist realism among a broad cross-section of composers gave way to growing disquiet and frustration at the increasing dogmatism and pressure by party officials and their allies in the musical world. Both parties made significant concessions to composer autonomy at the start of destalinization in 1953, but the SED handled this course correction much more successfully through a clever and judicious policy, in contrast to the excessive dogmatism and tactical mistakes committed by its counterpart in Poland. The SED could also count on a larger number of composers, both in absolute and relative terms, who sympathized more fully with its goals. (Tompkins 2013: 16)

Tompkins refers here principally to serious, state-supported music. However, his statements also concerned, to a large extent, popular music or at least its perception in neighboring countries. Polish audiences regarded German rock as bland, conformist, and innocuous and practically no star from East Germany became a star in Poland.

If East Berlin and East Germany were seen as a lucrative space to exploit by Polish pop-rockers, this was even more the case with West Berlin. West Berlin was regarded as a friendly and convenient place to go, due to its physical proximity and the network of people facilitating gigs of Polish artists. Among those who were the most frequent visitors to the city were Czesław Niemen, and the bands SBB and Kombi. However, these artists hardly sought to forge any deeper links with local musicians and music entrepreneurs. They were happy to be paid in hard currency, which they could exchange into Polish zloties on the black market or buy coveted music equipment.

7.3 Berlin as a Source of Knowledge and Prestige

Berlin is regarded as the main center of electronic music in Europe. For foreign artists this means that Berlin is the place where one can learn about new trends, meet its leading representatives, and forge connections with fellow musickers. Consequently, gaining recognition there equals achieving recognition in the "electronic world" at large.

The importance of Berlin as a source of knowledge was mentioned by many of my Austrian interviewees, who said that they travelled there to buy records and go to clubs. Some decided to stay there for longer. In the case of Viennese musicians, it was practically all of those whom I interviewed. One of the most significant examples is Susanne Kirchmayr, better known as Electric Indigo, who from 1993 to 1996 lived in Berlin and worked at Hard Wax, one of the leading institutions, promoting EDM in Europe, set up by Mark Emestus in 1989. Hard Wax consisted of a shop in the Kreuzberg district of Berlin and a distribution company. Needless to say, thanks to being in charge of sales, Kirchmayr became well connected with artists of similar interests, in Berlin and elsewhere. In this way, she overcame the main problem negatively affecting women's participation in electronic music, being excluded from the "boys clubs" of those trying their hands-on electronic instruments. For example, among employees of Hard Wax was DJ Hell, with whom Kirchmayr subsequently collaborated. During her Berlin years Electric Indigo produced her first compositions, some of which were released on German label Disko B, although based not in Berlin, but in Munich. Electric Indigo returned to her home town in 1996, in part because in Berlin she felt alienated. Although there was no language barrier, the contact with people living there was superficial. However, she retained close contact with Berlin. As she told me, Berlin remained very important for her, because she identifies with its club culture and it is still the city where she plays most often. Electric Indigo's connections with Berlin are also facilitated by her using a booking agency based in Berlin, Media Loca.

What concerns Electric Indigo is also, to a large extent, true about Patrick Pulsinger, a leading representative of Austrian techno. Pulsinger in fact is not Austrian, but comes from East Germany, although he relocated with his mother to Syria when he was a child. Unlike Kirchmayr, Pulsinger learnt his craft in New York, rather than Berlin, but once he returned to Austria and established himself there, Berlin clubs became his main destination. He also signed up to Media Loca, often played in Berlin clubs and recorded with Disco B, despite setting up his own label in Vienna, Cheap Records.

Other leading electronic musicians from Austria, Kruder and Dorfmeister, like Pulsinger, founded their own label in Vienna, G-Stone, but used a company from Berlin, !K7 Studio Records, to release their own records. !K7 was also the "home" for Dorfmeister's next project, Tosca, established with Rupert Huber. The cooperation with !K7 proved very fruitful, as it ensured international distribution for Kruder and Dorfmeister and Tosca. At the same time, productions of these two music entities, Kruder and Dorfmeister in the series *DJ Kicks* and Tosca's s *Suzuki* and *Delhi 9* belong to the most profitable in the history of this company. Kruder, Dorfmeister, and Huber have also been frequent guests in Berlin's venues, even though neither of them moved to Berlin; Dorfmeister relocated to Zurich and Kruder moved to Paris, although he also returned to Vienna (Mazierska 2019: 98–132).

Finally, a notable case of an Austrian electronic musician with close links with Berlin is Peter Votava, known as DJ Pure or just Pure, as well as half of the duo Ilsa Gold, set up with Christopher Just and very popular in Austria in the 1990s. Votava was moving between Vienna and Berlin, having projects in both cities, such as Wasted parties in Berlin, in collaboration with American DJ Jason Forrest, and finally settled in Berlin, where he made records for the label Staalplaat.

For electronic musicians from Austria the fall of the Berlin Wall meant greater opportunities to perform and a larger market to sell their music. For Poles, the change was even more dramatic, because it meant being able to move and work in a place which was previously off-limits to them: West Berlin, joined together with East Berlin. This opportunity, however, was not used immediately. Till the end of the

1990s for Polish electronic musicians Berlin was mostly the place to buy music instruments rather to seek employment opportunities.

One of the first Polish electronic musicians to break the mold is Jacek Sienkiewicz. Sienkiewicz is described as a pioneer of Polish techno, as well as being one of the first Polish musicians to set up his own record label Recognition. In the end of the 1990s, he started to send his tracks to the musical press and clubs and, to his surprise, they were reviewed by foreign journalists and picked up to be played in clubs. Among those who were enchanted by the productions of the young Warsawian was a well-known DJ and music producer Sven Väth. Väth suggested to Sienkiewicz to make a record for his label Cocoon Records. In the end Sienkiewicz recorded four records for Cocoon; the first of them being *Téchnè* (2002). Although Cocoon was based in Frankfurt, it was well known in Berlin and facilitated Sienkiewicz's entry to the clubs in the city, even made him consider the idea of moving to Berlin long term. Although in the end this did not happen, in the 2000s Sienkiewicz became an ambassador for Polish music in Berlin and Germany at large.

The next Polish electronic musician who made it in Berlin was Marcin Czubała, associated primarily with house, although he tried his hand in different genres. In his case, the role of facilitator was played by his father (Gzyl 2013), who organized events with German musicians in his hometown of Poznań—a fact to which I return in due course. Marcin Czubała's debut album *Dope* was released by German company Neue Heimat in 2001. Subsequently, he was linked to the Berlin label Mobilee, established in 2005 and owned by Anja Schneider and Ralf Kollmann. There Czubała released the album *Chronicles Of Never* in 2008 and in 2011 he curated part of a project titled *Back To Back*, which presents a selection of the best work from the last years of the company. It includes a record entitled *Marcin Czubala Exclusives & Collaborations*, which includes tracks of some of the most popular Polish electronic musicians, such as Novika and Catz 'n Dogz (Świąder 2015).

The last artists included on Czubała's compilation, Catz 'n Dogz, consisting of two DJs and music producers from Szczecin, Grzegorz Demiańczuk (Greg) and Wojciech Tarańczuk (Vojtek), associated mostly with house, also forged a career in which Berlin features prominently. This happened when, following a successful remix of the track "Who's Afraid of Detroit" of a producer from Detroit Claude VonStroke, they attracted his interest, which subsequently led to collaboration with him and opened the doors to Berlin's clubs. Eventually they moved there at the end of the 2000s (Bollin 2015: 51), albeit retaining close links with Poland.

Another Polish musician who forged a successful career in Berlin is Marcin Kozłowski, who uses the pseudonym DJ Highfish. Kozłowski released records on the Berlin label WMF Records.

Berlin also plays a major role in the career of one of the most talented and respected Polish female electronic musician, An On Bast (true name Anna Suda), based in Poznań. She started to play in Berlin in 2009, and by this point had gigs in almost all Berlin clubs, including Sisyphos, Watergate, Katerblau, Tresor, Challet, about blank, Golden Gate, and Mensch Meier. She also released records on Berlin labels, such as *Sundevit* for Acker Record in 2013 and *The Ballet Began at Eight* in 2018 for Pets Recordings.

There are more Polish DJs and music producers, who live and work in Berlin. As I was told by my informants, this does not mean that this scene has been easy for Poles. On the contrary, being invited to Berlin is more difficult than anywhere else in Europe—behind any Polish artist who succeeded in Berlin there are tens if not hundreds who failed.

When talking about Berlin as a source of knowledge for Polish musickers, it is also worth mentioning information about music in this city in the Polish music press. In magazines such as *Kaktus*, *Techno Party*, *Plastik*, and *Laif*, which were set up in the 1990s or the early 2000s, Berlin features prominently, indeed getting more space than cities in the United Kingdom or the United States. We can read there about Berlin clubs, star DJs, and record labels. For example, in *Laif*, in an issue from 2010, we find a five-page article dedicated to the previously mentioned, Berlin-based label! K7. We can learn there that the Polish branch of the record company BMG started officially to distribute records released by !K7. The author of this article, Piotr Nowicki, mentions that possessing such records was in Poland the source of specific cultural capital; it was a sign of belonging to a narrow circle of musickers who look for musical pleasures outside of mainstream techno and house. He also mentions that in Poland records from !K7 were very expensive, because the double CDs cost double in Poland (Nowicki 2010: 37). Of course !K7's records were also well known and respected in Austria, not least because K&D and Tosca released their works there, but I found the tone of this article particularly Polish; betraying a reverence which one would be unlikely to spot along the banks of Danube.

7.4 Berlin as a Model for Building Local Electronic Scenes

Prior to the 1990s, the Viennese popular music scene was rather small and inward-looking. There were few clubs where fans of music could meet and listen to their favorite music. Such a situation reflected the fact that Vienna was seen as the world capital of classical music. The city's authorities invested heavily to cultivate this image, in order to attract international tourists. Supporting popular music in Vienna was not a priority, was even seen by some as an obstruction to conveying the desired image. Historically, financial support of popular culture in Vienna has been low in comparison with that offered to high culture (Reitsamer 2011: 30). The second factor contributing to the scene being underdeveloped was the lack of major stars. Austrian stars, such as Georg Danzer were seen as parochial, even though their music often merited a wider recognition (Mazierska 2019: 35–36).

In the 1980s this situation changed to some extent due to Vienna getting its first global star, Falco (Mazierska 2013, 2019: 39–40). However, while Falco's successes gave some Austrian artists more confidence to try their hand in music, the "Falco's factor" did not play any major role in developing popular music culture in the city, not least because he was a global star who was more likely to perform in the United States and Japan than in Vienna. It was the successes of the Austrian electronic musicians of the 1990s, such as Patrick Pulsinger, Fennesz, and Peter Rehberg which allowed the development of local clubs with "nights" dedicated to specific genres, especially in Flex which became the center of electronic music in the city (Mazierska 2019: 55–80). Moreover, during the 1990s "municipal policy in Vienna developed a stronger interest in rock, pop and electronic music and embedded the opening of numerous bars and clubs into the Urban Wien Gürtel Plus gentrification project (1995–2000), which was aimed at restructuring a part of the Vienna Gürtel—a wall construction supporting an elevated train which divides the inner city districts from the outer suburban districts" (Reitsamer 2011: 31). Obviously, this was advantageous to artists, their audiences, and the Viennese popular music industry at large.

Although, as I mentioned earlier, many Viennese electronic musicians frequently travelled or even relocated to Berlin temporarily, Berlin was not used as a model to develop a local electronic scene; the city followed its own path, reflecting the city's specific circumstances. One crucial difference was the character of available spaces. Following Germany's reunification, which led to dramatic deindustrialization and depopulation of East Berlin and East Germany at large, created a surplus of places where music could be enjoyed, including large spaces and their semi-legal, underground atmosphere. Utilization of such spaces was cheap. In Vienna, this did not happen; space was limited, and their development was largely driven from above, by specific policies of the local authorities (Mazierska 2019: 57–59). Consequently, in popular opinion, the Viennese scene was more bourgeoise and laid-back in comparison with Berlin, with the downtempo productions of Kruder and Dorfmeister encapsulating its character. It was also Vienna, rather than Berlin, which pioneered the phenomenon of electronic musicians engaging with classical music traditions and perform in places normally reserved for classic and experimental artists. One early example was Patrick Pulsinger and Erdem Tunakan electronization of Tchaikovsky's *Swan Lake*, presented in Volksoper in Vienna and released in 1999 on a CD titled *Schwanensee Remixed*.

Berlin was more a model for developing electronic music in Polish cities, because the conditions in Poland were more similar to East Germany: both countries experienced rapid deindustrialization and the need to reinvent themselves, including in the area of culture. For East Germany and East Berlin it was, however, easier, due to its proximity to West Berlin and its openness to western influences, what can be unsympathetically described as cultural imperialism and neocolonialism.

I appreciated how important was Berlin for "electronic" Poland when I once looked at the "electronic map of Poland," published in one of the magazines, devoted to club music, probably *Laif*. In a nutshell, this map demonstrated that the closer a given town was to Germany, the more likely it was for it to have some electronic music festival and a network of clubs, playing electronic music, with the East of Poland being largely immune from such influences, instead developing its own version of dance music: disco polo.

In particular, Berlin acted as a model for Szczecin and Poznań. Szczecin was even called "little Berlin" and prided itself on being at the forefront of Polish electronic music. This started in the early 1990s with many young people travelling to Berlin to visit its clubs and take part in its Love Parade. The next stage was organizing similar events in Szczecin. In the documentary *Szczecin Calling*, directed by Nina

Pankiewicz, Adrian Janowski, and Wojciech Wyrwicki, we learn that the beginnings of Szczecin clubbing started in the early to mid-1990s. The precursors of this phenomenon were an agency called New Music Art, which organized events named Techno Dance Mission. They did not have a stable location, but were set up in different places, often abandoned warehouses or factories and attracted large crowds, on occasion several thousand people. As one of the oldest Szczecin "techno animators," Szymon Karpierz, reminisces, among DJs performing there were Tresor regulars and even guests from Detroit. At this time the electronic scene in Szczecin was not specialized; the best-known genres were techno and house, but it was not infrequent that a gig included hip-hop artists alongside representatives of techno. Many of the parties, again, as in Berlin, were illegal and had poor infrastructure; the sound systems did not work well; on occasion there were even no toilets. There was also no continuity; after several events the organizers had to move elsewhere when their place was discovered by the police.

After a decade or so this "time of pioneers" was over. The illegal events became replaced by legal parties and festivals; the new clubs got better facilities and equipment. The scene also became more specialized, although—unlike in some other places—the fans of different subgenres did not lock themselves up in their own microworlds. What remained was the close contact between musickers from Szczecin and Berlin. Nowhere in Poland are Berlin DJs as well-known as in Szczecin and the largest proportion of Polish DJs based in Berlin come from Szczecin. Among them, as mentioned earlier, are Catz 'n Dogz, who from Germany's capital shape their Polish career and animate music life in Szczecin, recently setting up there the Wooded City Festival with the hope that, as they said, "many people from Berlin will come" (Kowalka and Czarnecki 2018).

There are also cases when musickers from Berlin and Szczecin region collaborate on specific events. One such example is the festival Nagle Nad Morzem/Plötzlich am Meer, addressed principally to German fans of electronic music which till 2017 took place on a beach in Rogowo, about 15 km from Szczecin. This event, however, turned out to be controversial, largely due to a large amount of waste or, more precisely, human excrement, which the organizers were unable to utilize, and which stayed for a long time in barrels. There was also an accusation of not paying taxes, prompting the users of Internet forums to accuse Germans of behaving as colonizers (Kwiatkowski 2017; pw 2017).

In Poznań an important person bringing "Berlin to Poland" was Stefan Czubała, club owner and animator of culture. In the 1990s Czubała frequently travelled to Berlin, taking part in events organized by Tresor and the famous Love Parade. Subsequently he invited music producers from Tresor to play in Poznań, in total organizing over 160 events. Stefan Czubała also stood behind distributing electronic music "from Tresor," such as Jeff Mills, on cassettes. Consequently, Czubała attributes himself the role of somebody who brought techno to Poland and molded Poznań's scene in the image of Berlin. Twenty years later the Tresor name and brand does not cause such excitement in Poznań as it used to, but Poznań is still a place where one can often spot DJs from Germany's capital. Stefan Czubała's musical

taste also affected his son who, as previously mentioned, became a respected producer of electronic music and one who often performs in Berlin.

Łódź is located much further from Berlin than Szczecin and Poznań, but this city also borrowed from Berlin when trying to shape its electronic scene. In the case of Łódź the main event modelled on the musical life in Berlin was the techno parade—"Parada Wolności" (Freedom Parade), marching through Piotrkowska Street, the longest high street in Europe. A child of two managers of the Łódź club New Alcatraz, Sławomir Żak and Robert Jakubowski, it was meant to be merely an addition to the large techno event, organized regularly in the sports' hall, but its success encouraged the organizers to repeat it (Kaazetka 2001: 44). The first Freedom Parade took place in 1997, had five tracks with equipment and attracted 8000 visitors; 3 years later the number of visitors was between 28,000 and 30,000. The parade included a competition for DJs and a Mega Party in two sports halls (Kaazetka 2001: 47). Judging by its coverage in the press, this was the most important event in the calendar of Polish fans of techno from its beginnings throughout the 2000s. In common with the Love Parade, the Freedom Parade had political connotations: it celebrated the political freedom enjoyed by Poles after the fall of the Berlin Wall, including greater sexual and personal freedom, reflected in outrageous clothes and make-up.

To summarize the influence of Berlin on Polish musickers, it is worth mentioning the documentary film *Miłość do płyty winylowej* (*Love for a Vinyl Record*, 2002), directed by Maria Zmarz-Koczanowicz, which presents techno culture in Poland of the late 1990s, early 2000s. The film finishes with an image of Polish techno fans attending the Love Parade in Berlin. In this film Polish techno fans are part of a colorful crowd, engaged in a cosmopolitan event, where there are no *natives* and *guests*; everybody is European and equal. As I argued elsewhere, this image can be read as a symbol of Polish road toward the European Union and *returning* to Europe (Mazierska 2018: 167).

7.5 Collaborations and Textual Connections

Given the importance of Berlin for the careers of many musicians in Poland and Austria, one can suspect that their music reflects their journeys. Is this the case? The question is difficult to answer, as it is almost impossible to establish whether there exists something like a *Berlin sound* and what constitutes it. Those who believe in its existence claim that Berlin sound is impossible to emulate. It can be produced and heard only in this city, similarly as *Vienna sound* cannot be created in Berlin, Frankfurt, or Brussels.

Nevertheless, Berlin was not cited as an important source of inspiration for any of my informants from Vienna, who started their careers in the 1990s. They more likely admitted to being inspired by British productions: Depeche Mode, Sonic Youth, or krautrock bands, Kraftwerk, Can and Neu!; neither of which was from Berlin. Even the most Berlin-oriented of the Viennese stars, Electric Indigo, was unable to list a

single musician from Berlin whom she tried to emulate, only mentioning their general approach to the scene and music business, as represented by Mark Ernestus and Monolake, among others. This lack of recognized influences might reflect the fact that the successes of Viennese musicians, such as Kruder and Dorfmeister, Tosca, Pulsinger and Fennesz coincided with the rise of techno stars from Berlin or there was only a small lag between these phenomena. Moreover, I will risk the statement that the musicians from these two cities had different priorities. Berlin, due to its rich network of clubs, was conducive to developing a culture of clubbing and DJ-stars. Vienna, which had fewer and smaller clubs, prioritized music for listening, developing such subgenres as ambient and noise.

The situation changed in the last one and the half decades, the period which Robert Strachan describes as "convergent digitization," which arrived when a "number of different strains coming from earlier patterns of digitization converged upon the singular site of the personal computer" (Strachan 2017: 6) and the artists got more connected thanks to the Internet platforms which encourage networking and collaboration. One notable example of this phenomenon is a collaboration between the pop electronic duo HVOB from Vienna and a German dance and house music producer Oliver Koletzki, based in Berlin. HVOB started their career by releasing music on Soundcloud, where they were discovered by Koletzki, who contacted them and produced their first tracks. Subsequently, their debut album was released on the Berlin label Stil vor Talent. In this way a successful career was launched, leading to gigs all over the world (Brüggemann-Stepien 2013).

On the Polish side the closest to Berlin from this perspective is the previously mentioned Jacek Sienkiewicz, who produced tracks and records with a plethora of Berlin musicians such as Max Loderbauer and Ricardo Villalobos, a music producer born in Chile, but who spent most of his life in Berlin. With Loderbauer, best known from the band Sun Electric, Sienkiewicz recorded an EP *Ridges* (2015), which was recorded in Berlin and mixed by Villalobos. This record consists of only two long tracks, titled "East Ridge" and "West Ridge," which can be regarded as an allusion to the places from which these two musicians originate, as well as their trips to the Polish Tatra mountains and the Alps (Groyecka 2015: 49). These pieces betray influences of mountain folklore, Edvard Grieg and psychedelia, and reflect Sienkiewicz's own passion for mountains. Villalobos also remixed one of Sienkiewicz's most successful tracks, "Drifting" and Sienkiewicz's interpretation of Czesław Niemen's song "Pielgrzym" (Pilgrim). Conversely, Sienkiewicz's pieces are in the repertoire of such producers as Tobi Neumann and Chris Liebing.

Also, the previously mentioned An On Bast has in her portfolio collaborations with musicians from Berlin. For many years she has been working with the producer Douglas Greed, whom she met when she attended the Red Bull Music Academy in Melbourne in 2006. Another Berlin artist with whom she joined forces is the producer of deep house Zazou, producing together *Tunya* EP, which in my view belongs to the best in the career of the Polish producer. When I am writing these words, An On Bast is preparing herself for her next Berlin collaboration: playing in July 2019 a concert in Funkhaus with the Berlin duo INSTANT on the largest sequencer in the world.

7.6 Conclusions

There is no doubt that Berlin as a music scene strongly influences musickers from Austria and Poland. This results from the city's convenient geographic location, its place in postcommunist history, which was conducive to its becoming the main European center of electronic music and the fact that Germans and Austrians share the same language. For Austrians and Poles recording and performing in Berlin meant gaining knowledge and prestige and the chance to attract the largest possible audience. There are fewer examples of direct inspiration and influence on the character of the work of Austrian and Polish artists, but this might reflect the fact that such influence is difficult to establish and the artists themselves are unwilling to admit that they borrowed from their closest neighbors. The relationship between these three countries is asymmetrical: it matters more for Poles and Austrians to conquer Berlin than vice versa. It is likely that convergent digitization will weaken the electronic power of Berlin. Conversely, the growing importance of live music might lead to Berlin, with its dense network of music clubs, growing in importance. For the time being, however, we might expect more musicians from Austria and Vienna to travel to Berlin.

References

Bollin, P. (2015). Nic na siłę: Catz 'n Dogz. *Laif, 3*, 50–53.

Brüggemann-Stepien, T. (2013). Her voice over boys start through. *Music Austria*. Accessed May 20, 2019, from www.musicaustria.at/her-voice-over-boys-starten-durch/

Groyecka, D. (2015). Jacek Sienkiewicz: Ambient, jodłowanie i Detroit techno. *Laif, 2*, 48–50.

Gzyl, P. (2013). Początki nowej elektroniki nad Wisłą: jak wymyślano w Polsce techno i house. *Onet.Muzyka*. Accessed May 17, 2019, from https://kultura.onet.pl/muzyka/gatunki/klubowa/poczatki-nowej-elektroniki-nad-wisla-jak-wymyslano-w-polsce-techno-i-house/h7cpdqp

Kaazetka. (2001). Łódź techniczna tańczy. *Laif, 2*, 40–47.

Kowalka, Ł., & Czarnecki, D. (2018). 'Dużo się nauczyliśmy robiąc festiwal' – Catz 'n Dogz o Wooded City. *Muno.pl*. Accessed May 22, 2019, from https://muno.pl/author/danielczarnecki/

Kwiatkowski, M. (2017). Śmierdzące techno w Rogowie. *24 Kurier.pl*. Accessed May 29, 2019, from https://24kurier.pl/aktualnosci/wiadomosci/w-kurierze-smierdzace-techno-w-rogowie/

Mazierska, E. (2013). *Falco and beyond: Neo nothing post of all*. Sheffield: Equinox.

Mazierska, E. (2018). Disco polo and techno according to Maria Zmarz-Koczanowicz. In E. Mazierska & Z. Győri (Eds.), *Popular music and the moving image in Eastern Europe* (pp. 155–169). New York: Bloomsbury.

Mazierska, E. (2019). *Popular Viennese electronic music, 1990–2015: A cultural history*. London: Routledge.

Nowicki, P. (2010). Kultowa Siódemka. *Laif, 3–4*, 37–41.

pw. (2017). Nagle nad morzem zakotwiczy w Podczelu? *24 Kurier.pl*. Accessed May 30, 2019, from https://24kurier.pl/aktualnosci/wiadomosci/nagle-nad-morzem-zakotwiczy-w-podczelu/

Reitsamer, R. (2011). The DIY careers of techno and drum 'n' bass DJs in Vienna. *Dancecult*, (1), 28–43.

Small, C. (1998). *Musicking: The meanings of performing and listening*. Middletown, CT: Wesleyan University Press.

Strachan, R. (2017). *Sonic technologies: Popular music, digital culture and the creative process*. New York: Bloomsbury.

Świąder, J. (2015). Marcin Czubała. *Culture.pl*. Accessed May 16, 2019, from https://culture.pl/pl/tworca/marcin-czubala

Tompkins, D. G. (2013). *Composing the party line: Music and politics in early Cold War Poland and East Germany*. Purdue: University Press.

Chapter 8
"100% Expert!" Mastery and Equality in Darsha Hewitt's *Sideman 5000 Adventure*

Patrick Valiquet

Abstract This chapter examines the tutorial video series *A Sideman 5000 Adventure* (2015), in which Canadian-born artist Darsha Hewitt presents her research on early drum machine technology in a format that brings together for the first time her unique didactic and aesthetic interests. The work is presented in the context of Hewitt's immediate concerns as an artist and educator, with an emphasis on her staging of the creative encounter with obsolete hardware and her critical confrontation with normative standards of technical expertise. A concluding section then considers Hewitt's approach in relation to the pedagogical problems of equality and emancipation, bringing her work into dialogue with the educational philosophies of Pierre Bourdieu and Jacques Rancière.

In a 2015 series of videos documenting her restoration of a Wurlitzer Sideman 5000 drum machine, Berlin-based artist Darsha Hewitt blurs the lines between art, research, and education (Figs. 8.1 and 8.2). In one sense the project is archaeological, excavating a meticulously crafted, semi-mechanical ancestor of the sequencers and rhythm computers which structure so much of the music we hear today. The drum machine is effectively an instrument of control: it automatically measures out interconnected units of time, materializing a musical order beyond the limits of human precision. It is neither the musical function nor the sound of the machine that captures our attention, however. Adopting a persona reminiscent of online tutorial videos meting out instruction in everything from eye-liner application to astrophysics, Hewitt invites us to read the Sideman as a map to a lost set of assumptions about sound, music, and craft. She also poses some challenging questions about education as a component of artistic practice. What happens when the educational encounter is the form of the artwork rather than simply a device with which to mediate its effects? Should such artworks inculcate particular ways of thinking and acting, or should they leave their audience free to interpret anew?

P. Valiquet (✉)
University of Edinburgh, Edinburgh, UK
e-mail: patrick.valiquet@ed.ac.uk

A. Jóri, M. Lücke (eds.), *The New Age of Electronic Dance Music and Club Culture*, Music Business Research, https://doi.org/10.1007/978-3-030-39002-0_8

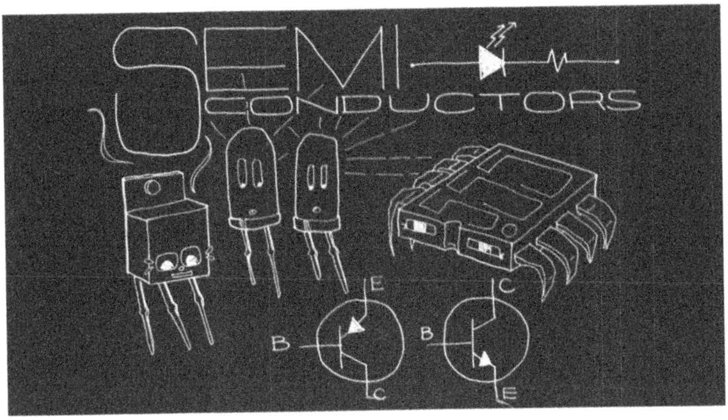

Fig. 8.1 Title card drawn by Darsha Hewitt, from her video *A Sideman 5000 Adventure* (2015) (Used with permission)

Fig. 8.2 Darsha Hewitt and the Wurlitzer Sideman 5000 drum machine, from her video *A Sideman 5000 Adventure* (2015) (Used with permission)

The staging of the didactic exchange in the Sideman videos invites the viewer to reconsider the significance of artistic and technical skills for the reproduction of social order. The idea that aesthetic expression should disclose knowledge or feeling in some way is often articulated on the basis of a semiotics of skill (Gell 1992). The selection and acquisition of particular skills for creative expression is also a cultural responsibility constrained by one's place in the social order with respect to class, race, or gender. In his *Politics*, Aristotle explicitly links the value of music education with the need for general moral discipline. Music for Aristotle imitated the natural forms of moral sentiments and qualities of feeling. Learning to make and appreciate music should enable one to acquire the right character while also honing one's ability to judge the dispositions of others (Aristotle 2007: 248–270). Many of the more

abstract and pluralistic forms of experimental music and art-making which have emerged since the late twentieth century still share this didactic fervor. The work of John Cage, for example, was guided by a clear project of political education. Central to the experimental and systems work that Cage's thinking catalyzed during the Cold War was the goal of improving the experimental listener: challenging her intellectually, expanding her range of cultural and scientific expertises, training her both perceptually and physically (Piekut 2012; Turner 2013). While many artists during this period took up teaching and theoretical production as a central part of their practice, however, relatively few featured pedagogy as the form or material of their work. Teaching and learning took place off-stage: a matter for books or classrooms, but not an essential part of the artwork or its reception.

The "circuit-bending" and hardware hacking movements which have emerged in recent decades turn this dynamic inside-out, promoting radical transparency in design, the principles of which are imparted to audiences through public workshops, open access publications, and social media (Ghazala 2004; Collins 2006; Richards 2013). Like their cybernetic forebears (Turner 2006; Halpern 2014) and their contemporaries in the open source software movement (Kelty 2005), contemporary open hardware activists regard democratic access to technological resources as an unconditional right. The convergence of Hewitt's creative and didactic projects is rooted in similar concerns, but also sets up a departure, enacting a formal challenge to the transparent, universal access of hacker ideology. The videos cast a new light on Hewitt's previous work, clarify long-standing influences, and pose new challenges for critics and audiences.

In one sense, Hewitt's Sideman videos seem to denaturalize the educational exchange, mounting it in a hyperaesthetic frame which amplifies its social undercurrents. As John Richards (2013) has written, the act of placing aesthetic attention on the experience of the electronics workshop rather than the object to be taken home brings such educational practices closer to the domain of relational art. Circuit benders might in this sense hail or coerce workshop publics into subject positions intrinsic to the form of a particular site-specific intervention (Bourriaud 2001). Richards' approach recalls classics in the genre such as the 2004 event Swiss Swiss Democracy by Thomas Hirschhorn, in which lectures, plays, and texts produced inside an installation elaborated upon and generated confrontations with its political content. Here and in similarly encounter-based artworks the political message is unambiguous and the audience is implicated in a participatory critique of current affairs or institutional norms (Hirschhorn 2013). The blur Richards allows between the form and content of his electronics workshops also sets up the kind of provisional recursive relationship that David Novak finds structuring the practice of noisicians in Japan. Zooming out from the technical construction of their performance setups, Novak extends the notion of feedback into a master metaphor for the Noise ethos, tracing its link to concepts of reciprocity and exchange in the late twentieth-century social sciences, and to noisicians' ongoing negotiations of their creative identities (Novak 2013: 140).

Hewitt takes a more heterogeneous approach, refusing to melt the ethical and the aesthetic into a single conceptual object. Instead of moving the encounter into the gallery, her work contributes constructively to the normal forms of participation and learning already used by the hacking and making communities in which her practice has its roots. The Sideman videos undermine the performances of mastery typical of sound engineering cultures not by quibbling with their content but by appropriating and revising their form. They model a style of learning in which technical expertise is not transferred from expert to novice, but emerges out of an egalitarian encounter with technological objects and systems. As such they also model a way past the gendered exclusions which so often structure the acquisition of technical skills, especially in musical contexts (Green 1997; McCartney 2006).

The candid, disarming approach to instruction is consistent with Hewitt's own teaching practice. Since her 2014 move from Canada to Germany, where she has held a series of academic positions in Weimar, Kassel, Karlsruhe and most recently Berlin, teaching has shifted to the center of Hewitt's professional life. Her interest in education can be traced back as far as her early contributions to the open source software projects Pure Data and Gridflow as a student of Alexandre Castonguay at the University of Ottawa. Hewitt's fascination with recycling and restoring obsolete technologies works in parallel with her focus on training and documentation. The pattern begins with the 2007 installation *Rotarian Choir*, produced in collaboration with Alexandre Quessy. Appliances are gathered into groups to play out cryptic choreographies. Hewitt finds the simplest imaginable ways of giving her objects voice—the mechanism of which is almost always transparent to the audience—and then lets them sing together as equals. In *Electrostatic Bell Choir* (2012) the result nearly approaches Nam June Paik's aesthetic, gesturing toward the grand psychedelic arrangements of meditating video screens by which he hoped to usher in a new electronic consciousness. In general, however, Hewitt's assemblages suggest starker interpretations. There are tangible parallels with the work of fellow Ottawa-born duo The User (Emmanuel Madan and Thomas McIntosh), for whom Hewitt once worked as a technician. From the *Coincidence Engine* installations (2008–2010) back to the first *Symphony for Dot Matrix Printers* (1998), The User has shown a similar fascination with chorusing as a way of accentuating the grain of the obsolete. But the mood here is distinctly dystopian. Choirs of clocks and office printers connote an unconsensual order. Their sounds harass us into compliance with generalized flows of power.

In contrast, the sites of Hewitt's interventions have always been much more personal. Nowhere is this more evident than in her *Feedback Babies* of 2014, which features a yawning, somnambulant chorus of Fisher-Price Nursery Monitors. Like the television and telephone installations, *Feedback Babies* refers to the scale and the concerns of the home, and in this sense Hewitt harks back to a long tradition of feminist critique. It is a penchant that connects her work thematically to that of Montreal-based performance art group Women With Kitchen Appliances, with whom Hewitt performed for a brief period in 2011. Their generic, faceless costumes and noisy reappropriations of cooking and cleaning devices impart a distinct sense of rage in the face of unequal domestication.

The Sideman 5000 was never a ubiquitous household object, to be sure. But the way Hewitt handles it draws attention to its intimate, furniture-like aesthetic appeal.

It is an accompanist, a buddy. It is endearing because of its idiosyncrasies. At times, she seems to be selling it to her viewers. She brings it down to a domestic scale and shows it to be banal, practical, and accessible. Her performance inhabits the same affective overlap between teaching and advertising you might detect in an "unboxing." The deflationary impulse originates in Hewitt's drawing: both her copious notebooks and the illustrations she uses in teaching (Fig. 8.1). These clearly betray the influence of Cold War popular science magazines and instructional guides such as those of Forrest Mims, with their bold, decorative lettering and fantastically anthropomorphized semiconductors (Mims 1986). If Hewitt's illustrations borrow heavily from this era of technological optimism, however, they also enact a revision of its social forms. Where mid-century hobbyist culture primarily addressed a public of white, suburban American men and boys, Hewitt's vision of the cybernetic era highlights its experiments in social organization and democracy. Viewed through a feminine historiographical lens, the canonical Foucauldian account of cybernetics as an "ontology of the enemy" (Galison 1994) breaks down to reveal a distinctly utopian tradition of artists and teachers inspired by the thought of themselves and their students as open systems. Hewitt herself has pointed to the American artist Sonya Landy Sheridan, whose "Generative Systems" courses at the Art Institute of Chicago in the 1960s challenged students to unlock the creative potential of basic office machines (Sheridan 2006). The generation of composer-educators who began their careers during the Cold War, among them Pauline Oliveros (1984) in the United States and Marcelle Deschênes (Valiquet 2017) in Canada, played a crucial role in institutionalizing electronic music pedagogies with a focus on receptivity, interdependence, and play rather than pure technical efficiency.

In her introduction to the 2010 book of interviews *Pink Noises*, Tara Rodgers weighs an essentialized femininity highlighting soft, irrational, or fuzzy qualities of experience against the possibility of a positive feminist historiography of audio engineering. She notes how many women "stake out philosophical positions that run counter to using dominant technoscientific priorities of precision and control as ends in themselves" (Rodgers 2010: 8), and thus invites us to look more closely at "how electronic music can (or has failed to) express possibilities for more imaginative and ethical encounters with technology and difference now and in the future" (ibid.: 10). We must keep in mind, however, that the same qualities have been used to implicitly devalue women's work in relation to dominant masculine norms of competition and creativity. Thinking of women in terms of "passivity, receptivity and maternality," writes Rodgers, traps them in a logic of "reproduction" which can become an obstacle to valorizing their work as "producers" (ibid.: 12). Reproductive technologies and technical practices, such as teaching, are generally ignored by audiences and critics. The standards of representation used to evaluate sound technologies in science and industry often perpetuate patriarchal assumptions about masculine originality and feminine transparency.

One of the opportunities for intervention, according to Rodgers, is to "account for reproductive sounds in all their temporal depth" and thus to "challenge the patrilineal lines of descent and the universalizing male claims to creation that have thus far characterized dominant discourses in electronic music" (ibid.: 15). This attention to the historically and culturally situated gendering of sounds does not originate in Rodgers' project, of course, but has been a shared strategy for feminist music scholars for decades. It links Zoe Sophia's (2000) study of "container technologies," Rebecca Leydon's (2001) work on the relationship between gendered listening positions and the use of "soft-focus" reverberation effects in certain "easy-listening" genres, and Andra McCartney's (2006) survey of the concepts of objectivity, modernity, and accuracy that help maintain gender boundaries in the electroacoustic studio. In Germany, it has informed interventions like Meike Jansen's (2005) anthology *Gendertronics*, which aims to enhance inclusion by privileging the body as both site of reception and as the means for productive action in electronic music, as well as advocacy and awareness-raising groups such as female:pressure. Insofar as the goal is to amplify feminine voices in the present, these strategies can be enormously helpful.

From a historiographical perspective, however, the implications are more complex. The main risk of this strategic essentialism is that it reinforces a "head and hands" division of labor in electronic music practice, separating the supposed abstractions produced by engineers and scientists from the emotional labor performed by listeners, players, and dancers, and thereby dissuading non-technicians from contributing as theorists or thinkers. The concentration of women in relatively invisible, "reproductive" professions like education, care, and administration may indeed echo ancient European cultural tropes identifying men with active reason and women with passive reception and affection (Lloyd 1985). The situation only seems so dire, however, to the extent that scholars and critics insist on excluding para-artistic practices like teaching and administration from the canon in the first place. The form of the category "artist" is exclusive all on its own, before we decide how to fill it with content. As teachers and administrators, women were of course never absent from electronic music production at all. Asking why they were excluded from positions of power can certainly be important from the perspective of restorative justice, but it is equally important to recognize their achievements in the positions they did hold. The relative importance of being recognized as a "producer" depends on the same gendered matrix that makes it seem like nothing special to be a secretary. As historian Marie Hicks (2017) has recently shown in her account of the retrospective defeminization of the British computing industry, there can be a reciprocal relationship between the value a profession is perceived to have for society and the value of the people perceived to be suited to performing it. As computer programming became more prestigious, it became more masculine; and as it became more masculine, it became more prestigious.

Pierre Bourdieu's sociological analysis of education gives some attention to the functions of grooming and gatekeeping associated with feminized roles, but adopts notions of care and reproduction different from those Rodgers seeks to reclaim. Although not explicitly linking education to the gendering of artistic professions, Bourdieu groups education with kinship and familial relations as ways of preserving existing orders of social and economic difference. Reproduction for Bourdieu is not undertaken intentionally, but rather animated by the subconscious, often mis-recognized *doxa* which bind together social groups across generations (Bourdieu 1977). The aesthetic and social forms that reproduction strategies take in cultural life are not experienced as coercive, but rather as freely enhancing feelings of pleasure and privilege (Bourdieu and Passeron 1964). Bourdieu's critique hinges upon the assumption that, whether one is undergoing or performing these educational or familial selection procedures, one is always in a sense consenting to one's own deception.

> These soft relations of exploitation only work if they are soft. They are relations of symbolic violence which can only be established with the complicity of those who suffer from it, like intradomestic relations. The dominated collaborate in their own exploitation through affection or admiration. (Bourdieu 1998: 111)

The emphasis here on the "soft" and "receptive" character of social reproduction underscores the uneasiness that has characterized most feminist readings of Bourdieu. As Terry Lovell puts it, Bourdieu is "bleakly pessimistic" when it comes to the sources of change available to those seeking equality (Lovell 2000: 27). He echoes structuralist forebears like Claude Lévi-Strauss in concentrating his thinking about women on their production as objects to be exchanged for social status or put to work in maintaining class boundaries through the accumulation of symbolic capital. This approach "rarely considers women as subjects with capital-accumulating strategies of their own which may be at odds with those of their family and kin" (Lovell 2000: 21). The challenge for critics has thus been to find value in Bourdieu's attention to the many constraints on gendered performance while also holding open the possibility of transformative social agency (McLeod 2005). Without assuming that subversions should be possible in all cases, it is still crucial to discover when and how gendered positionings *can* be consciously mobilized against a dispositionally determined *habitus*, and to whom such constructive boundary crossings are allowed within a given field.

Lovell illustrates the gap between reproduction and transformation by comparing the degree of subjective agency afforded by Bourdieu's theory of class with that presumed in Judith Butler's accounts of gender and sexuality (Butler 1990, 1993). Butler and Bourdieu develop contrasting readings of J. L. Austin's linguistic notion of "performativity." Butler argues that performative utterances can be "dislodged" in order to transgress authority structures, while for Bourdieu the degrees of freedom experienced by social actors are always "profoundly rooted" in authority, ironically perpetuating it by taking it for granted. Effectively, Butler locates agency in the act of performance, and thus finds all performances as equally fluid and potentially transgressive of the existing order, whereas Bourdieu locates agency in the underlying structure of economic domination, lamenting the fundamental inequality of access to transgressive actions and the inevitable condemnation of those without power to powerless forms of expression (Lovell 2000: 14–16). Readers like Lovell claim to seek a middle ground between the two: a critical performativity that is actively engaged in altering the social order which makes it possible.

A similar concern with recovering the potential for critical agency from Bourdieu's theory of social reproduction can be found in the work of French political theorist Jacques Rancière. Taking issue with the way Bourdieu reduces education to class reproduction, Rancière argues that the presumption of inequality as the starting point for education is in fact "the very means by which the actualization of equality is infinitely deferred" (Pelletier 2009: 148). In order to aim their critique at the "ineluctable reproduction" of domination, sociologists must presuppose a distinction between the capacities of the dominant and those of the dominated, dismissing the latter as "objects of study rather than intellectual subjects" (Pelletier 2009: 138; Rancière 2007). By characterizing social actors as incapable of recognizing their subordination to an immobile hierarchy, Rancière argues, Bourdieuian sociologists exclude the possibility of political change. The alternative, from this perspective, is to create forms of education in which critique from below is not only possible but essential for progress. Turning the tables on social reproduction means recognizing that, as Rancière argues, "the dominated do not remain in subordination because they misunderstand the existing state of affairs but because they lack confidence in their capacity to transform it" (Rancière 2004: 65). Equalizing actions are equally possible only in a social order which engenders equality, one where actors are presumed to be equal as a condition of possibility for their being actors at all. This presumption opens the door to what Rancière calls "dissensus," a term which encompasses not just direct "agonism" (Laclau and Mouffe 1985), but "an action taken by people declaring their capacity to alter the calculus of inclusion and exclusion that constitutes the formation to which they belong" (Moreno and Steingo 2012: 489).

In the 1987 book *Le maître ignorant* (The Ignorant Schoolmaster), Rancière makes this notion of dissensus the basis for an emancipatory philosophy of education, affirming the freedom of learners by shifting equality from the goal position to the starting point (Pelletier 2009: 142). Using historical allegory he challenges the educator to make equality a basic fact of pedagogical practice, rather than a reward promised only to the winners of an essentially unequal competition (Ross 1991: xix). Rather than presuming the student to be starting from the point of relative stupidity, and thus instructing from a position of superiority, the teacher in Rancière's allegory renounces his authority over the course of the students' explorations. Rancière's teacher—a French speaker in a Flemish classroom—is unable to communicate with the students about his own understanding of the material, so he lets them explore it for themselves and learn whatever they can. The shared text, in this case a bilingual edition of the eighteenth century didactic novel *Télémaque*, itself an important manifesto for equality through education, ceases to be a tool of distinction between them, one which the students must "absorb" in order to gain the symbolic capital appropriate to their position in society; instead, it becomes something that teacher and student can hold in common and learn from differently according to their interests. Allowed to "speak for itself," the text becomes the "egalitarian intellectual link between the master and the student" (Rancière 1987: 25). Mastery resides not in pressuring the student to follow a single "correct" path, but rather in empowering the student to invent a path of her own (ibid.: 58).

Rancière is not alone in imagining an ethos of pedagogy beyond the reproduction of structural inequality and the tragedy of Bourdieuian misrecognition. His allegory picks up long-established threads in the American pragmatist tradition, itself a considerable repository of feminist thought. Freedom in this perspective is not an inalienable property of human subjects that flourishes only when constraints are removed; in fact, without a generative matrix of social constraints, individual freedoms dissolve into unreflective habits and appetites (Addams 2002). Reproductive labor—the labor of people like teachers and administrators—should be recognized as the glue that holds our strategies for emancipation together. For theorists and historians, then, the challenge does not stop at valorizing the hidden work of women as "producers." The crux of the problem lies in breaking down the assumption that production has any value at all outside of reproduction. This is the question that gives critical power to Hewitt's engagement with education.

The friction between this outlook and the normal run of engineering education is obvious. Expertise ceases to depend upon rising in a preconceived social order and becomes a question of contingent needs and purposes unique to each individual. What may not be obvious is that the removal of the professional hierarchy also changes the meaning of the objects to which our expertise is applied. Nostalgic and dystopian uses of obsolete technologies—often boiled down to some version of the millennial turn toward an "aesthetics of failure" (Cascone 2000)—frame the old and inefficient as an ironic critique of technological progress. The obsolete machine stands as a reminder of technology's inevitable decay into uselessness: as faults accumulate over time, our everyday intentions and interactions break down to reveal their interdependency. As Hewitt explains early in the Sideman video series, however, this work is not about nostalgia. The contingency and interdependency of technological knowledge is not a crisis to be solved by some more universal form of mastery in the future. The challenges that this idiosyncratic machine presents to the student are still alive with possibility. Our tour through the inner workings of the Sideman is not about coming to terms with its original condition, nor is it about restoring it to perfection. Rather, it demonstrates that solving technical problems and becoming an "expert" is often simply a matter of opening the case and paying attention to what one finds inside.

Instead of struggling to expand the distribution of the dominant form of electronics mastery, or on the contrary trying to escape mastery altogether, Hewitt proposes an equal starting point from which each student can develop an expertise corresponding to her own concerns. The drum machine becomes a platform for what Donna Haraway (1991) has called "situated knowledges," shedding its aura of decaying order. Recall again the innocent, harmonious choreography of works like *Feedback Babies* and *Electrostatic Bell Choir*: the affective tone of these assemblages evokes not dismay or failure but calm, care and concern. Like the ignorant schoolmaster's bilingual volume of *Télémaque*, Hewitt's Sideman is a text in which multiple dissenting ideas and methods await anyone empowered to search for them.

References

Addams, J. (2002). *Democracy and social ethics*. Urbana: University of Illinois Press.

Aristote. (2007). *Politique: livres I à VIII*. Trans. J. Aubonnet. Paris: Gallimard.

Bourdieu, P. (1977). *Outline of a theory of practice*. Trans. R. Nice. Cambridge: Cambridge University Press.

Bourdieu, P. (1998). *Practical reason: On the theory of action*. Trans. R. Johnson. Stanford: Stanford University Press.

Bourdieu, P., & Passeron, J.-C. (1964). *La reproduction: éléments pour une théorie du système d'enseignement*. Paris: Les Éditions de minuit.

Bourriaud, N. (2001). *Esthétique relationnelle*. Dijon: Les Presses du réel.

Butler, J. (1990). *Gender trouble: Feminism and the subversion of identity*. New York: Routledge.

Butler, J. (1993). *Bodies that matter: On the discursive limits of 'sex'*. London: Routledge.

Cascone, K. (2000). The aesthetics of failure: 'Post-digital' tendencies in contemporary computer music. *Computer Music Journal, 24*, 12–18.

Collins, N. (2006). *Handmade electronic music: The art of hardware hacking*. New York: Routledge.

Galison, P. (1994). The ontology of the enemy: Norbert Wiener and the cybernetic vision. *Critical Inquiry, 21*, 228–266.

Gell, A. (1992). The technology of enchantment and the enchantment of technology. In E. Hirsch (Ed.), *The art of anthropology: Essays and diagrams* (pp. 159–187). Oxford: Berg.

Ghazala, Q. R. (2004). The folk music of chance electronics: Circuit-bending the modern coconut. *Leonardo Music Journal, 14*, 97–104.

Green, L. (1997). *Music, gender, education*. Cambridge: Cambridge University Press.

Halpern, O. (2014). *Beautiful data: A history of vision and reason since 1945*. Durham: Duke University Press.

Haraway, D. (1991). *Simians, cyborgs, and women*. New York: Routledge.

Hicks, M. (2017). *Programmed inequality: How Britain discarded women technologists and lost its edge in computing*. Cambridge: MIT Press.

Hirschhorn, T. (2013). *Critical laboratory: The writings of Thomas Hirschhorn*. Cambridge: MIT Press.

Jansen, M. (Ed.). (2005). *Gendertronics. Der Körper in der elektronischen Musik*. Berlin: Suhrkamp.

Kelty, C. (2005). Geeks, social imaginaries, and recursive publics. *Cultural Anthropology, 20*, 185–214.

Laclau, E., & Mouffe, C. (1985). *Hegemony and socialist strategy: Towards a radical democratic politics*. London: Verso.

Leydon, R. (2001). The soft-focus sound: Reverb as a gendered attribute in mid-century mood music. *Perspectives of New Music, 39*, 96–107.

Lloyd, G. (1985). *The man of reason: 'Male' and 'female' in western philosophy*. Minneapolis: University of Minnesota Press.

Lovell, T. (2000). Thinking feminism with and against Bourdieu. *Feminist Theory, 1*, 11–32.

McCartney, A. (2006). Gender, genre and electroacoustic soundmaking practices. *Intersections: Canadian Journal of Music, 26*, 20–48.

McLeod, J. (2005). Feminists re-reading Bourdieu: Old debates and new questions about gender habitus and gender change. *Theory and Research in Education, 3*, 11–30.

Mims, F. (1986). *Siliconnections: Coming of age in the electronic era*. New York: McGraw-Hill.

Moreno, J., & Steingo, G. (2012). Rancière's equal music. *Contemporary Music Review, 31*, 487–505.

Novak, D. (2013). *Japanoise: Music at the edge of circulation*. Durham: Duke University Press.

Oliveros, P. (1984). *Software for people: Collected writings 1963-80*. Baltimore: Smith Publications.

Pelletier, C. (2009). Emancipation, equality and education: Rancière's critique of Bourdieu and the question of performativity. *Discourse: Studies in the Cultural Politics of Education, 30*, 137–150.

Piekut, B. (2012). Sound's modest witness: Notes on cage and modernism. *Contemporary Music Review, 31*, 3–18.

Rancière, J. (1987). *Le maître ignorant*. Paris: Fayard.

Rancière, J. (2004). *Malaise dans l'esthétique*. Paris: Galilée.

Rancière, J. (2007). *Le philosophe et ses pauvres*. Paris: Flammarion.

Richards, J. (2013). Beyond DIY in electronic music. *Organised Sound, 18*, 274–281.

Rodgers, T. (2010). *Pink noises: Women on electronic music and sound*. Durham: Duke University Press.

Ross, K. (1991). Translator's introduction. In J. Rancière (Ed.), *The ignorant schoolmaster: Five lessons in intellectual emancipation* (pp. vii–xxiii, trans. K. Ross). Stanford: Stanford University Press.

Sheridan, S. (2006). Generative systems at the Art Institute of Chicago, 1970–1980. *Visual Resources, 22*, 315–324.

Sofia, Z. (2000). Container technologies. *Hypatia, 15*, 181–201.

Turner, F. (2006). *From counterculture to cyberculture: Stewart Brand, the whole earth network, and the rise of digital utopianism*. Chicago: University of Chicago Press.

Turner, F. (2013). *The democratic surround: Multimedia and American liberalism from World War II to the psychedelic sixties*. Chicago: University of Chicago Press.

Valiquet, P. (2017). Animating the object: Marcelle Deschênes and acousmatic education in Québec. *Organised Sound, 22*, 385–393.

Part III
Electronic Musical Instruments and Their Users

Chapter 9
Sound Visions and Visible Sounds: Electronic Musical Instruments and Their Power to Change

Benedikt Brilmayer

Abstract Electronics started to change the world of musical instruments as early as the 1920s. The first electronic instruments revolutionized the perception and understanding of the term instrument because they provided new ways of making accessible and controlling sound and timbre. Furthermore, new types of instruments started to develop into several subtypes during the 1950s and turned out to be quite heterogeneous in appearance, musical functionality, and, last but not least, playing technique. The preparing of analogue synthesizers before the actual concert as well as the programming of computer produced sounds and samples shifted the artistic work from the performance to its preparation. The use of computers enlarged the potential of instruments to be used like complete recording studios. Those features had, of course, tremendous influence on composing and producing music, and greatly changed music and the artistic aspects of composing. This chapter tries to shed light on those changes from an organological point of view, meaning that electronic instruments and their development could be seen from the perspective of not only functionality but also handling and playing. The ways of making functional features useable for the artist impacts her or his work and thoughts.

9.1 Introduction

Nowadays we are able to experience a multifaceted world of music. Due to the technological standards of reproduction devices, accessibility of music through several media forms, and the wide repertoire of recordings, we live in a potentially boundless musical world. Since all the recordings go through a process of editing in larger or smaller studios, it is legitimate to say that at least all recorded music strongly depends on some kind of electronic devices, which quite often cross, if not dissolve, the terminological boarders of musical instruments. The most prominent example for that is the computer. Also, music performed live is strongly

B. Brilmayer (✉)
Musical Instrument Museum Berlin SIM PK, Berlin, Germany
e-mail: brilmayer@sim.spk-berlin.de

A. Jóri, M. Lücke (eds.), *The New Age of Electronic Dance Music and Club Culture*, Music Business Research, https://doi.org/10.1007/978-3-030-39002-0_9

influenced by the use of electronic musical instruments. Not only characteristic instruments in the traditional term are present on stage and involved in music performance, but also the computer with specific software.

The influence of electronic musical instruments on today's musical world is strong. This fact, in regards to the relatively young group of musical instruments, still represents only one part of the ideas that finally led the Museum for Musical Instruments at the State Institute for Music Research of the Prussian Heritage Foundation in the decision to create a special exhibition on electronic musical instruments in 2017. An additional reason is the historical emergence and development of that group of instruments, which is strongly connected with the city of Berlin. An insight into that development is presented in the first part of this chapter. Further developments after 1950, which were not located in Berlin but still had some roots there, are described in the second part. Finally, the last step of breaking down the classical idea of musical instruments, mainly through digital technology, is outlined in the third part.

The technological progress in the past 125 years had a strong influence on musical instruments and added new potentials for approaching music both in its performance and production.

9.2 Emergence and First Developments of Electronic Musical Instruments

One cannot really answer the questions of where and when the very first electronic musical instrument was developed. However, one of the most valuable sources for early attempts of building musical instruments with the means of—at that time very new—electronic technology is provided by the German journal *Zeitschrift für Instrumentenbau* (*Journal for Building Musical Instruments*), which was published for over six decades, from 1880 until 1943. In its notes and articles can be found information on new patent applications—one, for example, filed by Ernst Lorenz (Nr. 33507) dated on March 12, 1886 (ZfM 11/VI: 139). It cannot be proved whether or not this patent was fully realized as an instrument or if it remained only an idea, but it shows how early the connection between building instruments and electronic technology was seen as a potentially fruitful one. Most certainly several traces of those ideas and even attempts at building real instruments could be found all over Europe as well as the United States. The first spectacular instrument, which is from today's perspective almost exclusively seen as the first success in building electronic musical instruments, is the so-called Telharmonium, later to be called Dynamophone.

It was invented by Thaddeus Cahill in the 1890s and he was granted a patent for it in the United States on April 6, 1897 (Weidenaar 1995: 28). The Telharmonium (and later the Dynamophone) was able to produce different timbres and could be played by means of a piano-like keyboard that was later replaced by an alternative keyboard with 48 keys per octave (Weidenaar 1995: 72, 104–109). For realizing different timbres, the instruments by Cahill used huge generators consisting of turning tonewheels. Both models of this instrument had enormous dimensions and were very expensive to build. Cahill can be credited as a visionary and great project manager, able to acquire money and creating a large-scale concept for refinancing his instrument. Roughly speaking, the Telharmonium was his demonstration instrument located in his building factory in Holyoke, Massachusetts, while the Dynamophone was the real instrument, placed in the so-called Telharmonic Hall in a hotel in New York (Weidenaar 1995).

Taking a closer look at this instrument from an organologist perspective—a musicologist specializing in musical instruments—the feature of sound production is the key for further analysis. The terminology of musical instruments strongly derives from the work of museums because museum-based musicologists coined and developed the scientific terms of musical instruments at the end of the nineteenth and in the early twentieth centuries. Until today the most influential ones are Curt Sachs and Erich Moritz von Hornbostel, who developed the so-called Sachs–Hornbostel scheme for categorizing musical instruments, first published in 1914 (Sachs et al. 1914). Sachs and Hornbostel distinguish musical instruments by means of their sound production. For that, the very first category is the type of body, brought into vibration to create sound, which leads them to four main categories: idiophones, membranophones, chordophones, and aerophones. The second category still refers to sound, particularly to the production of the vibration (plugging, striking, etc.). Further categories aim at construction characteristics, designating that system as a tool for museum-based work. Sachs and von Hornbostel did not include electronic musical instruments, as that group remained in a very experimental state until the 1920s. Later, Sachs and other organologists attempted the first steps of integrating them to the Sachs–Hornbostel system and took a closer look at the details of sound-production or construction characteristics (Sachs 1940; Draeger 1948).

As a first and important limitation for this chapter, it has to be kept in mind that here the focus lies on purely electronic musical instruments. The legendary Telharmonium or Dynamophone created sounds by spinning tonewheels, which, strictly speaking, resulted in labeling them as electro-mechanical instruments. Later, the famous Hammond organ used the same idea for creating tones and timbres, but with a significant reduction of dimensions (for more details see Weidenaar 1995; Brilmayer 2017a: 180–203). Purely electronic musical instruments could only be created at a certain stage of technological development, one that can be marked quite clearly with the invention of the vacuum tube. But why? The vacuum tube initially enabled some electronic steps and tricks to produce not only a single waveform but also a complex wave-shape, which is necessary to create not only frequencies (which would not be satisfying for musical purposes) but timbres, as well as a device for controlling the instrument (Brilmayer 2017b). From an organological point of view, by using a vacuum tube you do not have mechanically moving parts for sound production, which you actually have in all other categories of instruments, for example in a string, an air-column, a membrane, or the body of the instrument itself. So properly speaking, electronic instruments indeed only use moving electrons to produce sound.

So Cahill's inventions are not particularly interesting for this chapter because they are only electro-mechanic predecessors. But they were important for their contemporary music-interested technicians and technology-enthusiastic musicians and deserve to be mentioned at least. Especially because they inspired composers like the Berlin-based Ferruccio Busoni, who mentioned the Telharmonium in his book *Sketch of a New Aesthetics of Music* as an instrument being capable of outperforming the chromatic scale-system and leading into the sphere of micro-intervals (Busoni 1907: 29).

According to our present knowledge, the first purely electronic instrument that was realized and also played extensively, was the famous Theremin built by the Russian physician Lev Termen around 1920. By conducting research for an approximation alarm system, he stumbled over the principle of controlling pitch by accident. Producing sound had already been solved for his alarm system, but by noticing that the approximation of his body, or parts of his body (e.g., his arms and hands) influenced the pitch of his alarm system, the hobby musician quite quickly realized its potential as a musical instrument (Glinsky 2000: 23–24). Finally, this lucky accident resulted in what today can be seen as not only the first electronic musical instrument but also the first alternative controller, because the instrument used a completely new method to control pitch by approximation of the right hand to an antenna. This revolutionary playing technique granted a huge public success to the Theremin, despite the fact that its musical capabilities were very limited. It could produce only one timbre, one pitch at a time, and allowed for the control of volume in only an aimless manner so that between quick pitch-changes slight glissandi remained audible (Brilmayer 2017a: 186–191). The music played on the Theremin was almost exclusively classical music adapted for Theremin and piano. After 1927, Termen extensively traveled through Western Europe while residing in Berlin. Then, from 1929 onward, he traveled to the United States where the Theremin was produced by RCA and later (and still) by Robert Moog and his company.

The next important step for electronic musical instruments was the possibility to produce and control different timbres—as the next example, the Trautonium, clarifies. It also shows the importance and the forward-looking spirit of Berlin-based musicologists, composers, and technicians. Friedrich Trautwein was one of the most successful people in this field of invention, partially due to Berlin being one of the world's leading cities in electronics during the so-called Golden Twenties. For that reason a lot of people worked there on different forms of electronic instruments (Lertes 1933). Trautwein's instrument, however, was also revolutionary in several aspects: For example, it was very small and could be placed on a table. Moreover, it was capable of not only producing micro-intervals—here Trautwein, as other pioneers of building electronic instruments, followed esthetic thoughts of Busoni's Sketch (1907) mentioned above—but also to produce a wide range of timbres such as woodwind- and brass-like sounds as well as bowed string instruments. In addition, it was constructed in the Rundfunkversuchsstelle (Radio Research Section), founded in 1928 at the Berlin Academy of Music, where Paul Hindemith acted as artist in residence and adviser for musical aspects in developing the Trautonium (for further details see Brilmayer 2017a: 213–230). "Friedrich Trautwein, an engineer and pioneering radio technician, was appointed to lead the new research institute. The Trautonium, to which he gave his name, generates an initial vibration, rich in overtones, and filters these to produce the desired timbre" (Brilmayer 2017b: 26). This groundbreaking new principle of producing timbre today is called subtractive synthesis—as opposed to the, up until that point, commonly used principle of additive synthesis like we find in Cahill's instruments or in the Hammond organ, as well as in the French Ondes Martenot at that time.

Therefore, the Trautonium was an electronic instrument that could not only imitate acoustic instruments but could also produce completely new timbres. The young Oskar Sala, student of Hindemith, turned out to be a talented Trautonium virtuoso and started working for radiobroadcasts in the early 1930s. Also, he took the instrument one step further and opened it up to two new fields: producing sounds (no longer related to music) and working in the field of movie production. In 1933 he created the sound of an airplane-propeller for the German film *Stürme über dem Mont Blanc* (*Storm over Mont Blanc*). After World War II, working for movie productions was Sala's main assignment. However, opening up the field to create soundscapes was an important step for the new electronic musical instruments. Of course the Theremin and the Ondes Martenot were also used in film soundtracks as well as in concerts with original compositions. With the Trautonium's revolutionary potential for creating different timbres, electronic musical instruments became more than just musical, they gradually encompassed all sounds too. This aspect ultimately broke the chain of the classical term of musical instruments and would influence the design of electronic musical instruments as well as esthetic views on music.

The Trautonium had another big influence on the development of synthesizers in the 1950s. As Myles Jackson outlined in a lecture at the Museum for Musical Instruments in Berlin in March 2017, Robert Moog, a key figure for electronic musical instruments in the United States, at least knew of the Trautonium and perhaps even possessed one. He copied the Trautonium's architecture for timbre-creating, which consists of three steps. First, a frequency rich in harmonics is created; second, the harmonics are filtered according to desire; third, the created timbre is amplified and rendered audible by a loudspeaker. Thus the Trautonium can be seen as predecessor, or at least as a key source, for inspiration in Robert Moog's endeavor of designing the first synthesizer in the early 1950s.

Several authors emphasize the importance and range of Berlin-based inventions in the field of electronic musical instruments more explicitly then can be done here (Donhauser 2007: 67–126; Patteson 2016: 114). It is important to keep in mind that after first attempts in the field of electronic musical instruments, different steps were realized like creating frequency, creating timbre, and the designing of an instrument so that a player is able to control those aspects. Indeed, Cahill's Telharmonium and Dynamophone were huge steps in this field, although they remain in the role of an ancestor here because they were not purely electronic but electro-mechanic musical instruments. Lev Termen's Theremin was, though limited in musical dimensions, a huge success because of its revolutionary playing technique (playing without actually touching the instrument itself) being a predecessor for instruments with a so-called alternative interface. The Trautonium is actually one of the most successful examples of so many other inventions made during the 1920s and 1930s all over the electrified world. It enabled complex musical performance with dynamic keyboard expression (soft to loud), vibrato, glissando, intonation, a great ambit as well as the potential for micro-intervals and, last but not least, different timbre. Also, with Oskar Sala's engagement it quickly found its way into radio broadcasts and movie productions next to the classical field of musical instruments used in concerts. The most prominent example for this would be Oskar Sala's soundscape for Alfred Hitchcock's movie *The Birds* (1963), but he actually produced several hundred film scores as well as soundscapes (Donhauser 2007: 226–230). In the 1920s and 1930s however, the new group of electronic musical instruments started to gain a foothold primarily in terms of the classic use of musical instruments: by adapting classical compositions or receiving the attention of composers who composed solo and concerto pieces for the new inventions. However, before they could penetrate almost every musical genre and even shape the sound characteristics of another genre like they do in EDM, the Second World War and the ensuing years put a sudden and severe end to that auspicious field of instruments.

9.3 The Synthesizer Was Not Alone

After the war, it took several years until there were further developments in the field of electronic musical instruments, and at that point there were a lot of different subdivisions within this group of instruments. Claviolines and Combichords were conceived as timbre-enlarging devices for smaller groups of musicians and/or pianists during the late 1940s and early 1950s. Also for pianists or groups of musicians without a drumset, a device called Sideman was created during the late 1950s. It was the first commercial drum machine. But those inventions were to be overshadowed by the development of the first modular synthesizers.

Both Robert Moog and Donald Buchla started working on synthesizers independently. The key element was the realization of modifying signals by voltage control. "In the mid-1960s, Donald Buchla at Berkeley/California and Robert Moog in New York made the principle of voltage control usable for serially produced musical instruments" (Feser 2017: 29). First models did not have any known input device—like a keyboard—for controlling pitch, which shows that the creator's focus was on shaping and creating new timbres and sounds. Only later did both designers start to equip their instruments with a keyboard, both for practical as well as for commercial reasons. But synthesizers could also be controlled or played by an electric guitar, like Franz Zappa did. So the design and the potential for interconnecting different modules provided some basic characteristics for these kinds of instruments. Moog's design seemed to be created with the thought that melodic playing was an important factor. Whereas Buchla's instruments provided the potential for more automated sound-controlling processes and manual interactions to those (Feser 2017: 29).

With their numerous module plates mounted next to each other in huge locker-like racks, connected by wires and with their control nobs and switches, their look appeared to fit into the common picture of a classical musical instrument quite oddly. Naturally their sounds were associated with the sphere of science fiction, and several synthesizer sounds were used in film and radio broadcasts. But they also opened up new sound dimensions in music, for example as Pink Floyd or Tangerine Dream explored in their music. In addition, the progressive rock music band Emerson, Lake & Palmer used the sounds of their Moog synthesizer very extensively to substitute acoustic instruments and to create new timbres for their album *Pictures at an Exhibition* (1971).

In the first half of the 1970s, a new version of synthesizers appeared and presented a counterpoint to the development of huge synth-racks on stage. Moog and Buchla as well as EMS—a London-based synthesizer-company founded by Peter Zinnovieff in 1969—developed small transportable and much cheaper devices. Soon the so-called Minimoog gained some fame with its prefixed modules, filter banks, and integrated keyboard, and most likely influenced future synthesizer designs (Feser 2017: 30). A new way of connecting and at the same time avoiding cable clutter was introduced by EMS (Electronic Music Studios) with the VCS-3. A patch matrix enabled the player to connect modules and a small joystick enabled operating within a selected parameter. Buchla presented his Music Easel, a suitcase with an integrated keyboard. The new and infinite potential of creating sounds that are provided by a huge modular synthesizer creates a problem in conjunction with that freedom: the problem of controlling. Without the option to somehow save the preset for one special sound, the infinite potential remained locked behind the time-consuming (at least in terms of live-performance) need to change wiring or switches. Against this background, it is no surprise that Pink Floyd did not buy one but sixteen Minimoogs (Supper and Ungeheuer 1995: 1760).

Next to the commonly known development of synthesizers, instruments like the Wurlitzer Sideman, ancestor of drum machines, or the Clavioline only played a small role in the world of music during the 1960s. However, another instrument for providing musicians with a range of timbre turned out to be quite successful. In the way of its process of creating sound and timbre, it represents an antipode to the synthesizer design and philosophy. Synthesizers indeed produce sounds and timbres by means of oscillators in combination with filters, other oscillators, a sequencer, and so on. The Mellotron, however, was not a synthesizer. It could not produce and alter waves, but it could reproduce recorded sounds by using short parts of audiotape. Therefore it is a sample-based instrument—in short, a sampler.

By taking a look at the big radio-broadcast studios which emerged after the war, the synthesizer and the sampler can be seen as representatives of two different and very popular ways of making music. The more synthesizer-like approach can be seen in the work of the Cologne-based Studio für elektronische Musik (Studio for Electronic Music), founded and led by Herbert Eimert in 1951. The studio was originally equipped with a Melochord built by Harald Bode (also a Berlin-based pioneer in the late 1920s and 1930s) and an electronic Monochord by Trautwein. But only 2 years later, those instruments were not in use by Karlheinz Stockhausen because he specifically demanded a sine wave generator for his work (Supper and Ungeheuer 1995: 1755). Instead of having an instrument doing all the timbre work, he experimented in the field of timbre design with the use of (recorded) sine waves. The Paris-based Club d'Essai, founded by Pierre Schaeffer as Studio d'Essai in 1943, worked under very different esthetic premises. Recorded sounds were the original material for his *Musique conrète*, the actual process of composing started only after the recordings were finished by altering tape speed as well as cutting (Supper and Ungeheuer 1995: 1753). Of course, both esthetic concepts used tape, but the main focus lay on the creation and nature of the original material. In Cologne this is realized by wave oscillators for creating sine waves, just like the synthesizer does. In Paris the original materials were real-life audible events, which were processed by using a state-of-the-art tape recorder. For that reason the Mellotron, in comparison to the synthesizer, can be seen as an antipode in providing a musician with the potential of playing in a different timbre.

Of course, the Mellotron has an ancestor: the instruments by Harry Chamberlin, who built and sold his instruments from the end of the 1940s onward in the United States. Chamberlin's idea came to Great Britain, where a producer of high-quality audiotapes started to build Mellotrons in the 1960s. It could be equipped with different audiotape cartridges, containing three different timbres on short tapes, one tape for each key. In fact we all know the Mellotron, even if we are not aware of it—if you ever listened to the song *Strawberry Fields* by The Beatles you heard the flute intro, which Paul McCartney played on his Mellotron. In the following years, the sampler turned out to be an important tool for music studios.

Beside those two groups of electronic musical instruments, synthesizers and samplers, a third and highly specialized group made its step onto the stage of music and music production. Today this third group is known as drum machines and is widely disseminated in different subgenres of electronic (dance) music. The group's ancestor, the Sideman, has already been mentioned, but it was more than one decade later that drum machines were used in recordings, while on stage they had to wait until the 1980s. Probably the first recording of a studio LP that contained sounds of a drum machine was *There's a Riot Goin' On* by Sly and The Family Stone in 1971 (Pelleter 2017: 42), where a Rhythm King by Maestro was used. Later—and now for the first time we get to EDM—the connection of an instrument to a location (drum machines and dancefloors) will turn out to be style forming, especially for the genres of house and techno. Here we can think of the legendary drum machines like the Roland company's TR-808 and TR-909 because of their characteristic sound. At first those analogue sounds were not able to withstand the competition that came with the first digitally working devices. "'Eight-Oh-Eight' and 'Nine-Oh-Nine' owe the techno, house and HipHop DJs that the initial failure could be overcome and meanwhile be turned into legendary status" (Pelleter 2017: 42).

Drum machines play preprogrammed or live-programmed rhythm patterns instead of melodies or harmonies and create their sounds either by means of analog circuitries or digitally sampled sounds. The sole role of substituting drum sets led to completely new interfaces on which musicians were able to use those instruments for their artistic ideas. For that reason, drum machines as well as synthesizers revolutionized the aspect of playing on instruments completely. This characteristic will mostly disappear after the next huge step in the development of electronic musical instruments. But first, from the late 1950s until the late 1970s—and further on—electronic musical instruments became an integral part of pop music and music production in general: They earned their place on the stage of music.

9.4 Dissolving the Instrument, Electronic Devices in Music

The abovementioned synthesizers and drum machines introduced a new characteristic of playing musical instruments. For opening up new musical possibilities, like creating and shaping timbre, aspects of handling those instruments became critical. This fact can also be observed by taking a look at the abovementioned early electronic musical instruments. Cahill's instruments looked like huge organs, with their organ console being where all the stop knobs are located to control the different pipe ranks with their characteristic timbre.

A modular synthesizer had to be wired according to the musician's desire, so actually playing on them consisted of two different steps. To make music, the first step was to set up all the connections required for timbre, and the second was to actually play the melody or harmony. So changing the wiring and all the settings of the rotary switches, at least live on stage, had to be choreographed in some way with the band (or many synthesizers had to be on stage, not just one).

The first step of setting up the instrument also applied to drum machines but in a slightly different way. Their handling was not as complex as the wiring of a synthesizer, but the drum pattern had to be set up on machines like the Roland TR-808 or TR-909. Of course earlier models only used presets where musicians could add some drum hits or claps by means of separate buttons. Those extra sounds could be used freely and independently from the parallel-running preset beat pattern, or even solo without a running pattern. With the introduction of the sequencer and its reduction in size so that it fit into the relatively small dimensions of the abovementioned models, the process of setting up the beat could be performed live on stage. All in all, playing an electronic musical instrument differs greatly in the feeling of liveness and virtuosity compared to acoustic instruments. This aspect gains even more importance with the rise of computers and their application in music.

Although the development of computer technology had already taken important steps since the 1950s and also saw the first compositions for software, it took several years until computer technology was sophisticated enough to be directly combined with musical instruments. "Since ca. 1975 digital technology was implemented in analogue synthesizer technology" (Supper and Ungeheuer 1995: 1760, translated by the author). This fusion first took place in the late 1970s when the Fairlight CMI (Computer Music Instrument) by the company Fairlight and, parallel but independently from that, the Synclavier by New England Digital appeared on the market. Their first models were not equipped with keyboards. They "were able to digitalize sounds, transpose them and make them playable on a polyphonic keyboard. In combination with subtractive synthesis with filters and modulators and with a simple FM synthesis, subsequently a series of sampling synthesizers with digitalized sounds as basic material were developed" (Harenberg 2017: 62). Both instruments completely relied on digital reckoning for all processes needed to realize any sounds. But with the Fairlight CMI especially, the computer seemed to be an add-on. With the computer's power at hand, however, both instruments were able to synthesize as well as sample sounds. In addition to that, built-in sequencers allowed the saving of composed music and, of course, editing it in a way that had only been possible in studios until then. On the Fairlight's monitor (which was highly sophisticated for that time) by means of a light pen, sound waves created by the synthesizer as well as waves from samples could be edited in real time. Beside the light pen, a computer keyboard was required—similarly to the Synclavier. Finally, the aspect of computer-extended instruments turned those instruments into a working station, like a miniature sound studio. On one instrument almost every part of the music as well as the work processes were united at the musician's command.

Especially in the 1990s, computer software turned out to become the key aspect superseding the musical instrument the keyboard, thus revolutionizing the concept and term of musical instrument. A digital device in combination with a certain software turned out to be able to produce music completely. "From the 'discovery' that computers can be used for music up to the present variety of different musical styles as well as internationally successful music software companies, this development followed manifold steps in technical and cultural formation" (Möllenkamp 2017: 56). For electronic musical instruments, the subgroup of software instruments is most likely the widest spread group nowadays. Composers do not have to be educated musicians anymore. Theoretically everyone can handle computers, learn how to use software, and at the same time compose and even fully produce music. Live programming or live sampling was possible with the help of some 1980s computer systems like Atari, Commodore, and Amiga (see Harenberg 2017: 63). After two decades of progress in computer technology, new aspects of interface rose with touchscreens and smart phones as hardware. Software, of course, also developed further and turned the possibilities from live coding to live performance, rising the computer up from the state of being a component of an instrument to virtual studio technology on stage.

Electronic musical instruments in their variety of manifestation are key elements of today's popular music. Some instruments like drum machines can be seen as indicators of specific genres of EDM such as house or techno.

9.5 Conclusions

Electronic musical instruments emerged in the time of electrification of the human environment during the turn of the twentieth century. In the beginning they remained instruments in a classical sense: They were coherent tools with sound or timbre-producing circuits, and interfaces for controlling the circuitry that enabled more or less musical characteristics, as could be seen in the comparison of the Theremin and the Trautonium. Since the first attempts of building electronic instruments, the realization of new musical features, like timbres and micro-intervals, was an inspiring factor, as was briefly discussed above. Timbres and micro-intervals greatly influenced the newly developed interfaces that were developed in order to control them. On the one hand, new layouts of control knobs and pitch-control devices were needed; on the other hand, all those new interface designs had to be learned by the musicians themselves.

This problem can be illustrated by taking a look at the Trautonium again. By being developed at a research institute with the aim of mass production and marketed by the Telefunken company (Brilmayer 2017a: 234–251), the Trautonium provided the musician with an interface that was as intuitively playable as it was easy to handle in regards to musical characteristics like timbre shaping, tuning, intonation, and so forth. Trautwein's own proposals of different interfaces mainly focused on pitch control alone, comprising a version of a piano keyboard as well as probably the first theoretical idea for a wind control device (Trautwein 1930: 27). It took some decades until wind controllers were produced and disseminated. In short, wind controllers are woodwind-like devices that collect data from the airstream created by the musician and turn it into control information for a sound-producing device like a synthesizer or a computer, equipped with the appropriate software. According to the argument of being playable by everyone, with the Trautonium an interface was designed that consisted of a single string over a metal plate that the musician could play in the same way as a piano. But at the same time it was able to produce micro-intervals by sliding on the string for only millimeters.

Even during the time of great developments in electronic musical instruments during the 1960s and 1970s, the problem of musicians having to learn new interfaces still remained viral. The first synthesizers by Moog and Buchla are famous examples of actually letting the musician decide by him- or herself what kind of interface should be added to the sound-producing device. The widely spread keyboards of the 1980s and 1990s only indicate how broadly recognized the piano keyboard was as a musical interface.

The synthesizers, as well as samplers and drum machines, finally revolutionized the term musical instrument in the aspects of interface and virtuosity. By shifting priorities from live performance to preperformance preparations on the synthesizer's huge module-racks—by the need for wiring and presetting control knobs and switches—performing music remained second to presetting its desired characteristics. Computers and software enabled even more people to make music and at least posed the potential of completely replacing traditional music interfaces. At the same time, they let musicians reach out for new esthetic ideas and, last but not least, to establish new musical genres and styles especially in the field of popular music. In return, new esthetic ideas have always inspired people, and they will continue to inspire people to create new tools to realize them. "How influential the role of popular music styles was for the growing differentiation of electronic instruments can be discerned, among other things, in the variety of rhythm machines, which from the 1980s on could experience a large boom" (Jarre 2017: 10). Rhythm or drum machines pushed the aspect of creative freedom even more and were necessary in the teleological progress of esthetic and musical ideas. The nowadays much-appreciated model of the TR-808 was a commercial flop in the beginning because of its comparatively bad sound characteristics. Therefore, it was sold for a low price and only then did it begin to circulate widely. Later, it was actually used for its characteristic—and formerly badly perceived—sounds. Nowadays it is still widespread, although not primarily as a real instrument but as a software emulation.

Electronic musical instruments show how powerful creative minds can handle tools for achieving their artistic goals, as well as how unpredictable it sometimes is to anticipate what aspect of new tools, or in this case musical instruments, will turn out to be critical for their success. In relation to the upcoming emulated instruments on touch screen devices, Ulrich Schnauss makes the following statement: "Can the Minimoog's plain functional design really be improved by a touch screen? But isn't it this very technology that, for example, finally makes the sound capabilities of a Synclavier available for a circle of people beyond a small elite? Isn't it the lack of availability of presets and stock sounds that virtually force the musician on the modular system to find [their] own forms of expression? Or does the unlimited range of today's immediately available examples before any single cable is patched, any single controller is turned, inspire us?" (Schnauss 2017: 13).

This short insight into the development of electronic musical instruments shows the enormous potential of this comparatively young group of musical instruments. This potential is reflected in the wide range of different approaches to the design and realization of new instruments, which provide musicians with great freedom in composing new music. For the future it will be very interesting to observe technological progress and how it will be turned into new (electronic) musical instruments and new music, respectively. The Museum for Musical Instruments at the State Institute for Music Research of the Prussian Heritage Foundation in Berlin decided to devote a special exhibition to the cosmos of electronic musical instruments, which originally was scheduled to run from March 25, 2017 until June 25, 2017 but was extended until August 27, 2017 due to its huge success. The decision for such an exhibition project was not only inspired by the abovementioned features of organology (as the science of musical instruments is called in musicology), but also by the collection that this museum already had, which is strongly connected to the early developments of electronic instruments, especially the Trautonium. The radio research section was located at the same institution as the collection of musical instruments was, which today is Berlin University of Arts. Furthermore, Berlin became a center for electronic music during the 1970s and developed an internationally influential club scene. Those historical facts added to the most interesting musicological aspects and led to the earlier mentioned exciting research and exhibition project *Good Vibrations: A History of Electronic Musical Instruments*.

References

Brilmayer, B. (2017a). Das Trautonium. *Prozesse des Technologietransfers im Musikinstrumentenbau.* Augsburg. Retrieved May 12, 2019 from https://Opus.Bibliothek.Uni-Augsburg.De/Opus4/Frontdoor/Deliver/Index/Docid/4059/File/Brilmayer_Diss.Pdf

Brilmayer, B. (2017b). Electronic musical instruments: How electricity came to music. In C. Restle, B. Brilmayer, & S. Hardjowirogo (Eds.), *Good vibrations: A history of electronic musical instruments* (pp. 23–27). Berlin: Deutscher Kunstverlag.

Busoni, F. (1907). *Entwurf einer neuen Aesthetik der Tonkunst.* Berlin: Berliner Musikalien Druckerei. Retrieved May 12, 2019 from https://busoni-nachlass.org/edition/essays/entwurf/entwurf1907?q=#29.

Donhauser, P. (2007). Elektrische Klangmaschinen. In *Die Pionierzeit in Deutschland und Österreich.* Böhlau: Wien.

Draeger, H.-H. (1948). *Prinzip einer Systematik der Musikinstrumente.* Kassel: Bärenreiter.

Feser, K. (2017). Modular – semi-modular – non-modular, voltage-controlled synthesizers between complexity and playability. In C. Restle, B. Brilmayer, & S. Hardjowirogo (Eds.), *Good vibrations: A history of electronic musical instruments* (pp. 29–33). Berlin: Deutscher Kunstverlag.

Glinsky, A. (2000). *Theremin: Ether music and espionage.* Urbana: University of Illinois Press.

Harenberg, M. (2017). Sound visions: The CX5M and the revolution of sound production. In C. Restle, B. Brilmayer, & S. Hardjowirogo (Eds.), *Good vibrations: A history of electronic musical instruments* (pp. 61–65). Berlin: Deutscher Kunstverlag.

Jarre, J.-M. (2017). Welcome note. In C. Restle, B. Brilmayer, & S. Hardjowirogo (Eds.), *Good vibrations: A history of electronic musical instruments* (pp. 10–11). Berlin: Deutscher Kunstverlag.

Lertes, P. (1933). *Elektrische Musik.* Dresden: Theodor Steinkopff.

Möllenkamp, A. (2017). Sound visions: The CX5M and the revolution of sound production. In C. Restle, B. Brilmayer, & S. Hardjowirogo (Eds.), *Good vibrations: A history of electronic musical instruments* (pp. 55–59). Berlin: Deutscher Kunstverlag.

Patteson, T. (2016). *Instruments for new music: Sound, technology, and modernism.* Oakland: University of California Press.

Pelleter, M. (2017). Beating time: Futuristic histories and past futures of the drum machine. In C. Restle, B. Brilmayer, & S. Hardjowirogo (Eds.), *Good vibrations: A history of electronic musical instruments* (pp. 41–45). Berlin: Deutscher Kunstverlag.

Sachs, C. (1940). *The history of musical instruments.* New York: Norton.

Sachs, C., & von Hornbostel, E. M. (1914). Systematik der Musikinstrumente. Ein Versuch. *Zeitschrift für Ethnologie, 43*, 553–590.

Schnauss, U. (2017). Good vibrations – Mixed emotions. In C. Restle, B. Brilmayer, & S. Hardjowirogo (Eds.), *Good vibrations: A history of electronic musical instruments* (pp. 12–13). Berlin: Deutscher Kunstverlag.

Supper, M., & Ungeheuer, E. (1995). Art. Elektroakustische Musik. In L. Finscher et al. (Eds.), *Die Musik in Geschichte und Gegenwart* (Vol. 2, pp. 1717–1765). Bärenreiter: Kassel.

Trautwein, F. (1930). Elektrische Musik. In *Veröffentlichungen der Rundfunkversuchsstelle bei der Staatlichen akademischen Hochschule für Musik 1.* Berlin.

Weidenaar, R. (1995). *Magic music from the telharmonium.* Metuchen, NJ: The Scarecrow Press.

ZfM, Anonymous: Illustrated Patent-Review. (1886). *Zeitschrift für Instrumentenbau 11*, 139. Retrieved May 12, 2019 from http://daten.digitale-sammlungen.de/~db/bsb00004232/images/index.html?id=00004232&nativeno=139

Chapter 10
The Discourse Community of Electronic Dance Music Through the Example of the *TB-303 Owners Club*

Anita Jóri

Abstract The aim of this chapter is to introduce the model of the discourse community of electronic dance music using a case study of the Facebook group *TB-303 Owners Club*. This model is based on the discourse community theories of John M. Swales and the analytical system of computer-mediated discourse analysis put forward by Susan C. Herring. The methodology presented in this study is new in research on electronic dance music cultures. It can help us to understand the fine details about online community building and social identity construction via language use. Here, discourse is seen as language in use and as a tool for expressing identity. Therefore, different examples are examined of how identity construction works through discourse and how discourse influences these mechanisms. Furthermore, the results of this study add up-to-date information to the research on computer-mediated communication, with a special focus on the communication processes of social media.

10.1 Introduction

The present chapter introduces the model of the discourse community of electronic dance music through the case study of the Facebook group *TB-303 Owners Club*. This model was extensively discussed in my dissertation (Jóri 2016) and this chapter is an extended excerpt of it.

Electronic dance music has a highly diverse profile in terms of its aesthetics and audiences. Therefore, the parent discourse community of electronic dance music is a multilayered entity: it includes all people that are interested in electronic dance music and willing to communicate on such topics.

From the perspectives of subcultural studies or popular music studies, musical communities are mainly developed by the group members' interests in different music genres. So these groups of individuals are mainly organized into a community

A. Jóri (✉)
Berlin University of the Arts, Berlin, Germany
e-mail: a.jori@medienhaus.udk-berlin.de

A. Jóri, M. Lücke (eds.), *The New Age of Electronic Dance Music and Club Culture*, Music Business Research, https://doi.org/10.1007/978-3-030-39002-0_10

(or a scene, subculture, etc.) by the music genre they are interested in, they work with, or they listen to, etc. Therefore, the global electronic dance music scene is a huge category that consists of smaller [local, translocal or virtual (Peterson and Bennett 2004)] scenes. The members of these scenes are diverse; they can be musicians, fans, promoters, flyer designers, and so on. By introducing linguistic discourse analysis into electronic dance music cultures, one can also see how these musical communities are articulated and formed by the actual discourse between their members. Therefore, the model of the discourse community of electronic dance music shifts its interest from community building via the members' common interest, way of clothing, signs of being connected (etc.) to their actual language use.

Moreover, with the concept of discourse community, one can define the mechanisms of community constructions not only by the music genres and their communities, but also by their other special interests (e.g., the discourse community of fans and users of analogue synthesizers) or their profession (e.g., flyer designers', music or event managers' discourse), etc. These smaller groups would then become the sub-discourse communities or sub-sub-discourse communities (as one could name them after music genre, subgenre, sub-subgenre, etc.—see more in McLeod 2001).

In order to introduce the model in question, I will analyze the discourse behaviors of the members of the abovementioned Facebook group with regards to community and identity constructions with the help of different methods and approaches of computer-mediated discourse analysis.

10.2 The Model of the Discourse Community of Electronic Dance Music

The definition of discourse community (henceforth DC) is originally adopted from leading relativist or social constructionist thinkers' works like Perelman and Olbrechts-Tyteca's (1969) *The New Rhetoric*, Kuhn's (1962) *The Structure of Scientific Revolutions* and Fish's (1980) *Is There a Text in this Class?* More specifically, it was developed from the concepts of speech community and interpretative community (Borg 2003).

The linguist John M. Swales articulated his main ideas on DC in his milestone book *Genre Analysis. English in academic and research settings* in 1990. His model of DC was influenced by the sociolinguist Nystrand's (1982) earlier work, *What Writers Know: The Language, Process, and Structure of Written Discourse*, which was an investigation into written discourse. From Swales' perspective, DC can be defined as a group of people who share a specific set of discourses that represent basic values as well.

Swales (1990) proposed six defining characteristics that identify a group of individuals as a discourse community. Based on his ideas, the following points can be stated for the discourse community of electronic dance music:

1. It has a common public goal: communication on electronic dance music and related topics.
2. It has mechanisms of intercommunication: e.g., emails, web discussion forum posts, phone calls, etc.
3. These mechanisms were set up to provide information about electronic dance music.
4. It has more genres in the communicative furtherance, e.g., Internet genres (blogs, forums, websites, etc.) and multimodal texts (flyers, posters, cover art works, etc.).
5. It has a specific lexis (e.g., *pattern, MIDI, loop,* etc.).
6. Its common knowledge is based on the topic of electronic dance music and the members have different levels of knowledge (Jóri 2012).

I propose the following categories of discourse community to describe the discourse community in question: The discourse community of electronic dance music is the (1) parent discourse community (Swales 1990 also uses this classification). The parent discourse community includes all (2) discourse communities (and sub- or sub-sub-discourse communities, etc.) discussing any kind of EDM-related topics. An example could be the discourse community of the music genre acid house—still a huge group of people all around the world who communicate on this type of music and related topics—which would be ordered under the parent DC. Another example is the legendary instrument Roland TB-303, a tool to produce acid house music; so members of the DC often exchange information about this tool. A whole discourse—and at the same time a community—in different forms (e.g., on web discussion forums, in fan groups, etc.) has been developed around this machine. Therefore, another (sub-)discourse community can be established that is specialized in the communication on such topics. This DC is also closely related to acid house communities. As we can see, it creates a DC by its special interest in an instrument, but at the same time it remains part of the parent discourse community.

The process of identity construction as a discursive phenomenon can also be observed. It also means that individuals who form a music-related discourse community construct their identities during their discursive activities, for example, in chat rooms, web discussion forums, Facebook groups, etc. In this sense, multiple linguistic codes and characteristics explain musical identities in a discursive event.

Research on music-related identities in discourse analysis is a relatively new field and there are only a few scholars who deal with this topic. Here, I will name only a few important works related to the subject of this study.

An early work of Sue Widdicombe and Robin Wooffitt (1995) *The language of youth subcultures* uses a combination of discourse and conversation analysis methods in order to take a closer look at punks', goths', and rockers' language use to construct subcultural identities and group memberships.

Several papers exist on the questions of hip-hop identity and discourse. For example, the collection of papers, *Global Linguistic Flows. Hip Hop Cultures, Youth Identities, and the Politics of Language*, edited by Alim, Ibrahim and Pennycook (2009), deals with the topic of hip-hop identity from very different points of view. Another example is Androutsopoulos' (2007, 2008) work, which examines German-speaking hip-hop websites and discussion boards to demonstrate how methods of discourse-centered online ethnography can help to analyze computer-mediated communication. He also analyzes language style, genre, and member identities on this hip-hop related language sample.

On the topic of EDM, I found just one work; Andrew Whelan's (2008) book *Breakcore: Identity and Interaction on Peer-to-Peer* which is thematically very close to the present study. It examines breakcore—one of the genres of EDM—identity in chat room conversations. However, the author does not use a specific method to analyze the discourse pieces.

In my research I am interested in building up a methodology of linguistic discourse analysis that can be used for analyzing the language use of music-related communities.

10.3 Research Methods Based on Computer-Mediated Discourse Analysis

The main methodological framework of this chapter is Computer-Mediated Discourse Analysis (henceforth CMDA). Based on Susan C. Herring's (2004) CMDA framework—which is organized around the four domains of language: structure, meaning, interaction management, and social phenomena, the present study implements the following methods in its analysis in order to analyze a period of conversation of the Facebook group *TB-303 Owners Club* (Table 10.1).

The first two domains of language—structure and meaning—are analyzed together, because they are close to each other in the scope of this research: through analyzing the structure of the group's language, one can understand the negotiation of meaning too. Here the study takes a closer look at the (1) special lexis, (2) the technical terms, (3) the specific community reference words, (4) the personal pronouns, and (5) the compensatory strategies. Examining (1) the special lexis of the sample brings us closer to the group-specific lexis, which is understood here as a signifier of community sense: the group members understand them in a specific way that cannot be understood by an out-group person. These terms are analyzed with the help of content analysis and semantics. The same can be said about the used (2) technical terms: they are also group-specific and signifiers of the common ground of a community. They also signify the members' level of knowledge on the community's common topic. These are examined with the help of terminology studies. The (3) specific community reference words (e.g., friend, mate) are also examined in order to take a closer look at the in- and out-group language. For that, the classical content analysis is taken as an analytical method. (4) Personal pronouns (I, we, and they) can indicate community identification and individual and group identity. The frequency of their usage is analyzed with the help of descriptive statistics and content analysis. This study is also interested in the same community

Table 10.1 Explored issues and used analytical methods

Language domains	Phenomena type	Explored issues	Analytical method
Structure and meaning	Special lexis	Group-specific lexis, signifiers of community sense	Content analysis and semantics
	Technical terms	Common ground; knowledge	Terminology studies
	Specific community reference words	Reference to group: In- and out-group language	Content analysis
	Personal pronouns	*I* and *we* vs. *they*: signification of individual vs. social identity	Content analysis and descriptive statistics
	Compensatory strategies	Expressions with other tools (not text): their community markers	Multimodal discourse analysis
Interaction management	Concern structures	Signifier of respecting the other members; initiation response	Conversation analysis
	Participation	Special roles in a community; power relations and their roles in community construction and sustaining	Descriptive statistics and conversation analysis
Social phenomena	Interpersonal discourse behaviors	Showing divergence or convergence; friendship building; signifier of community partnerships; a way of showing interest in one another; introduce a new topic, vocation and/or avocation; tools of sustaining a community	Conversation analysis and membership categorization analysis
	Information exchanges	A way of showing interest in one another; showing mutual influence; sense of belonging	Conversation analysis

and identity construction phenomena in multimodal texts—emoticons, pictures, videos, etc. as (5) compensatory strategies—which are analyzed with the help of multimodal discourse analysis.

At the level of interaction management, the (1) concern structures and (2) participation of the community members are examined. Within (1) concern structures, the study takes a closer look at the frequency of linking and quoting. They refer explicitly to the content of a previous message in one's response, which can be understood as an initiation response. They also create an extended conversation exchange, as Rasulo (2008) mentions, because they incorporate juxtapositions with two turns within a single message. These concern structures are therefore signifiers of respecting the other members and this respect also helps to construct communities and friendships. With the help of descriptive statistics, the rates of the members' (2) participation are examined in the conversations. It is intended to figure out if these rates are balanced, harmonic, or hierarchic within the community.

Finally, at the level of social phenomena, the study is interested in the (1) interpersonal discourse behaviors and the (2) information exchanges. (1) Interpersonal discourse behaviors show divergence or convergence; they signify the community partnerships and reconstruct the level of interest in one another (Rasulo 2008). They can introduce a new topic (for example, by asking a question) and they are also representative of friendship building. Moreover, self-representation and convergence toward community identity and partnerships can be also evidenced by participants' use of interpersonal discourse behaviors (Rasulo 2008). Additionally, the features of (2) information exchanges represent how to show interest in one another and they are evidence of mutual influence, establishing presence or significance and sense of belonging (Rasulo 2008).

Based on these explored issues, different coding categories and subcategories were constructed for linguistic analysis, which I will not explain in detail here but instead will highlight some of them in the next part of the text.

10.4 The *TB-303 Owners Club*

10.4.1 Facebook Groups

Facebook groups and their contents are created by the members of the groups (Facebook users); therefore, they have user-generated content only. Members can comment and post within the group; with the aim—as promised on the website: "to discuss anything with just the people you want" (Facebook, Facebook Groups n.d.). Facebook groups normally have an *exclusive* character, because in most cases only the right people can be part of it: "You can make each space special to share the right stuff with the right people" (Facebook, Facebook Groups n.d.).

A Facebook group can be (1) public, (2) closed, or (3) secret. To the (1) public groups anyone can join and there is no data restriction, everybody has access to all the posts and has the right to post even without being a member. To the (2) closed groups, one has to be added or invited by a member and only these members can read its content and post. The (3) secret groups have the most strict privacy settings: a person has to be added or invited to the group; only current and former members can see the group's name and its group description (all other users would not know that this group exists at all); only current members can see who is in the group, the group tags, etc. (see more in Facebook, What are the privacy options for Facebook groups n.d.).

Members can be blocked (with a restriction of rights) or removed from a group (e.g., in case of inappropriate behavior), or they can leave or unfollow groups.

A Facebook group is a very interesting form of online community building: one can easily recognize group membership identity markers in members' posts and their language use that I will also illustrate in the analysis of the *TB-303 Owners Club*.

A Facebook group is a subgenre of asynchronous chat (Crystal 2006) or message board (Bishop 2009), because members of a Facebook Group can post their messages anytime and people can react to them, again, anytime later.

There are two types of text genres used in Facebook groups: posts and comments. Members of Facebook groups can leave posts on the group's timeline. Facebook group posts can differ in length and content: just like forum posts, they can include not only plain texts, but also for example, hyperlinks, pictures, emoticons, GIFs, memes, etc. In most of the cases, they have multimodal characteristics. Apart from the content of the post one can see the member's name and profile picture of the member, who posted it as well as the date it was posted. A Facebook group post functions as a forum thread: the person who posts initiates a discussion topic. However, it should be mentioned that a reaction or comment to a post is not obligatory and they are often left uncommented.

Aside from leaving a post in a Facebook group, members have the possibility to react and comment on posts. If we stay with the comparison of forums, comments function as forum posts after a thread. A whole discussion can start with these comments. Under a comment, other members can answer and comment on comments.

10.4.2 TB-303 Owners Club

The *TB-303 Owners Club* is a restricted public Facebook group in terms of its topic and membership. It is dedicated exclusively to owners of Roland TB-303 bass line only. As it is written in the group description:

Remember, this group is for TB-303 owners only.

1. You must submit a photo of your TB-303 to be allowed to join this club.
2. You can specify to keep your photo private if you do not want anyone to see your unit.
3. If you have a friend that you know has a TB-303 please suggest this group to them (TB-303 Owners Club n.d.).

So new members are accepted only if they submit a photo of their TB-303—including its serial number. As it is a public group, anyone can read its content. Currently, it has two administrators and 989 members (data from 2019 July).

The Roland TB-303 ("Transistor Bass") is one of the most influential instruments in the history of electronic dance music. Of the monophonic analogue bass synthesizer, only 10,000 units were manufactured between 1982 and 1984. It was originally produced to guitarists for bass accompaniment that helped them practicing alone, but it never became popular among them because of its inauthentic sound.

Later, Chicago house producers discovered a creative way to use this instrument by applying its built-in effects to its programmed sound patterns. The result was the so-called *acid sound* that led to the establishment of a completely new music genre: acid house. This *wrong* way of using an instrument also represents the "creative perversion of technology" (Vitos 2014) by these early producers.

In the 1980s, the instrument was relatively cheap to acquire because of its failure amongst the original target group. Its current price is between € 2000 and € 3000, depending on its current condition. The TB-303 became a mythical and must-have piece of equipment among acid house[1] and acid techno[2] producers. Aside from this group, there are also many analogue synth fans and instrument collectors who own it as a prestige object without practicing music production.

The reasons for its high price today are complex, and here it can only be speculated: (1) it has a historical value for musicians who want to produce the original acid sound; (2) this corresponds with the phenomenon of nostalgia or vintage as a key role in making something more popular or valuable; and the other reason is that (3) only 10,000 units were produced.

Even if many software and hardware clones (even analogue ones) exist today, most of the musicians and fans only believe in the original machine and consider the clone sound to be noticeably different (Reynolds 2013).

With the chosen Facebook group comments, I want to illustrate some characteristics of the language use of individuals who take part in the discourse of TB-303. This discourse is especially important because of the aforementioned creative use of the instrument. The original manual did not include those "new" functions discovered by the EDM musicians; therefore, the members exchange experience in order to learn how to use their instrument in these new ways.

The discourse, in part through the community's specific lexis, helps to keep the group together, building friendships, connections, creating opinion leaders, and sharing ideas and thoughts.

10.4.3 The Language Use of the TB-303 Owners Club

All posts and comments of the Facebook group were analyzed between April 1 and April 30, 2016. During this period of time, the members of the group posted 31 posts and added 87 comments to these posts. The topics of the posts are various: some of them are specific questions about the TB-303 functions; some are about the music produced partly with the help of the Roland TB-303; a few are about own music, etc.

By analyzing this Facebook group, I was interested in how a discourse community is constructed around a specific technological item. How can this object determine the identity of a discourse community?

Within the domains of structure and meaning, the frequently used music- and machine-related adjectives were analyzed. I found the following examples for music-related adjectives: ***grimy acid house; pulsating hi-hats and cymbals; crafty percussion****; great acid; deep and late night vibes; creates* ***motion that fluid and full; driving kick drum****; fantastic tones;* ***sweeping builds****; intense dopeness.* Within these

[1]Acid house is a subgenre of the genre house music developed in the mid-1980s in Chicago, USA. The style is defined primarily by the squelching sounds of the famous analogue bass line TB-303.

[2]Acid techno is also one of the subgenres of techno that developed out of acid house. The sound of TB-303 is a very important landmark of the subgenre, but aesthetically it is considered darker and harder than acid house.

examples (highlighted in bold) one can easily recognize many structural metaphors (Lakoff and Johnson 1980; Kövecses 2010). In structural metaphors, the source domain provides a rich knowledge structure for the target concept (Kövecses 2010). In every case, the target concept is the music itself. It is not a surprising phenomenon because talking about music can generally be very difficult and consequently, one often uses metaphors or metaphorical expressions in order to express one's thoughts on music (see more in Jóri 2015).

The same phenomenon can be seen in the case of using machine-related adjectives. The members of the Facebook group used the following adjectives for different music production equipment (but mainly for their Roland TB-303s): *robust; healthy; great; absolutely beautiful; mint; strident and proud*. These adjectives can be also understood as metaphorical expressions because some of them—e.g., *healthy; proud*—sound strange being used on a machine; they would normally be used to describe a living being. Here we can clearly see examples for the phenomenon of how users of the TB-303 give human characteristics to their machines and emphatically project emotions onto them. The phenomenon can be explained through the members' passionate—often even fetishist—feelings toward their instrument, which I would like to illustrate with the help of a quote from a web discussion forum, *Vintage Synth Explorer*:

> THE ANALOG ROLAND ORCHESTRA: GRAND SILVER PLASTIC MACHINE. ACID.
> WAY TOO EXPENSIVE BUT WORTH EVERY CENT. I MEAN SURE YOU CAN HAVE A WAYS CHEAPER EMU AND FAKE BUT ISNT IT GOOD TO TURN THE REAL KNOBS. YEAH. PEOPLE WHO WANTS THAT SOUND, BUY ACIDLAB BASSLINES - THE BEST EMU OF THIS BUT IF YOU WANT TO HAVE THIS FEELING YOU HAVE TO GIVE SOMEONE 1500 DOLLARS OR 1000 EURO[3] AND YOU GET IT. ACID PURE. YOU CAN WATCH THIS SILVER BOX FOR HOURS AND SHE WILL LOVE YOU AND YOU WILL TURN HER KNOBS AND SHE WILL LOVE YOU AND YOU WILL LOVE HER.
> NICE RELATIONSHIP.
> I LOVE MINE AND I M HAPPY AND IT WAS WORTH 1000 EURO. (Vintage Synth Explorer n.d.)

This brings us to the next interesting case I want to discuss in this analysis: when members use anthropomorphic expressions on their machines: *small silver family; our little friends; one of my guys, little sister; beautiful baby*. In these examples, the TB-303 is treated as a friend, a family member, or as an own child. As one of the users wrote in a comment, *Family + 303 = Love*.

Another good example from the collected sample is the following post: One of the users posted an image about his new-born baby together with a TB-303. The post received all together 92 Facebook reactions—that can be *Like, Love, Haha, Wow, Sad,* or *Angry*—from the other members (Fig. 10.1).

They are compensatory strategies to express feelings about a post or a comment: to like or love, to find something funny, astonishing, sad or infuriating. In the

[3]The comment is from 2008. At this time the 303's price was much lower than at present.

Fig. 10.1 Facebook reactions (Facebook, Reactions Now Available 2016)

Fig. 10.2 Comments under the post (TB-303 Owners Club n.d.). Here a screenshot of the comment was pasted to keep the original usage of the compensatory strategies (emoticons)

abovementioned post, the 92 members used the "Like" and "Love" reactions and 13 of them also congratulated him in the form of a comment underneath the post. In these comments, many members were joking: first, they expressed their congratulations for the *beautiful* machine, and only then for the baby (Fig. 10.2).

With these examples I can illustrate the fact that some of the TB-303 owners treat their machines as humans and that they are big fans or enthusiasts of their objects. The members express their fanaticism also through their numerologies: they remark and collect things that have some kind of connection with the number 303. As a user writes, *My son Eliah was born last friday at 3.03 in the afternoon…acid baby.* A comment under it says, *my son was born 03.03.2013…in the morning. it's also an acidline!!!* and someone else adds, *karma, and my girl was born in room 303 @ hospital.*

While analyzing the community's language use in the domains of structure and meaning, it is easy to see that the community often uses technical terms that are mainly connected with the functions of the synthesizer or they are related to music production generally: *knob; mod; modded; sequencer; groovebox; remix; programming mode; mix; noise ratio; low notes; compressor; high ratio; long release time; loop.* These terms are also examples of expertise in the community. Members with a higher level of knowledge on the topic obviously use these terms with more self-confidence.

The group also uses many specific community reference words that are signifiers for holding the community together. These terms were categorized into four types: the ones that are related to (1) the Roland TB-303; to (2) music genres (scenes); to (3) relationships; and to (4) the Facebook group itself. (1) Statistically, the group only mentioned the term TB-303 (or its different variations: *Roland TB-303; TB-303; 303; TB303; tb303; tb-303,* etc.) 13 times, but this number would be much higher if I added the aforementioned metaphors used for the synthesizer and its referential pronouns (e.g., *it, he, she, this, that*). (2) Another typical community reference word is the music genre that the members produce with their machines (*acid*), which can refer to the genres of acid house and acid techno. Surprisingly these terms were used only 13 times in the sample, but one can still believe that it is part of the in-group language use, as mentioned before, showing that the members of this Facebook group are part of the acid house and acid techno *virtual scenes* (after Peterson and Bennett 2004).

To show another example of terms that help to build the community together, I also want to focus on ones that relate to friendships and relationships between the members. Of these, the following were used all together 15 times in the sample: *mate; bro; friend, man, guys, member, group, Facebook Group.* The fact that these terms are often used in the comments proves that the members treat the community as a *friendship* community.

By analyzing the use of singular and collective personal pronouns, I wanted to find evidence for collective identity. I predicted that the group would use the collective *we* frequently. This cannot be proven from this sample, because the community used *we* and *our* only nine times. In contradiction, the members used *I* and its related forms *me* and *my* all together 65 times. So, from the personal pronouns *we* cannot be presented as evidence for collective or group identity.

As mentioned before, one type of compensatory strategy to express emotions and thoughts is the Facebook reaction. Now I must add some points on the other types of strategies used by the members: emoticons, pictures, and *Facebook stickers*.

I found different types of emoticons in the sample; some were Facebook's own graphics—for example in the screenshot above—and some of them took the form of the classical emoticon, such as *:)*. For the scope of this study, it is not necessary to separate these types from each other: I consequently counted all of them together and found that the members used them only 22 times in the analyzed sample. This was a surprisingly low number and I seek to explain it with the focus of the group (TB-303) possibly being considered a *serious* topic. One can also support this theory with the fact that members used the most emoticons and Facebook reactions in the aforementioned post about the baby. It is not surprising that in the case of such a personal and emotional topic, the members use more compensatory strategies. Of the five used Facebook stickers, three were also emoticons (three different smileys) and two were types of *like icons*. Four of them were used by the same member, so one can understand this as her/his habitual behavior and not as a general group feature.

From the eight pictures that were posted, six illustrate own TB-303s and other music production equipment and two of them depict something else. This indicates that the group members post their pictures about their TB-303s as a tool to show their machines proudly to the others. As mentioned in the introduction of the group, one of the requirements of being added to the group is that one has to send her/his own bass line with serial number to the administrator. This can be in the form of a private message, or s/he can publicly post in the group. So many members post these pictures publicly in the group timeline.

In the domain of interaction management, I was interested in the concern structures via linking, quoting, tagging, and using hashtags and in the features of the members' participation.

Within linking, I can separate (1) hyperlinks from the Internet and (2) sharing an earlier Facebook post from another Facebook site (this can be a member's own profile, an institution's/organization's profile, another Facebook group, etc.). In most of the cases the group members linked music or music videos external to Facebook.[4] Linking and sharing music with each other is a tool for expressing knowledge in the discourse community and at the same time motivates the other members to react: they might *like* it as a Facebook reaction, start a discussion, and/or express their opinions about it.

The group members did not quote anyone in their posts and comments. This may be due to the functions of the website: quoting is more common on web discussion forums, where one can directly answer someone else's comment while keeping the original text. On Facebook this function is not available.

By tagging a person within a message, her/his public Facebook profile can be directly accessed by clicking on the person's name. In this case, there was a hyperlink function linking the person's own profile, but users who tag another person in a comment often do it in order to address the message to a person directly. In a Facebook group, tagging can be also understood as a tool for community construction, because addressing someone in a message encourages the addressee, who receives a notification about having been tagged, to be an active part of the group and react to the post. From the eight cases where someone was tagged, seven were the latter mentioned type of tagging: to address someone directly.

Using a hashtag (#) on Facebook also implies a hyperlink function that collects all posts that use the same hashtag-word. In the scope of this research, hashtag-use can be thought of as an expression of knowledge, because a person who uses a hashtag is aware of the fact that thousands of other people can be reached by her/his post.

Remaining in the domain of interaction management, I took a closer look at the rates of the participation. Forty-one members—one of whom is the administrator himself—participated in the conversations during this month. The powerful role of the administrator within the group is notable: he accepts or rejects new members. As mentioned, only those who send in photos of their TB-303s can become part of the group. After "B.B." checks these photos, a person can be accepted or rejected to be the part of the Facebook group. The administrator is normally an active member of the group, but within this 1 month, he only made three posts and added one comment to others' posts. Another interesting point about the administrator is that although I expected his posts to be the most popular, since he is the most powerful member of the group, this cannot be proved from the sample. I considered those posts that received at least 10 Facebook reactions on their posts as popular. For example, the aforementioned post about the baby received 92 reactions. The administrator's two posts only received 6 likes.

The activity of the members was coded as follows: (1) *active* if this person made at least 10 comments or posts; (2) *moderate* if s/he left between 4 and 9 comments or posts; (3) *occasional* if someone made 1–3 comments or posts; and coded as (4) *no activity* if s/he left no comments or posts. From the total 119 activities (posts and comments), at least 10 conversation pieces can be considered active. The results

[4]Mainly from YouTube or Soundcloud.

were the following: only 2 members were in the *active* category, 8 in the *moderate*, and 31 had *occasional* activity. This also means that the rate of the activity is balanced out between the members: statistically from a total of 119 activities, the average activities per person would be 2.9. This is nearly what the members actually show in their activity, because as mentioned, 31 of them had between 1 and 3 comments and/or posts. I consider this a balanced conversation among the participants, which also points to the *harmonic* relationship between them.

This balance and near harmony could also be seen in the analysis of the domain of social phenomena. There was literally no disagreement among the members in this 1 month. This is not surprising, as this group was created for the owners and fans of TB-303s.

The members of the group often post a piece of their own, someone else's music, or—as mentioned before—a photograph of their music production equipment. In these cases, the others normally give feedback to the person who posted it, which can take the form of a Facebook reaction (mostly a *like*) or a written text: *that's all you need mate!! It's brilliant!!; Lovin it.; Intense dopeness.* These posts can also be considered as invitations, as the member who posts these comments knows that others might answer or give feedback concerning it—so gaining attention may be the basic main motivation. The community members often ask for information about their machines from each other:

> Give me a short description if you are able.
> Any tt303 owners know how to access tb303 style programming mode?
> Anyone knows where I can download those sheets to write your notes in.
> Does anyone make those plastic coverings (...).
> Is there any routine maintenance that needs (...).

Regarding information exchange, I can presume that in most of the cases, they provide knowledge. I include here not only those posts and comments that provide exact knowledge via their written texts, but also those symbolic posts that share, for example, a single link to a music video or track, because this also expresses that the person who posted them is informed about it and "owns" knowledge on such things.

The majority of biographical information shared in the group relates to personal equipment. This takes the form of photography with or without a short description. The phenomenon of sharing photos of music production equipment was also considered as a representation for establishing a sense of belonging: they belong to those people who own these machines and they probably have the same taste of music and interest in music production.

To sum up the language use of the *TB-303 Owners Club*: one could see evidence for community and ideology construction through the special jargon (mostly on the TB-303), their cooperative discursive behaviors (no disagreement or conflict), the special knowledge they share with each other (about music production, using instruments, etc.) and the characteristics of member participation in the conversations (balanced out and harmonic).

10.5 Conclusions

The aim of this chapter was to introduce the model and methodology system of the discourse community of electronic dance music. Therefore, I highlighted the potentials of looking at these communities with the help of linguistic discourse analysis.

This methodology can open up a new perspective on research of electronic dance music. By looking at the communities of EDM as discourse communities, the research focus can be shifted from sociological and cultural features of the communities to the actual analysis of discourses and language use within these groups.

Therefore, my research in general and this study see discourse as language in use and as a tool for expressing identity. This study also presented different examples of how identity construction works through discourse and how discourse influences these mechanisms. Moreover, on further consideration of the model of discourse community, the processes of community construction could be described through the selected sample.

This methodology system can help us understand the fine details about online community building and social identity construction via language use. Furthermore, it brings us closer to an ethnographic analysis of computer-mediated communication.

To reiterate some examples of the outcomes of this chapter, the linguistic data of the Facebook group *TB-303 Owners Club* showed that the use of special terminology indicates social identities: as mentioned, they are a signifier of in-group language and partly hold the community together. The participants of the discourse community identified themselves to be part of this social group by using community-specific terminology. Furthermore, social identities and community constructions became clearly visible by analyzing the interactional management of the data.

Social phenomena showed that the community members were intent on building community partnerships and showing interest in one another by their interpersonal discourse behaviors such as thanking, asking for information, inviting feedback, offering advice, and joking. Additionally, the features of information exchange represented mutual influence and established significance and sense of belonging (e.g., by sharing biographical information).

This analysis could have been much longer and detailed, but for the scope of this chapter, I wanted to introduce the potentials of this kind of methodology system through a couple of short examples. Hopefully this example will encourage other (applied) linguists to bring their awareness to music-related online communities to see how interesting samples can be found and analyzed.

References

Alim, H. S., Ibrahim, A., & Pennycook, A. (Eds.). (2009). *Global linguistic flows: Hip hop cultures, youth identities, and the politics of language*. New York: Routledge.

Androutsopoulos, J. (2007). Style online: Doing hip-hop on the German-speaking Web. In P. Auer (Ed.), *Style and social identities: Alternative approaches to linguistic heterogeneity* (pp. 279–320). Berlin: de Gruyter.

Androutsopoulos, J. (2008). Potentials and limitations of discourse-centred online ethnography. *Language@Internet* 5. Retrieved July 12, 2018 from https://www.languageatinternet.org/articles/2008/1610

Bishop, J. (2009). Enhancing the understanding of genres of web-based communities: The role of the ecological cognition framework. *International Journal of Web Based Communities, 5*(1), 4–17.

Borg, E. (2003). Discourse community. *ELT Journal, 57*(4), 398–400.

Crystal, D. (2006). *Language and the internet*. Cambridge: Cambridge University Press.

Facebook, Facebook Groups. (n.d.). Retrieved June 21, 2017 from https://groups.fb.com

Facebook, Reactions Now Available. (2016). Retrieved June 12, 2018 from http://newsroom.fb.com/news/2016/02/reactions-now-available-globally/

Facebook, What are the privacy options for Facebook groups? (n.d.). Retrieved June 26, 2018 from https://www.facebook.com/help/220336891328465

Fish, S. (1980). *Is there a text in this class? The authority of interpretative communities*. Cambridge, UK: Harvard University Press.

Herring, S. C. (2004). Computer-mediated discourse analysis: An approach to researching online behavior. In S. A. Barab, R. Kling, & J. H. Gray (Eds.), *Designing for virtual communities in the service of learning* (pp. 338–376). Cambridge, NY: Cambridge University Press.

Jóri, A. (2012). On the discourse community of electronic music. *Sound Studies Lab*. Retrieved August 10, 2018 from http://www.soundstudieslab.org/on-the-discourse-community-of-electronic-music/

Jóri, A. (2015). A metaforikus nyelvi kifejezések vizsgálata a "funkkal szaggatott androidtechno" területén. In A. Jóri & M. Folmeg (Eds.), *Világ és nyelv szenvedéllyel* (pp. 288–297). Budapest: Tinta könyviadó.

Jóri, A. (2016). *On the discourse community of electronic dance music*. Doctoral dissertation. Faculty of Humanities, Eötvös Loránd University, Budapest.

Kövecses, Z. (2010). *Metaphor*. Oxford: Oxford University Press.

Kuhn, T. S. (1962). *The structure of scientific revolutions*. Chicago, IL: University of Chicago Press.

Lakoff, G., & Johnson, M. (1980). *Metaphors we live by*. London: University of Chicago Press.

McLeod, K. (2001). Genres, subgenres, sub-subgenres and more: Musical and social differentiation within electronic/dance music communities. *Journal of Popular Music Studies, 13*, 59–75.

Nystrand, M. (1982). *What writers know: The language, process, and structure of written discourse*. New York: Academic.

Perelman, C., & Olbrechts-Tyteca, L. (1969). *The new rhetoric: A treatise on argumentation*. Notre Dame: University of Notre Dame Press.

Peterson, R. A., & Bennett, A. (2004). Introducing music scenes. In A. Andy Bennett & R. A. Peterson (Eds.), *Music scenes: Local, translocal, and virtual* (pp. 1–15). Nashville, TN: Vanderbilt University Press.

Rasulo, M. (2008). *The role of participant discourse in online community formation*. Rome: Aracne.

Reynolds, S. (2013). *Energy flash: A journey through rave music and dance culture*. London: Faber & Faber.

Swales, J. M. (1990). *Genre analysis: English in academic and research settings*. Cambridge: Cambridge University Press.

TB-303 Owners Club. (n.d.). Retrieved August 10, 2017 from https://www.facebook.com/groups/tb303ownersclub/

Vintage Synth Explorer. (n.d.). Roland TB-303. Retrieved June 20, 2018 from http://www.vintagesynth.com/roland/303.php

Vitos, B. (2014). Along the lines of the Roland TB-303: Three perversions of acid techno. *Dancecult* 6. Retrieved August 15, 2017 from https://dj.dancecult.net/index.php/dancecult/article/view/460/462

Whelan, A. (2008). *Breakcore: Identity and interaction on peer-to-peer*. Cambridge: Cambridge Scholars.

Widdicombe, S., & Wooffitt, R. (1995). *The language of youth subcultures: Social identity in action*. New York: Harvester Wheatsheaf.

Chapter 11
The Human Modular Synthesizer: The Musical Design and Live Performance of Elektro Guzzi's *Pentagonia*

Josef Schaubruch

Abstract This chapter investigates the Austrian band Elektro Guzzi performing techno live on stage. It focuses on their specific constellation of musical production, musical design, and live performance as key elements of electronic dance music. Methodologically, the chapter combines focused ethnography (Knoblauch, *Sozialforschung/forum: Qualitative social research, 6*(3), 44, 2005), musical analysis (Butler, *Unlocking the groove: Rhythm, meter, and musical design in electronic dance music*, Indiana University Press, 2006), and performance analysis (Sanden, *Liveness in modern music: Musicians, technology, and the perception of performance*, Routledge, 2013; Auslander, *Liveness: Performance in a mediatized culture*, Routledge, 2008 and *The Oxford handbook of new audiovisual aesthetics*, Oxford University Press, 2013; Butler, *Playing with something that runs: Technology, improvisation, and composition in DJ and laptop performance*, Oxford University Press, 2014). The combination of these analytical approaches provides new insights into the challenging musical practice of the performance of liveness, as exemplified by Elektro Guzzi.

11.1 Approaching Elektro Guzzi's *Pentagonia*

"Elektro Guzzi is a human modular synthesizer which plays ingenious technoid sounds with a classic guitar-bass-drum-setup" (Elektro Guzzi 2017)—it is with these words that the Austrian music group Elektro Guzzi announce themselves on the cover of their recent release *Parade*. As additional press information and several interviews (Dancity Festival 2011: 1.57–2.46 min; Breuer et al. 2014a, b; Udvardyová 2016; Brooks 2017) suggest, they describe themselves as a band that play techno live on stage; an appraisal which is also mirrored by music journalists (Teichs and Wick 2012: 0.30–1.16 min; Bath 2014).

J. Schaubruch (✉)
Leuphana University of Lüneburg, Lüneburg, Germany
e-mail: josef@schaubruch.com

A. Jóri, M. Lücke (eds.), *The New Age of Electronic Dance Music and Club Culture*, Music Business Research, https://doi.org/10.1007/978-3-030-39002-0_11

Reflecting on their introductory statement, it does not seem unusual that techno is created in multiple ways or is presented with varying degrees of liveness. However, it does perhaps seem like a "strange concept to produce techno without a computer, synthesizer or sampler," as Teichs and Wick questioned (2012: 0.30–1.15 min). Techno is noticeably associated with a framework (albeit flexible), which is largely determined by its electronic world, manifesting itself in the art of producing and performing music by electronic artists such as DJs and live acts.[1] Elektro Guzzi's approach deviates substantially from this framework, because it has radically different implications: as classically trained instrumentalists, they depend primarily on the possibilities of their (acoustic) musical instruments and are restricted by the conditions of the creation of techno in real time. Therefore, it seems they lack the electronic world (respectively *techno*logical world) that is fundamental to the genre of electronic dance music, particularly as it is characterized by early definitions (Peel 2001; Butler 2006).[2]

For this reason it is questionable why Elektro Guzzi is considered as techno. It can be assumed that the musical design and its forms of production and performance by electronic artists can be viewed as parameters, that—temporally—define a genre. According to this, a sound and social event associated with techno will have a certain specificity. This specificity can then be helpful to examine whether it corresponds to Elektro Guzzi or not.

Thus, firstly, this chapter investigates how Elektro Guzzi's positioning within the genre of techno can be explained on the level of their musical design. The presented musical analysis can provide possible answers to this question. Based on transcriptions, the production practice and sound aesthetics, as well as the temporal and

---

[1]I use the term electronic artists to describe DJs and live acts. I describe a DJ as "a person who puts together a continuous musical program by selecting, combining, and manipulating tracks [. . .] with two or more turntables and a mixing board" (Butler 2006: 326). For the term live act there are also other common terms, e.g., "live PA" (Butler 2006: 33, 70f., 326) or "laptop performer" (Butler 2014: 6f., 13). I use the term live act to refer to a performing artist, who "manipulates studio technology in real time to (re)create his or her own music" (Butler 2014: 13).

[2]I understand genres as "a set of musical events (real or possible) whose course is governed by a definite set of socially accepted rules" (Fabbri 1982: 52). Brackett (2016: 6–13) discusses this much cited definition, which Fabbri reinforced several times (1999: 7; 2012: 188), in detail in the context of current genre debates.

In the following I will primarily use the term techno as a subcategory of electronic dance music. Firstly, because techno (or, less often, technoid music) is the preferred term within the musical scene focused upon within this chapter. Both the musicians and the music journalists who write about them use this term: "We've always [. . .] called it techno and we still do. Because that's where it comes from and that's what we want" (Hammer in Breuer et al. 2018). Secondly, the term electronic dance music, especially in its abbreviation EDM, is rather associated with mainstream pop (Rietveld 2013: 2; Butler 2014: 5), while the music examined in this chapter is more associated with underground culture. Thirdly, the chapter utilizes the approach of Butler, who ascribes his study to electronic dance music in general, but consciously uses the term techno in his more detailed analysis (Butler 2006: 25). Regarding the difficulty of genre names within electronic dance music see McLeod (2001) and Lena (2012: 78).

formal design of the studio version of *Pentagonia*—a track of their album *Parquet* produced with Patrick Pulsinger in 2011—are examined as an example.

Secondly, the chapter interrogates how the positioning of Elektro Guzzi within the genre of techno can be understood from the perspective of performance and its underlying dimensions of liveness, which the band present to their audience. Theoretical considerations on liveness can enlighten the performances of Elektro Guzzi, acting as a useful approach to better understanding the mediatized environments of electronic dance music. Hence, Elektro Guzzi's music performance at Heidelberger Frühling (2014) will be considered with respect to various approaches to liveness. Furthermore, the analysis is based on the method of focused ethnography (Knoblauch 2005). In this way, the analysis is enriched by my participant observations of this concert (and another one from 2018 in Potsdam) and several interviews with the band (three guideline-based expert interviews in April, August 2014/June 2018 conducted by myself as well as interviews by music journalists).

11.2 The Process of Production and Sound Aesthetics of *Pentagonia*

To systematically reflect upon the production process and sound aesthetics of *Pentagonia*, both aspects will be examined on the basis of the functions, which characterize the individual work phases involved. Butler (2006: 60–62) distinguishes synthesizing, processing, sampling, and sequencing: (1) synthesizing includes the production of sound using analog or digital signal sources, (2) processing describes the operation of processing sound, (3) sampling means the use of samples or the procedure of sampling itself, and (4) sequencing refers to the structural organization and storage of individual sounds.

However, Butler's (2006: 70–95) perspective is affiliated with a mediatized interface environment, e.g., with laptop, drum machines, controllers, etc. Since Elektro Guzzi's recording of *Pentagonia* was based on output signals from their acoustic instruments and they almost exclusively use neither electronically produced sounds (e.g., through synthesizing modules) nor prerecorded sounds (e.g., presets, samples from sample libraries, field recordings) for conceptual reasons, Butler's approach seems to be only applicable to a limited extent. Nevertheless, Elektro Guzzi pursue a technoid sound aesthetic as it is shaped by the common electronic devices of techno on all functional levels: this is reflected accordingly in all of these levels in *Pentagonia*. This is apparent from both the interviews (see Breuer et al. 2014a, b, 2018) and from the analysis of their approach to production, as shown in the following.

It is worth considering the process of production of *Pentagonia* and the underlying intentions of Elektro Guzzi, as Jakob Schneidewind, the bassist, explains:

> We don't do any edits or overdubs. We did not even record the new album (...) on the computer, but, like back in the good old days, on a tape recorder. We didn't even have the possibility to edit anything afterwards. We ruled that possibility out consciously. (Schneidewind in Teichs and Wick 2012: 5.32–5.58 min)

Bernhard Hammer, the guitarist, remembers the production of *Parquet* similarly:

> In the beginnings, we really tried to record the music like it is and not to cut so much and to edit so much, afterwards, in the post-production. (Hammer in Breuer et al. 2018)

The original sound has to be sufficient from the beginning with the intention that nothing (or, rather as little as possible) should be edited afterwards. More specifically, the band state that their material gains appeal via the manner in which it is played (see Hammer in Teichs and Wick 2012: 6.13–6.46 min). Thus, *Pentagonia* can be considered as a snapshot of their studio session in a state of "non-take-twoness" (Sanden 2013: 5) as it also exists on stage, based on musical instruments. Their profile description on Facebook (without author n.d.) strengthens the absence of machines to praise their live performance:

> Though their sound most certainly suggests that Bernhard Hammer, Jakob Schneidewind and Bernhard Breuer also decided to become machines, they strangely enough don't use any (it took several confirmations in mails and personal meetings and a rehearsal video to convince that they don't). (. . .) There is no computer backup material they prepared earlier, no loops and things, no overdubs. However hard it is to believe, what you hear is 100% live.

This further indicates that Elektro Guzzi's approach seems to raise questions. However, this impression could be revised, by taking into account their musical background as musicians and (live) instrumentalists who share a passion for electronic music, and especially for techno. For them, their approach feels more like a natural process than a dogmatic concept (Dancity Festival 2011: 0.30–1.37 min; Teichs and Wick 2012: 1.16–2.01 min; Breuer et al. 2014a, b, 2018). Elektro Guzzi are particularly interested in a repetitive sound that is "nearly mechanical, despite being played live" (Teichs and Wick 2012: 2:23–3:22 min). Their live performance enhances the sound by creating a "certain lack of definition," which enriches the music sonically, temporally, and formally because it gains a more human feel, which provides a certain kind of groove, energy, and magic (Teichs and Wick 2012: 4:01–4:56 min, 8:33–10:03 min).

Without disagreeing with this statement, it nevertheless seems evident to argue that their approach limits their possibilities. In Table 11.1, which transfers Butler's main functions of the production of electronic dance music to the production and sound aesthetics of *Pentagonia*, I attempt to demonstrate how they respond creatively to these limitations (or rather: their self-imposed restrictions) and thus expand their possibilities.

The synthesizing of the electric guitar and electric bass (only called guitar/bass in the following) is caused by the strings and is thus acoustic (chordophone). The drums and percussion instruments also produce acoustic signals (idiophonic and membranophonic), which trigger external devices. Since these acoustic signals trigger peripheral oscillators, but are initiated and controlled by the musicians, the synthesizing can also be denoted electronically (electrophone), for instance, by enriching the acoustic sound with electronically generated sounds (ring modulation) or by modulating frequencies of electronic sounds (frequency modulation). Thus, the acoustically generated signal remains the starting point, which passes through a complex signal processing path that provides further opportunities for processing

Table 11.1 Elektro Guzzi's adaptations of Butler's main functions of the production of electronic dance music in relation to their musical instruments[a]

Function (rows)/ musical instrument (columnes)	Electric guitar	Electric bass	Drums/percussion instruments	Electronic devices
Synthesizing[b]	• Electro-acoustic chordophone (strings) • Idiophone (wooden corpus)		• Idiophone (bells, cymbals, etc.) • Membranophone (drumhead)	Electrophone (transducer, analogue/digital modules and components)
Processing	• Preparations of the instruments (e.g., use of magnetic fields above the sound pickups; addition of objects like attaching metal clips to the strings to change the overtone structure and to disturb the magnetic field of the pickups; placing cymbals on drumheads; attaching coins to cymbals, etc.) • Various playing techniques and different tunings (e.g., use of a cello bow, playing the guitar strings with felt mallets; use of sticks, brushes, rods, shaker sticks, mallets for timpani; tapping, flageolet playing, palm mutes, bendings, etc.) • DIY-percussions[c] • Audio signal processing[d] (primarily as stompboxes) (a) Effects for influencing dynamics (compressor, gate) (b) Effects for spectral processing (equalizer, filter/envelope shaping, octaver, harmonizer, pitch-shifter/detuner, frequency modulation, organ emulator, distortion/overdrive) (c) Effects for influencing time (delay, reverb, chorus, ring modulation)			
Sampling	• Capturing sounds, acoustic snapshots (e.g., freezing-effects)			
Sequencing	• Organization of signals (division, merging, redirection) • Control of effects as a repeating sequence			

[a]Regarding the instrumentation see also Archiv österreichischer Popularmusik (n.d.)
[b]The instrumental description is inspired by the revision of the Hornbostel–Sachs classification by the MIMO consortium (2011)
[c]Elektro Guzzi built a construction for the simulation of hall effects, which is played with a stick on a tensioned spring. It is based on the technology of the spring reverb, which produced a reverb mechanically, before electronically produced reverbs were used
[d]The digital processing of sound events is based on a classification by Stange-Elbe (2015)

(see Fig. 11.1). For example, Bernhard Breuer, the drummer, processes his sound in two ways: firstly, the acoustic sounds are microphoned, amplified, and altered in sound by effect devices (e.g., the Boss-DD 20 Giga Delay, the Pigtronix Disnortion, see Fig. 11.1) connected to a mixing console; secondly, triggers are mounted to components of the drum set, which convert acoustic signals into piezoelectric signals, which then control various drum synthesizers (e.g., the Clavia Nord Drum, the Jomox MBase, see Fig. 11.1), which in turn add electronically generated sounds. These electronic sounds are manipulated in a manner determined by the possibilities of the devices.

Elektro Guzzi also use the technique of sampling by freezing acoustic components of the signal chain, which they can then process as repetitive cycles.

Fig. 11.1 Elektro Guzzi's instrumental setup (see Parkin 2013 (left) and Heidelberger Frühling 2014 (right))

The sequencing phase is apparent in devices that sequence additional effects, such as independent effects devices. In addition, devices are used to process the signal paths (splitting, merging, redirecting), thus organizing the sound. While the guitar signal remains a single signal, the bass signal is split into two signals, which then pass through several effect devices as a low-frequency bass signal and a high-frequency effect signal. Within this signal chain, the signals are then deeply processed depending on how the effect devices work (e.g., by altering their envelopes, their frequencies, their dynamics, etc.).

This is illustrated in *Pentagonia* with regard to bass and guitar (see Fig. 11.1 and elektroguzzi 2011): The split bass signal is distorted by various effect devices (e.g., by the Pigtronix Disnortion) and is enriched by synthetic overtones in quint and octave intervals (by the Moogerfooger-FreqBox). The signal is then modified by a compressor (the Philosophers King) and triggers an effect device of the guitar which can modulate its own sounds along with the rhythmic signal of the bass. Thus, the soundscapes of the guitar are synchronized with the rhythm of the bass. At the end of the chain, the envelope curve of the bass signal is changed and its frequency is influenced by a low-pass filter (by the MF-101 Moogerfooger Lowpass Filter) using a foot pedal.

The guitar tuned to a D minor chord (in D-A-D-F-A-D) is played with a felt mallet and strokes on the corpus (in relation to the pattern A, see Fig. 11.4). Hammer plays additional flageolets and struck chords, which are processed with a delay (Boss-DD 20 Giga Delay), a reverb and a ring modulation (the Electro Harmonix Ring Thing). In addition, the duration of the reverb is controlled by a footswitch and included in the rhythmic design (the pattern B, see Fig. 11.4).

Elektro Guzzi thus adapt the sound aesthetic of techno by developing a powerful and inspiring live setup based on acoustic instruments that are coalesced with external electronic devices.

In addition to this, the instrumentalists integrate various playing techniques and object preparations to influence the sound. I describe these creative strategies as (1) imitation, (2) experimentation, and (3) conflation/potentiation. (1) The strategy of imitation is used to replicate technoid sounds and their specific processing. This is illustrated in *Pentagonia* for example by the pattern A/B of a prepared tom (with an attached brush) which aims to imitate the effect of noise (see Breuer et al. 2014a, b).

The other sounds in *Pentagonia* can be traced back to the imitation of typical "electronic synthesized and sampled instrumentation" (Collins et al. 2013: 102), such as synthetic models of drums and percussion instruments as well as bass and synthesizers, for example in the form of a Roland TR808 or TR909 and a TB303 (see Fig. 11.2). However, Elektro Guzzi's synthesizing does not statically aim to reproduce instrumental sounds. They alter them via a process of modifications of instrumental characteristics. Rick Snoman characterizes these modifications as crucial in the production of techno:

> Ultimately, the key technique for techno is experimentation with effects and processing. Heavy compression, bit-crushers, distortion, saturation, phasers, delay, reverb and automation of all these parameters over any number of bars provides the foundation for this genre of music. (Snoman 2014: 372f.)

(2) In addition, Elektro Guzzi emphasize that their tracks emerge from improvising and exploring new sounds in an ongoing process of experimentation, which takes significant rehearsal and preparation time.[3] For instance, Schneidewind explains that the band develop musical possibilities over time, allowing their work to become more complex:

> How our sound can become more multilayered, despite only having three instruments, by putting several layers on top of each other. We are trying to fathom and further our instruments' limits. (Schneidewind in Teichs and Wick 2012: 6:47–8:25 min)

This also explains, why their setup is constantly changing,

> because otherwise it would quickly become boring for us. Only our instruments are constant as the only acoustic sound generators and signal generators. But the peripherals are developing, so you add a device and take others out for it. (Hammer in Breuer et al. 2014a, b)[4]

(3) In accordance with their self-conception as a "human modular synthesizer," a further strategy Elektro Guzzi use can be described as a strategy of conflation and potentiation, which is a result of the interconnection between individual musicians and between the musicians and their electronic devices. This not only affects guitar and bass, as already described above; the drummer is also linked to the others:

> The other guys trigger drums or I trigger their machines (. . .) the sounds melt together in different ways. We send each signal through every other thing. (. . .) Especially, what we did for the last record, I triggered their sounds and stuff like that. And they treated my sounds and we played like this and felt much more like one thing, one synthesizer, which we are always searching for. (Breuer in Breuer et al. 2018)

---

[3] The profile description on Facebook (without author n.d.) also emphasizes this: "The Band started in 2004, taking 5 years to shape their skills before ever entering the studio. This may explain why they have been one of the few acts so convincing that they got a tour of Japan and appearances at Barcelona's Sonar and Berlin's Berghain booked before any recording was even promoted." (see also Teichs and Wick 2012, 8:28–8:32).

[4] This process indicates why they experiment also with samplers and sequencers (e.g., the Elektron Octatrack DPS-1, Roland TR 808, see elektroguzzi 2017). They emphasize several times the importance of advancement and therefore exploring various approaches and setups, e.g., the tempting possibilities of the studio environment (Hammer in Breuer et al. 2018).

This strategy is highlighted by the signal processing in particular, which enables Elektro Guzzi to adapt typical simultaneous "multiple complementary layers" (Collins et al. 2013: 114).

> With the delay pedals synchronized to our tempo, it sometimes sounds almost like a loop, but these are all just effect loops on signals that we produce live. (Schneidewind in Breuer et al. 2014a, b)

The band alters sounds in order to simulate the complexity and aesthetic design of techno with the help of effect devices, as described above (for example, the intense use of delays, Schneidewind in Breuer et al. 2014a, b). The band's analogy of a modular synthesizer can be seen in Elektro Guzzi's subdivision into different types of synthesis, which are then processed, sampled, and sequenced by external devices. The fact that a modular synthesizer, in contrast to Elektro Guzzi, is one single instrument, however, correspond to their intention to create a compact sound, where "one can no longer reconstruct who does exactly what" (Breuer et al. 2014a, b) and the instrumental functions are dissolved within the context of the band.

11.3 Musical Design in *Pentagonia*

11.3.1 Rhythm and Meter in Pentagonia

Butler identifies four common even rhythms in electronic dance music (2006: 82, Table 2.1; see also Collins et al. 2013: 117) that are reflected by *Pentagonia* par excellence. As Fig. 11.2 demonstrates, all four rhythms occur in exactly this form and in the typical texture:

With regard to rhythm and its instrumental representation, bass drum (as four on the floor-pattern) and hi-hat (as offbeat) are exactly the same as described by Butler (2006). The rhythm of shaker also corresponds to his model (even if the rhythm is not represented here by the hi-hat). The remaining rhythms from Fig. 11.2 all represent a backbeat that varies in its instrumental representation (as snare drum,

Fig. 11.2 Even rhythms in *Pentagonia*

woodblock, tom, and guitar. The guitar also varies tonally). These rhythms are combined differently in the development of the track. In this combination the bass drum, the hi-hat, and one of the backbeat patterns play almost continuously and thus create a repetitive groove. In addition, the snare drum (pattern C) and tom (pattern B), both rhythmically identical, represent syncopated rhythms (Butler 2006: 85–89) that fit complementarily into the temporal design (see Fig. 11.4). On the sixteenth level, syncopations are additionally represented by the bass, and the pattern B of the snare drum and woodblock. It is worth noting that these rhythms are very constant. The four basic rhythms and syncopated complements dominate the temporal design, and rhythmic variations are rare.[5]

The meter seems to be clear, *Pentagonia* is in 4/4 time with 130 bpm.[6] As the even rhythms have already indicated, the time is largely divided symmetrically (the cycles of repetition varying from one sixteenth note to four whole notes, see Fig. 11.4). Even if some patterns begin with a pause, suggesting asymmetrical divisions, the first beat remains clearly marked. Nevertheless, the temporal design functions as a tool to create variety within a repetitive context, to which the parameters of melody and harmony are subordinated. Thus, forms of ambiguity and metrical dissonances emerge, that indicate an interpretative multiplicity which is typical for electronic dance music (Butler 2006: 117–177). In *Pentagonia*, metrical disorientations are intensified after the removal of the bass drum, which has clearly marked the meter beforehand. Diverging metrical tensions, which were already latently present as different divisions of time, then increase in their effect, as the following example illustrates. The bass pattern in particular enriches the division of time. It is characterized by an asymmetrical cycle of repetition (5/8), resulting in two phenomena of metrical dissonance: Firstly, it leads to a grouping dissonance (G 5/2, 1 = ♪) with the Bass Drum.[7] Secondly, this grouping dissonance (theoretically) leads to a further grouping dissonance (G 20/4, 1 = ♩) after five 4/4 bars due to its alignment (Fig. 11.3).[8]

The two grouping dissonances occur simultaneously and on a different metrical level. This creates (theoretically) an embedded grouping dissonance (Butler 2006: 158).[9] The grouping dissonance at the lower level is embedded by the grouping

---

[5]Butler describes a third type as diatonic rhythm. The fact that these do not exist here (and no other ones either) underlines the dominance of the other two types.

[6]For detailed considerations on the 4/4 in electronic dance music see Butler (2006: 76f., 113–116).

[7]A grouping dissonance is a "[t]ype of metrical dissonance created through the nonalignment of two or more layers with non-congruent cardinalities. The layers involved in a grouping dissonance, unlike those found in a displacement dissonance, will align at periodic intervals" (Butler 2006: 326).

The G indicates the phenomenon of grouping dissonance, the 5 and the 2 the cycles of repetition with the smaller numeral of an eight note; the 4 and the 20 refer to the numerals larger quarter notes (Butler 2006: 155–166).

[8]In consideration of the interpretive multiplicity of temporal experience (Butler 2006), I thank Schneidewind for pointing out his bass pattern as a 5/8.

[9]An embedded grouping dissonance is "[t]he simultaneous presentation of more than one grouping dissonance at multiple metrical levels." An embedded grouping dissonance "arises when the cycle of a lower level dissonance is incommensurate with the meter, thereby generating a higher-level

Fig. 11.3 Grouping dissonance in *Pentagonia* (bar 1–6, 0–0.11 min)

dissonance at the higher level, which has a larger cycle of repetition. Therefore, the bass, which consists of only one note, establishes an alternative time experience that does not change with the unfolding of the track. Nevertheless, the guitar and the consistent four on the floor-pattern played by the bass drum seem to insist on the 4/4 time spans. The 5/8 time signature is clearly subordinated to these.[10] They mark metrically sensitive parts of the track clearly, such as the beginning and the end, and thus inhibit other temporal phenomena like turning the beat around (Butler 2006: 141) and an ambiguity of beginning (Butler 2006: 125–129). Even the pause of guitar and the bass drum in bars 82–90, which increases the presence of the 5/8 bass pattern, question the previously assumed metrical interpretation only temporarily, because up to this point the 4/4 time signature has been clearly constructed. This is also due to the fact that the duration of the simultaneous patterns is short and dropping the beat is confirmed again exactly after eight bars so that the 4/4 continues consistently. For this reason, it is not plausible to argue for an ambiguity of metrical type in Butler's sense (Butler 2006: 129–133).

I would like to emphasize here that a multiplicity of temporal experience arises from a conflation of rhythms evoked by humans and machines. Thus, delay effects in *Pentagonia* are not obtained solely by playing instruments. While only even rhythms are played by the guitar, the resulting rhythm is a more complex one, because the stompboxes expand the temporal experience. Through signal processing with electronic devices, the rhythm that is subsequently heard can thus dynamically fill the time gaps in the texture. This is achieved through the use of machines. On the other hand, the rhythmization of the reverb in pattern B of the guitar is caused by the guitarist himself, as well as the 5/8 pattern that is played by the bassist himself (and not by machines). This is also similar to the manner in which he triggers the

grouping dissonance that unfolds at the same time as the lower-level dissonance" (Butler 2006: 326).

[10]I therefore speak only about a theoretical grouping dissonance.

soundscapes of the guitar rhythmically. Signal processors are less an idiosyncratic persona, they merely function as a strategy of potentiation regarding the sound aesthetics and the rhythmical possibilities.

In summary, the temporal design of *Pentagonia* reveals an orientation toward the stylistic conventions of techno. The track indicates typical rhythms and texture as well as metrical dissonance like the grouping dissonance described above and, for instance, the typical displacement dissonances (Butler 2006: 139) between bass drum and hi-hat (D2 + 1, 1 = ♪) and bass drum and snare drum (D2 + 1, 1 = ♪). However, these metrical dissonances are sensitively employed in their complexity, which corresponds to the function of dancing intended by Elektro Guzzi.

11.3.2 Form in Pentagonia

The formal structure of *Pentagonia* is built upon patterns as the smallest structural unit. As a larger time span, the patterns form one single sequence, since the track is characterized by a high degree of repetition with only minimal changes. On the level of sound, the patterns of shaker and woodblock are rarely distinctive enough to establish their own sequence; on the level of time, the patterns of snare drum and toms vary only slightly, while the patterns of bass, bass drum, shaker, woodblock, and hi-hat do not change during the whole track. Guitar patterns A, B, and C operate on a higher structural level and evoke the perception of multimeasure patterning most directly. There are several reasons for this: firstly, the guitar patterns encompass the longest cycles of repetition (the others consist mainly of a whole note at most). As a result, when removing one of the guitar patterns, only patterns with shorter cycles of repetition remain, which cannot form their own sequences. Secondly, they differ most clearly in their sound design, whereby the single sequence A is varied in sequences A′ and A″ (see Fig. 11.4).

Larger formal sections are also formed by an orientation toward two- and four-bar patterns. They are constituted by changes in the pattern mixture by adding patterns (bars 16, 24, 34), removing (bars 24, 68, 82), varying (bars 42, 54), and resuming (bar 90). All changes are realized after two or four bars, whereby the orientation to four-bar patterns in particular shapes the formal structure. Thus, changes begin after four rather than two bars and at the beginning of a structural sequence (sequence A comprises 32 + 2 bars, sequence A′ 48 bars, sequence A″ 48 bars).

The formal organization toward a four-bar structure is therefore mainly negotiated between guitar and drums, while the bass pattern remains a rhythmically unchanged constant. Sequence A starts directly with all three instruments and then consistently builds up a four-bar structure up to bar 32. This structure is interrupted by the beginning of sequence A′, because the initiating pattern of the woodblock starts after only two bars (and not after four bars). The woodblock manifests a new, secondary four-bar structure, in which the changes also occur consistently after 4 (respectively, after 8 and 12) bars. It is then the guitar that interrupts this newly constructed four-bar structure with its removal after bar 68 (and not after bar 66) and thus establishes a tertiary four-bar structure in which the patterns also begin after

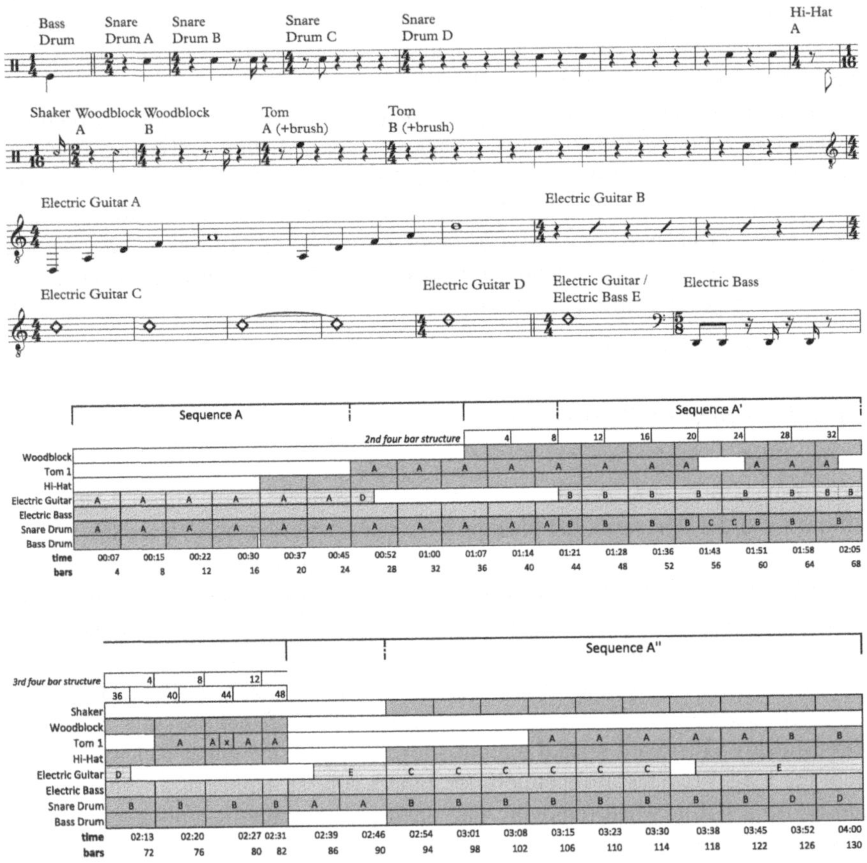

Fig. 11.4 Formal structure and sound palette/loop lengths of *Pentagonia*. The formal structure and its underlying patterns is oriented toward Butler (2006: 259–261) and documents the arrangement and its building blocks. The figure corresponds to four bars on which the track is based. Several patterns per instrument can be distinguished by different letters; white marks pauses. Variations within a pattern are marked by a cross; different sound representations of rhythmically identical patterns are regarded as independent patterns. The dashed lines indicate alternative divisions within these sequences, depending on the parameter which constitutes the division (e.g., the beginning and ending of the patterns of the guitar). The dashed lines indicate alternative divisions within these sequences, depending on whether the pattern of the synthesizer is based on structuring low-frequency patterns (bass/bass drum) or on the chronological course of the synthesizer patterns. To keep it short, the "sound palette" is not based on Butler but on Collins et al. (2013: 117). Thus, the division into rhythmic sound, articulative sounds, and atmospheric sounds is omitted. The cycle of repetition is indicated by the time signature. It is oriented to the first point in time at which a pattern repeats itself. In all, my analysis should be considered as an interpretation (e.g., my proposed sequencing is only one of several possible ones, since the sequences are very similar due to the many constant patterns)

four bars (with the tom pattern). The tertiary structure is then interrupted after bar 82 (and not after bar 80) by the drums, which correspond exactly with the secondary four-bar pattern that the drums had established 48 bars earlier. The drums thus initiate the last sequence A″, whose four-bar structuring is then continued uninterrupted to the end of the track.

As these considerations suggest, I am arguing that the formal structuring is crucially influenced by the improvisation of Elektro Guzzi, in which the structure results from interaction with each other.[11] Instead of a detailed prearranged structure that determines when each formal section begins and ends (as in a precisely defined intro/outro, breakdown or build up), these must be collectively anticipated.

This is also shown by the fact that the transitions between four bars are rarely marked, with little anacrusis orientation and articulative patterns, which reinforces the impression of repetition rather than initiating new formal sections. Instead, new four-bar structures and sequence variants are formed by adding or removing patterns, to which the musicians can then react. The modular and symmetrical structure of the track is arguably the result of (and hence also supports) this interactive negotiation of the sequences and their underlying patterns. Therefore, structure is an entity that establishes itself at the moment of the concert rather than a predetermined factor influencing the progress of the track. In contrast, track-specific patterns such as those of the guitar, which constitute the core of the track, are predetermined as fixed ideas. *Pentagonia* can thus be considered as a reconstruction of these track-specific layers. Its improvised nature also suggests that the track does not represent the preplanned prototypical form of an EDM track (as Butler 2006: 222 and Snoman 2014: 278 point out), but rather Butler's model A (Butler 2006: 207, 229), in which a sequence is improvised in real time (see Fig. 11.5). It is more like a snapshot of the studio recording taken from a live set, in which a previously defined set of patterns is varying.

In *Pentagonia*, improvisation seems to be not only a consciously chosen approach, but also a necessary consequence of the restrictions that Elektro Guzzi impose on themselves with their intention of playing live. Since, for example, they interact with effect devices in real time and this takes varying durations, these are not determined beforehand but communicated according to the particular situation. Again, this type of

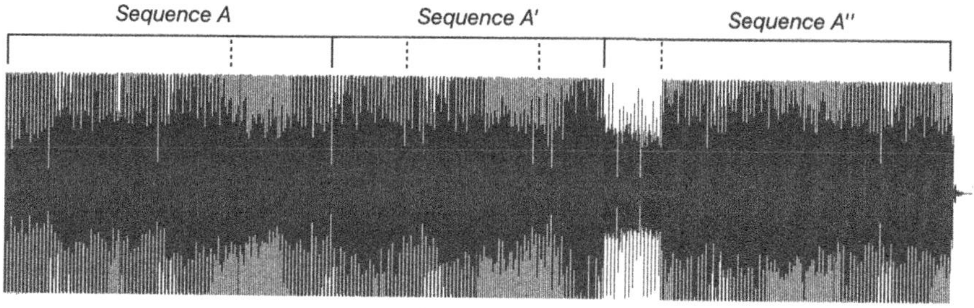

Fig. 11.5 The formal structure transferred to the waveform of *Pentagonia*

[11]According to this, the interruption of sequence A′ by the drums is meaningful: the adding of the woodblock in bar 34 has established a four-bar meta-plane, which is completed exactly after 48 bars and thus does not lessen but rather reinforces an orientation toward four-bar structures.

improvised interaction is very compatible with the repetitive form, as patterns can be freely combined and effortlessly continued cyclically without causing unwanted breaks (see Breuer et al. 2014a, b). In addition, Elektro Guzzi deliberately avoids predetermined structuring in order to preserve improvisation and the character of playing live: as soon as structures are entrenched through multiple rehearsals or concerts, these are dissolved to maintain the magic of the musical moment (Breuer et al. 2014a, b). As explained above, these particular reconstructions of the track in the live performance are characterized by four-bar structures, which are seemingly internalized by Elektro Guzzi, since they fulfill the conventions of the musical design of techno.

However, this does not exclude deviations. Irregular structuring also emphasizes the possibility of failure and thus highlights the real (live) character of the moment of the concert. It prevents a formal structuring that is too mechanical (Hammer in Breuer et al. 2014a, b). As such, the formal design reflects the performance of Elektro Guzzi, which is examined regarding its dimensions of liveness in more detail below.

11.4 Shadings of Liveness in *Pentagonia*

Taking Sanden's definition as a starting point, liveness can be understood as "a flexible concept with different shades of meaning for different musickers in different times and places and in different musical contexts" (Sanden 2013: 6). As Fritsch and Strötgen (2012: 48–50) specify, liveness is a term used to qualitatively describe the relationship between a performer and an audience in a musical performance. Within this framework of a musical performance, I use the term to describe not only a modality of perception (Sanden 2013: 31–33) from the perspective of the audience; furthermore, I would like to highlight the point of view of the performing artists, from which liveness can also be understood as a modality of how a performance is performed. Taking Sanden's multi-perspective theory of liveness into account, the following dimensions can be applied to Elektro Guzzi's performance at Heidelberger Frühling in 2014.

Elektro Guzzi's performance is perceived as live because it takes place as a musical event limited by time and space (see "temporal liveness" and "spatial liveness" in Sanden 2013: 35). This can also be considered as the "classic liveness", defined by Auslander (2008: 61) as "physical co-presence of performers and audience; temporal simultaneity of production and reception; experience in the moment."[12] Elektro Guzzi do not differ in this respect from most performances by electronic artists (or live entertainment in general), since the performers on stage (or in the DJ booth) and the audience in front of the stage share co-presence in time and space.

The "liveness of fidelity," however, helps to further describe their performance ("Music is live when it is perceived as faithful to its initial utterance, its unmediated

[12] Auslander (2016) also refers to these two dimensions in a more recent explanation of the term live performance as "an event in which two sets of people (performers and spectators) are co-present in the same place at the same time."

(or *less* mediated) origins, or an imagined unmediated original," Sanden 2013: 11). The performance is perceived as live because the tracks are based on musical material originally made by themselves (in contrast to performances of DJs, who primarily play musical material of others). Moreover, it is assumed that the tracks are performed largely with "classical instruments" (see Butler 2014: 105f.), which can be described as a contrast to (mediated) interface environments, the likes of which are usually essential in the context of live techno (especially for live acts). However, the interface environment is not nonexistent, but simply relocated and less visible for the audience. The electronic equipment is placed on the floor and on the side next to the drums, so that less electronic musical instruments are apparent at first sight. Drums, guitar, and bass dominate the stage design. Fidelity is constituted by presenting the music as an entity that can be traced back to the three instrumentalists, who initially create acoustic sounds which are then modified by them. The fact that they play familiar musical instruments (theoretically) facilitates the traceability of which musician is responsible for which sound at what time. Elektro Guzzi can thus be perceived as crucial agents of the entire music, as it is presented in the performance.

Elektro Guzzi's performance also distinguishes them from electronic artists, because their performance offers "corporeal liveness": "Music is *live* when it demonstrates a perceptible connection to an acoustic sounding body" (Sanden 2013: 11). Elektro Guzzi embody techno through the process of interacting with the acoustic sounding bodies of their musical instruments, which suggests that the resulting sound is caused by them—quite in contrast to electronic artists, where this is not the case by definition (see the introduction above). Such traceability can also be possible here, although the sounding bodies are rarely acoustic, but rather electronic (Sanden 2013: 39).[13]

The performance also makes Sanden's (2013: 10f.) "interactive liveness" and "liveness of spontaneity" perceptible. Even if the sonic performance is based on preexisting compositional ideas reflected in the recorded tracks, its recreation is always improvised. As described above, Elektro Guzzi interact with each other on stage (albeit less with the audience), which provides a certain unpredictability that stimulates the musical performance of the band in a special way (no one concert is like any other). The entire performance consists of a continuous sound stream in which previously agreed musical patterns are transformed into something unique. Unpredictability is also reflected on the corporeal level, since the movements of Elektro Guzzi are not fixed choreographies. Instead, they move spontaneously and "in the moment," while their bodies and their musical instruments seem like a unit that by and large remains stationary. Announcements to the audience are also rare and unplanned.

However, the latter forms of interaction and spontaneity are (at least) equally possible in mediatized performances of electronic artists. Electronic artists do not

[13]For the relationship between sound and movement in electronic dance music, see also Ferreira (2008).

have to produce sound physically, so they can respond to an audience with flexibility regarding the way they select and present sounding material. Thus, the dimensions of fidelity and corporeality are particularly distinctive, and are referred to by Auslander as an audio/visual economy of musical performance. Auslander describes this perspective as traditionalistic since it expresses the understanding of musical performances in which the configuration of what is seen and what is heard is causal. Especially in mediatized performances of electronic dance music with laptops and various electronic devices, the relationship between these two paths is nontransparent, since the performers' actions with the interface environment and their caused effects may be less familiar and identifiable (and, maybe most importantly, less relevant) to the audience.

Taking this traditionalist perspective into account, Elektro Guzzi's presented cause-and-effect connection (respectively agent–agency connection) can be interpreted as an answer to reconstitute this economy. They adapt traditionalistic values of a classic live performance by presenting a sound environment, whose elements suggest that they can be traced back to the traditional musical instruments they play. However, the final sound results from an electrification through their electronic devices, whose interplay is complicated enough that only a few, if any, of the audience will understand immediately which musician produces which sound at which time (even Elektro Guzzi do not know this sometimes).[14] Elektro Guzzi thus offer a cause-and-effect connection that suggests that their musical performance is live, although the connection is difficult to reconstruct. Auslander also stresses that for the most part the musical audience probably do not have "a very fine-grained sense of instrumental causality" and "does not really understand exactly how the sound is produced, but wants to believe it does nevertheless" (Auslander 2013: 607). Elektro Guzzi thus display the ideological character of "the traditionalist's emphasis on visible causality in musical performances" (Auslander 2013: 607). However, Elektro Guzzi's audio/visual economy is more a by-product of playing techno with their learned musical instruments than a "conscious decision" or the intention "to start a counterculture" (Teichs and Wick 2012: 1.16–2.01 min).

11.5 Conclusions

The foregoing considerations have approached Elektro Guzzi's *Pentagonia* as a constellation of sound events, and their production and performance in the rehearsal room/studio and on stage, in order to be able to trace their stylistic categorization as techno.

Despite the reduction that a musical analysis entails it can be stated that *Pentagonia* strongly corresponds to the musical conventions of techno tracks

[14] In this regard, the intention of being a "human modular synthesizer" is relevant again: "that one can no longer reconstruct who does exactly what" (Breuer et al. 2014a, b).

concerning time and form. Therefore, regarding the musical sound, an orientation toward genre conventions can be ascertained, which explains why the track is considered as techno music.

However, Elektro Guzzi's presented dimensions of liveness differ from the performances of electronic artists in electronic dance music. The musical entities involved in such performances are usually prerecorded and transformed electronically during the performance (Butler 2014: 42–54). In the production and performance of *Pentagonia*, Elektro Guzzi exclude such provisional fixed objects and originate all musical sounds in real time. This means that they neither play completely without any electronic devices, nor that they are less relevant: they are merely shifted or out of sight.[15] Thus their performance deviates from the genre-typical mediatization of techno performances. Elektro Guzzi's performance can instead be perceived as a traditionalization of performances of electronic artists in electronic dance music by reconstituting an audio/visual economy, which suggests a fundamental traceability of musical (inter) actions. I advocate here strongly for a positive connotation of the term traditionalization, since it intensifies the aesthetic experience associated with classic liveness (and, ironically, regarding the tradition of electronic dance music performance, Elektro Guzzi's approach appears rather innovative than traditional). It can also be stated that Elektro Guzzi's approach reflects liveness in complex ways at various levels: not only regarding the temporal and formal design of the music, but also regarding creative strategies and improvisation, as well as the fusion of human and machine, emphasized in their term "human modular synthesizer".

In conclusion, *Pentagonia* can be perceived as techno because the track represents the musical codes of this style, as Butler points out. Elektro Guzzi's resemblance to techno can also be explained by the fact that they, due to their more human-than-machine-based approach, may well have figured out stylistic conventions by themselves. The citation of this elaboration in *Pentagonia* makes their readability as techno possible in the first place. Ultimately, I wish to stress that prototypes of a genre, as this chapter suggests, must be seen in the wider context from which they emerged. It is important to take the historicity and sociocultural context of such prototypes into account since the characteristic dispositions of a genre are in constant shift (Brackett 2016: 13).[16] In this perspective, *Pentagonia* can be seen as a

[15]On the contrary, it should be noted that the degree of electronic devices plays a crucial role due to the influence on their sound aesthetics. For example, the tactile energy is achieved by amplifying the sound through the PA and directing it to the audience and the band. Moreover, the sound engineer (FOH) also optimizes (and expands) the sound, even if he is not visible to the audience. Even if the sound originates from the acoustic instruments and is modified by electronic devices only afterwards, the resulting sound is significantly electrified by a mediatized environment.

[16]A historically informed examination of genre definitions of electronic dance music/techno may illuminate this: Recent definitions in particular point out the growing diversity, dynamics and even the dichotomies of electronic dance music cultures (Rietveld 2013: 2; Butler 2014: 16). Therefore, it seems to be useful to understand electronic dance music as "one of the great cultural-musical hybrids of the past century" (Kirn 2011: ix) which encompasses a network of related musical styles (see Butler 2012: xii). For this reason, the term can be viewed as an "umbrella term" (Rietveld 2013: 2) for a "metagenre" (McLeod 2001: 60), to which Elektro Guzzi can be attributed.

contemporary iteration of stylistic conventions, which enriches them with a (new) way of performing live.

References

Archiv österreichischer Popularmusik. (n.d.). Elektro Guzzi. Retrieved August 09, 2018 from http://www.sra.at/band/40638

Auslander, P. (2008). *Liveness: Performance in a mediatized culture*. New York: Routledge.

Auslander, P. (2013). Sound and vision: The audio/visual economy of musical performance. In J. Richardson, C. Gorbman, & C. Vernallis (Eds.), *The Oxford handbook of new audiovisual aesthetics* (pp. 605–621). Oxford: Oxford University Press.

Auslander, P. (2016). Afterword: So close and yet so far. The proxemics of liveness. In *Experiencing liveness in contemporary performance: Interdisciplinary perspectives* (pp. 295–298). New York: Routledge.

Bath, T. (2014). Threshold people: An interview with Elektro Guzzi. Retrieved August 04, 2018 from http://thequietus.com/articles/16892-elektro-guzzi-interview

Brackett, D. (2016). *Categorizing sound: Genres and twentieth-century popular music*. Oakland: University of California Press.

Breuer, B., Hammer, B., & Schneidewind, J. (2014a). Interview with the author, 3 April [not published, trans. by the author]. Heidelberg, Halle 02 (at Heidelberger Frühling).

Breuer, B., Hammer, B., & Schneidewind, J. (2014b). Interview with the author, 30 August [not published, trans. by the author]. Wien, rehearsal room/recording studio Elektro Guzzi.

Breuer, B., Hammer, B., & Schneidewind, J. (2018). Interview with the author, 2 June [not published]. Potsdam, FreiLand (at Lalonova Open Air).

Brooks, C. (2017). Music interviews. Elektro Guzzi. Retrieved August 04, 2018 from https://thepartae.com/elektro-guzzi/

Butler, M. J. (2006). *Unlocking the groove: Rhythm, meter, and musical design in electronic dance music*. Bloomington: Indiana University Press.

Butler, M. J. (Ed.). (2012). *Electronica, dance and club music*. Surrey: Ashgate.

Butler, M. J. (2014). *Playing with something that runs: Technology, improvisation, and composition in DJ and laptop performance*. Oxford: Oxford University Press.

Collins, N., Schedel, M., & Wilson, S. (Eds.). (2013). *Electronic music*. Cambridge: Cambridge University Press.

Dancity Festival. (2011). ELEKTRO GUZZI – interview at DANCITY FESTIVAL 2011. Retrieved May 20, 2019 from https://www.youtube.com/watch?v=pWgfq89zCGc

Fabbri, F. (1982). A theory of musical genres: Two applications. *Popular Music Perspectives*: 52–81. Retrieved May 24, 2019 from https://www.tagg.org/xpdfs/ffabbri81a.pdf

Fabbri, F. (1999). Browsing music spaces: Categories and the musical mind. Retrieved May 24, 2019 from http://www.tagg.org/others/ffabbri9907.html

Fabbri, F. (2012). How genres are born, change, die: Conventions, communities and diachronic processes. In S. Hawkins (Ed.), *Critical musicological reflections. Essays in honour of Derek B. Scott* (pp. 179–191). Farnham: Ashgate.

Ferreira, P. P. (2008). When sound meets movement: Performance in electronic dance music. *Leonardo Music Journal, 18*, 17–20.

Fritsch, M., & Strötgen, S. (2012). Relatively live: How to identify live music performances. *Music and the Moving Image, 5*(1), 47–66. Retrieved May 20, 2019 from http://www.jstor.org/stable/10.5406/musimoviimag.5.1.0047.

Guzzi, E. (2017). Parade. Denovali Records, den272, Germany. [Sticker attached on the front].

Kirn, P. (2011). *The evolution of electronic dance music*. Milwaukie: Backbeat Books.

Knoblauch, H. (2005). Focused ethnography [30 paragraphs]. *Forum qualitative Sozialforschung/ forum: Qualitative social research, 6*(3), 44. Retrieved June 10, 2019 from http://www.qualitative-research.net/index.php/fqs/article/view/20/43.

Lena, J. (2012). *Banding together: How communities create genres in popular music*. Princeton: Princeton University Press.

McLeod, K. (2001). Genres, sub-genres, sub-sub-genres and more: Musical and social difference within electronic dance music communities. *Journal of Popular Music Studies, 13*, 59–75.

Musical Instruments Museum Online (MIMO) Consortium. (2011). Revision of the Hornbostel-Sachs classification of musical instruments. Retrieved May 27, 2019 from http://www.mimo-international.com/documents/Hornbostel%20Sachs.pdf

Parkin, C., & Red Bull Music. (2013). Elektro Guzzi: Creating music by mimicking machine sounds | sounds like. Retrieved May 20, 2019 from https://www.youtube.com/watch?v=L89Sy0TrbKI

Peel, I. (2001). Dance music. In S. Sadie, J. Tyrrell, & G. Grove (Eds.), *The new Grove dictionary of music and musicians* (p. 909). Oxford: Oxford University Press.

Rietveld, H. (2013). Introduction. In B. Attias, A. Gavanas, & H. Rietveld (Eds.), *DJ culture in the mix: Power, technology, and social change in electronic dance music* (pp. 1–14). New York: Bloomsbury Academic.

Sanden, P. (2013). *Liveness in modern music: Musicians, technology, and the perception of performance*. New York: Routledge.

Snoman, R. (2014). *Dance music manual: Tools, toys, and techniques*. Burlington: Focal Press.

Stange-Elbe, J. (2015). *Computer und Musik. Grundlagen, Technologien und Produktionsumgebungen der digitalen Musik*. Berlin: De Gruyter.

Teichs, R., & Wick, H. (2012). ELEKTRO GUZZI (Slices Feature). Retrieved May 20, 2019 from https://www.youtube.com/watch?v=HEo9LgkR3oU

Udvardyová, L. (2016). Jakob Schneidewind talks about his bands Elektro Guzzi, Demi Broxa and Monochord. Retrieved May 20, 2019 from http://shapeplatform.eu/2016/interview-jakob-schneidewind/

Without author. (n.d.). Retrieved May 27, 2019 from https://www.facebook.com/pg/elektroguzzi/about/

Discography and Videography

elektroguzzi. (2011). Elektro Guzzi – Pentagonia. *YouTube*. Retrieved May 20, 2019 from https://www.youtube.com/watch?v=iWviLy1BiCs. Published 24 October 2011 [music video].

elektroguzzi. (2017). Elektro Guzzi – Achse Dachse. *YouTube*. Retrieved May 27, 2019 from https://www.youtube.com/watch?v=gxX24pk98eo. Published 22 October 2017 [music video].

Frühling, H. (2014). Elektro Guzzi in Concert – 3.4.2014. *YouTube*. Retrieved May 20, 2019 from https://www.youtube.com/watch?v=Xu2SHy1i7mM. Published 13 April 2014 [live performance].

Guzzi, E. (2011). Pentagonia. On *Parquet*. Macro M27.

The manufacturer's authorised representative in the EU is Springer Nature Customer Service Centre GmbH, Europaplatz 3, 69115 Heidelberg, Germany. If you have any concerns regarding our products, please contact ProductSafety@springernature.com

Printed and bound by CPI Group (UK) Ltd, Croydon, CR0 4YY
30/09/2026
02225467-0016